A TEXT FOR CLASS USE

FUNDAMENTALS

Enduring Convictions of the Restoration

By F. Henry Edwards

HERALD PUBLISHING HOUSE
Independence, Missouri

Copyright, MCMXLVIII
HERALD PUBLISHING HOUSE
Independence, Missouri

All rights in this book are reserved. No part of the text may be reproduced in any form without written permission of the publishers, except brief quotations used in connection with reviews in magazines or newspapers.

FIRST EDITION
First Printing, September 1936
Second Printing, January 1937
Third Printing, August 1939

SECOND EDITION
(Extensively Revised)
First Printing, January 1948
Second Printing, August 1956
Third Printing, February 1960

Printed in the United States of America

To my parents, Latter Day Saints for nearly sixty
years, who lived in the spirit of Zion
while in a distant mission, this
book is affectionately
dedicated.

Foreword

THIS book attempts a brief statement of some of the fundamental beliefs of the Reorganized Church of Jesus Christ of Latter Day Saints. Lack of space has made it necessary to omit other topics which might well have been discussed, and has made it impossible to give elaborate discussion of such topics as have been included; but I hope that the book will at least indicate some of the rich values of our faith and will help in the movement to cause our people to "Know the Church."

The book is not primarily intended for cursory reading, but for study. In religion, as elsewhere, the richer values elude us unless we are willing to dig for them. The weekly assignments for reading, however, are quite brief, and should not place an undue burden on those who take their church school work seriously. Students will do well to use with each lesson the lesson helps furnished in the appendix. These helps are suggestive only and should be elaborated by both teacher and student.

As might be expected, these studies have been enriched by all who have ministered to my understanding of the Restoration Movement. It is not possible, therefore, to acknowledge my indebtedness except in the most general way. My gratitude for the help given is nevertheless deep and sincere.

I am constantly more aware that our Heavenly Father seeks to reach us through each window of the soul. I believe, therefore, that hearts as well as minds should be prepared for the adventure of understanding which each study period should furnish.

F. Henry Edwards.

Table of Contents

	Page
Chapter I—Foundations of Belief	9-13
Chapter II—God, the Father, Almighty	14-37
Chapter III—God Seeks to Make Himself Known	38-49
Chapter IV—Jesus Christ Our Lord	50-73
Chapter V—The Holy Spirit	74-88
Chapter VI—The Antiquity of the Gospel	89-95
Chapter VII—Priesthood	96-110
Chapter VIII—Sin and Forgiveness	111-140
Chapter IX—The Church	141-152
Chapter X—The Lord's Day	153-160
Chapter XI—The Sacrament of the Lord's Supper	161-166
Chapter XII—The Place of Prayer	167-174
Chapter XIII—Apostasy and Restoration	175-211
Chapter XIV—The Gifts of the Spirit	212-253
Chapter XV—The Scriptures	254-260
Chapter XVI—Marriage	261-287
Chapter XVII—The Kingdom of God	288-309
Chapter XVIII—Conditions of Progress	310-325
Chapter XIX—The Future Life	326-356
Chapter XX—The Church of Jesus Christ	357-365

Chapter I

FOUNDATIONS OF BELIEF

We need the guidance of sound convictions—These are achieved in worship—True worship draws on the best in man—Our convictions are tested in action.

Lesson One

"WHAT DOES IT MATTER what a man believes so long as he does what is right?" "It is not your creed I am concerned with, but your conduct." "What you do counts, and how you do it, and in the long run nothing else is of importance." Such statements as these are characteristic of our day, and indicate a widespread impatience with mere theorizing. But they are totally misleading.

No man ever achieves distinction in a worthy field who does not believe some great truth with all his heart and mind. It was the quality of his belief in the Union that led Lincoln on to greatness; it was the urgency of his faith that sent Columbus westward until he found the New World. So, also, the quality of our beliefs and the tenacity with which we hold them determines the course of our life today.

It has been said that all we need to do to straighten out the tangles in our modern life is to follow the Golden Rule. This sounds good, but this, too, is misleading. The Golden Rule requires that we shall do unto others as we would have them do to us. But suppose I am a drunkard, a thief, and a liar. Then, if I apply the Golden Rule, I will supply my neighbor with liquor, I will give him opportunity to steal, and I will protect him in his lying. Surely, this is not the true meaning of the Golden Rule. The Golden Rule is only truly golden if it refers back to golden standards.

What we believe matters tremendously, not as a substitute for right doing, but as a guide in right doing. I do not know whether I am doing right in turning west when I leave home, unless I know where I want to go. I do not know whether I am doing right in hitting a golf ball straight down the fairway unless I have some idea what lies over the hill and where the cup is. I do not know whether I am doing right when I give up my life belt to a woman or a child unless I have some feeling regarding the value of human life and the requirements of honor. No matter what the situation, I do not know what is right unless I have a working idea of the total purpose of things, of where I am going, and why I am going there.

Sound convictions regarding the final purpose of life underlie all sober life plans. No one can map his life effectively who lacks assurance about the purpose of life itself; that is one reason why religion is so very important. Religion is the one interest of mankind which has to do with ultimates: with God and Man, with Time and Eternity, with Life and Immortality. Moreover, such sound convictions as we are now discussing draw on all that a man is and has. They arise in the depths of the soul. And here, again, religion is important, for his religion relates itself to a man's very self: to his heart and mind and conscience and will.

The enlarging of our experience which we achieve when we enter the realm of religion is won in the act of worship. Worship does not decry any of the other approaches to understanding, such as thought, observation, and experiment. But it goes beyond them. It recognizes the severe and narrow limitations of unaided reason, and gives opportunity for the soul to venture out beyond the border of mere human understanding to the place where the voice of the infinite sounds clear and true above the clamor of little things. In sane, heartfelt, and expansive worship, we come closer to the truth of things as they are than in any other field of experience.

The approach to understanding by way of worship is frequently decried, but there is no valid reason why it should be. Indeed, the primacy of worship appears to demand recognition, since it includes the best that there is of every other approach to the truth. There appears to be only one fundamental reason why this primacy is denied, and that is, that no man is at home in a genuine worship experience who is not a good man. The riches of understanding are not available to anyone who is merely clever, but only to those who are morally worthy. To be petty, unclean, and self-centered is no preparation for insight into the grandeur which environs us.

The fact that religion operates beyond the field of precise measurement does not mean that religious belief must be forever tentative. Religious convictions can merge into certitudes as strong as the certainties of mathematics. And these certitudes are not weakened by the fact that they are achieved in a larger field than that occupied by pure reason. There are some things that simply cannot be proved by logic. By no process known to mathematician or logician can it ever be proved that it is better to be noble than to be paltry, or that it is finer to be generous than to be selfish, or that it is nobler to be brave than to be a coward, or that "behind the dim unknown, standeth God within the shadow, keeping watch above his own." By the wise provision of Divinity, truths of this nature must be discovered. Certainty in these fields is available only to men and women who take the initiative and make the great adventure. It was for this reason that Jesus said to the men of his own generation, "Do, and you shall know" (I John 7: 17). For the same reason the Master says to our generation, "Follow me, and you shall learn in experience." If any man really wants to know the truth about God, his best course is to devote himself to some Godlike cause and to discover God as a working comrade.

Belief operates in a larger sphere than reason, but it does well to check up by the aid of reason. A young man who is carried off his feet by his passion for an attractive young

[11]

woman and refuses to consider the reasonable objections of his friends, is a fool. The doctor who glimpses a possible cure for a dangerous disease and risks men's lives without properly testing his intuition, is a charlatan. The man who sees that the most damnable deeds in all history were done by conscientious people whose intentions were good but whose understanding was warped, and who still launches out into life on the strength of beliefs which have not been tested, is the kind of fool who will pay for his folly in losses which last through all eternity. It is a major tragedy to be without the guidance of deep convictions. It is a tragedy almost as great to give allegiance to ideals which dissipate devotion because they are not grounded in truth.

Intelligence must check up on intuition, not apart from the spirit of worship, but under the influence of that spirit. The wise man will observe with care the influence of his faith on his performance. But the question is not whether faith promotes our material success. It is, rather, whether our faith brings soul satisfaction; whether it puts us to work on the side of the best that we can dream; whether it gives us joy in the midst of the struggle; whether it gives us courage to endure. It is useless to hold sound convictions timidly. Their value is in life; and they become stronger and more sure as life is made rich and meaningful in experience because of them.

Sound convictions rest on sound living. They have to do with healthy minds and healthy bodies and healthy spirits. They are not the product of thought alone nor of feeling alone, but of the highest thought and feeling uplifted and illumined by the Spirit of God. They may be received, in the first place, on the basis of tradition and authority, for a man may reasonably borrow spiritual capital to start him out in life just as he borrows money for his education. But, however they are initiated, <u>convictions are not sound until they are one's own, the fruit and inspiration of one's best self in action under God.</u>

Study Outlines

Foundations of Belief

Lesson Purpose

To impress the importance of believing rightly and translating this belief into action.

High Points of the Lesson

Some theory of the total purpose of life is essential to success. What we believe about God and about human destiny matters more than what we believe about anything else.

Belief is the verdict of our best experience, including the impressions of the Spirit.

Inherited beliefs are not to be despised as starting points.

Questions and Discussion Topics

(1) Discuss briefly the relative importance of belief, opinions, and convictions. Is it true that a great man is a man of great convictions?

(2) Why is religious belief supremely important?

(3) How do we decide what to believe in business, in school, in personal relations? What additional guides to belief are available in the field of religion?

(4) When are your beliefs most trustworthy, when you are living well or when you are living badly? What lessons do your answers teach?

(5) What factors are likely to make a person doubt the promises of God? At what point does doubt become sin? Why?

(6) If a man finds himself doubting things upon which he has relied all his life, what would you advise him to do?

(7) What are your most significant beliefs? What effect do they have in your life?

(8) You have a good friend who is totally unconcerned about religion. He says it does not matter what a man believes so long as he is a "good sport." What would you say to him?

What the Lesson Means Today:

We need a working faith in times of crisis; in bereavement and disaster. It will be too late to build such a faith then. Nor can we then rely very strongly on a faith borrowed from someone else. Now is the time to learn to see things steadily and to see them whole.

Chapter II

GOD, THE FATHER, ALMIGHTY

God Is—He is our Father—He is Almighty—He created the world through his Son.

Lesson Two

I—GOD IS

WE are very proud of the tools with which our generation faces the business of living. This is the atomic age, and its realities and possibilities stagger our imagination. Our powerful telescopes and microscopes, our majestic bridges and huge skyscrapers, our express trains and swift liners and winged planes, our cables and radios and wire photos, and the thousand-and-one other devices which our day has perfected all combine to testify of our power and to prophesy yet greater power which will soon be within our grasp. <u>It is not because of lack of brains that we are yet distant from the millennium, but because somehow—in spite of our colossal achievements in other fields—we have not yet organized the spiritual forces of the universe. Our personal relationships do not match our scientific achievements.</u>

As has already been indicated, it is for just this reason that religion is so very important to the modern man, for religion is concerned with those spiritual forces which make for justice and peace and which set before men, both individually and collectively, an inclusive purpose which is eternally worth-while. Science, invention, commerce, and government are fascinating pursuits for this life. They satisfy the deepest needs of all. And they give us no sense of adjustment to the final purpose of life. Only religion can do that, and only such religion as brings us into personal

[14]

relation with One who can fuse all our smaller purposes into one great purpose, big enough for eternity, and generous enough to warm the hearts of all mankind.

The fundamental concern of all religion is with God. We cannot have religion without God. We can have morals and rules and a sense of duty. But the programs of the moralist, ingenious as they are, fail to pierce to the deeper well-springs of human action. Because we are concerned, therefore, in causing the great advances of our modern world to minister to the deepest needs of man, we must go beyond duty, beyond morality, and beyond patriotism, and must consider the claims of religion—the claims of God— in our lives. Whatever our final decision may be, it is important that we shall consider well the reasons for believing in God or for failing to do so. And it is important that we shall consider such questions with our whole selves, noting carefully how we think and feel about them when we are living at our best, and testing them in light of our finest experience. After such an approach, here are some of the reasons why I believe in God:

(1) I believe in God because the loving activity of Divinity is the best explanation I can find for the universe and for our place in it.

(2) To believe in God does not put an end to all questioning. There still remain many problems and difficulties which challenge my understanding. But belief in God answers more questions more satisfactorily and inspiringly than any other belief. Confronted with such a world as ours, populated by such people as we are, the miracle of unbelief is greater than the miracle of belief. It requires more credulity not to believe in God than it does to believe in him.

Belief in God, I will admit, is not capable of scientific demonstration. That is due to the limitations of science rather than to the absence of evidence. I cannot prove by science demonstration the love of my mother, the fidelity of my wife, the beauty of a sunrise, or the sweetness of com-

[15]

munion between friends. But of the existence of these things I am as sure as I am that two and two make four.

At the headquarters of the church at Independence, Missouri, is an imposing General Conference Auditorium. Scores of men participated in its construction—carpenters, masons, plumbers, painters, glaziers, steel workers, electricians, and a host of others. If each of these had come to work when he pleased and had taken up his task where he pleased, the work would never have been brought to its present state of completion, and we would have said that such chaos indicated the lack of intelligent and purposeful direction. But from the beginning, the progress of the Auditorium showed organization and leadership; the foundations were laid, the walls rose in their places, the great central auditorium took shape, the beams came together; and as we looked at the growing perfection of the building, the order and purpose revealed therein bore testimony to the intelligence and skill of the architect and the builder.

In similar fashion, whoever looks beyond the immediacy of the present to the great scope of universal activity perceives the emergence of a great structure. In building this, the men of every generation have their place. Some are not well-trained. Others do not have in mind the ultimate purpose of their work. But despite these things, a glance at the records of the past shows that behind all our apparently unco-ordinated activity is a farsighted and well-integrated purpose, and that men are gradually moving from savagery to fellowship, from individualism to co-operation, from ignorance to understanding, from selfishness to love. Humanity goes toward its divine goal as a ship goes steadily toward its predetermined port. Dare we say that no captain directs its destinies?

When I was a boy, I could not understand all the reasons which prompted my father's discipline. But my love for him and my assurance of his love for me gave me a certain confidence in his guidance, and in later years my growing understanding confirmed my earlier trust in him. In much the same way my first steps in the great Christian adventure were founded on trust in the love of God which I found all around me; but this trust is being vindicated as I see that the great disciples of God are producing men of intelligence and spiritual courage and steady assurance. The ways of Divinity are majestic beyond my comprehension; I have caught a fleeting glimpse of the glory of the Father—and I believe in God.

I believe in God, furthermore, because my observation of human nature at its best demands such a belief.

One of the most evident signs of the progress of humanity is the increased sensitiveness of the public conscience. Not many years ago, the basic idea of penal administration was punishment. Now we are gradually coming to realize that we owe even criminals a chance to "make good," and instead of incarcerating them as a punishment, we are now trying to educate them in preparation for their full participation as citizens. In past years everything was justifiable in time of war; now we are trying to guarantee limitations of these horrors, the best limitation of all being no war at all. Many practices upon which we should now look with loathing were taken as a matter of course by our forebears. The conscience of civilization is becoming increasingly sensitive, and men are finding within themselves an ever more insistent impulsion toward right doing.

This awakened conscience is not entirely a creature of environment. While it has been influenced by the progress made by men and nations and has reflected that progress, conscience has also been a major factor in that growth. The most powerful influence making for right doing on the part of men of every race and creed has been a certain compelling sense of moral accountability which was ever present within them. The greatest heroes of spiritual history have been the men who were most responsive to the inner voice which was constantly challenging them to greatness. Even the

[17]

multitudes who once killed the prophets, have later been found acknowledging and accepting the great truths which the prophets proclaimed. In spite of our prejudices, the Light shines in the darkness, and it cannot be put out.

As I read the story of the great men of the past and note the enduring glory of those who were most fully responsive to the call of Divinity, I believe in God. But as I look into the beckoning future, and see that the only hope of humanity is that more and more of these men shall rise in the majesty of true nobility, I find that more than ever before I must believe in God.

Then again, I believe in God because Jesus, the world's greatest specialist in spiritual affairs, believed in him. One of the fruits of the modern interest in education is an increasing respect for the man who speaks with authority. Indeed, this has now spread far beyond the academic circles in which it had its birth and is rapidly becoming characteristic of our times. Now, as never before, the man of authority is being granted his rightful place of pre-eminence. The conclusions of Mr. Einstein, written on a few sheets of paper but representing the fruitage of years of hard work, are read with respect by physicists the world over, for he is a recognized authority in this field.

In the field of religion, faith in authority is equally sound, especially when we can test the conclusions of this authority for ourselves. So we turn quite naturally to men and women of matured spiritual judgment when we need advice on matters of spiritual importance. But even when these good friends have done their best for us, we look beyond them in search of One who can speak with final certitude.

In our search for God, particularly, we do not want mere opinion. We want to know. And, anticipating our desperate need, Jesus stands forth with credentials which mark him as the spiritual authority par excellence. He says that he is as sure of God as he is of his own existence. And as he speaks, we are somehow sure that he really does know.

Jesus faced life in its most dispiriting aspects. He lived in close touch with physical, mental, and spiritual degeneracy. Those who should have supported him were among his most bitter enemies. His highest ambitions for men, born of his great love for them, went utterly disregarded. He went to ignominious death unaccompanied by a single friend of nobility and vision. Yet he still turned to God in every crisis as the Great Companion. The matchless splendor of his life and death can only be explained on the basis which he himself has given—that God was with him.

Jesus never argued about God. He took the fact of God and the love of God for granted and lived them into assurance. After the initial adventure of faith, he needed faith no longer, for his trust had been verified in experience. No other evidence can nullify such a demonstration. The skepticism of a thousand cannot outweigh such testimony on the part of one who knows. Jesus believed in God. Jesus made men believe in God because he demonstrated to them beyond all doubt what the love of God means when it is incarnate among men.

I believe in God. This is infinitely more important than merely believing *about* God. Many an outstanding man owes his present position of distinction to the fact that some other man believed in him enough to give him a start in life. The outstanding facts about him were probably obvious to everyone, but the quality of the man who was behind these facts, and the rich promise of his life, were only realized by a few. The facts *about* him were comparatively unimportant. The thing that mattered was that he was the kind of man who would justify his friend's belief *in* him.

We believe in men, sometimes in spite of what we know about them, because through contact with them we have come to recognize an inner quality which is not apparent to the casual observer. I believe in God in the same way, because of personal experience with him. The test for the existence of God and for the spiritual quality of his nature is not argument about him. Nor, in the final analysis, is it the testimony of others. The final test is for me to act as though God is all that the greatest spiritual heroes of the ages have said that he is, and then to await the results of this action in my own life. I believe in God because my slightest approach to him has brought such response as has given abundant evidence of his love and power. I do not yet believe in him as much as I expect to believe because I have not yet been able to discipline myself to such intimacy with him as I some day hope to achieve. But, my faith grows with my spiritual stature. Indeed, my faith is the mark of my spiritual stature. That is true of every man.

STUDY OUTLINES

GOD IS

LESSON PURPOSE

To urge some of the major reasons for believing in God.

HIGH POINTS OF THE LESSON

Our thought of the purpose of life must take God into account. No wise man ignores the spiritual realities in determining his life purpose.

Belief in God is reasonable. God is our best explanation of the world about us. He is our best explanation of moral progress, even though this progress is so spasmodic. He is the best explanation for Jesus, who is so unique as to demand explanation.

QUESTIONS AND DISCUSSION TOPICS

(1) Name some of the evidences of planned order in the universe. Do these evidences cause you to believe in God? Does it explain this order to say that it is "natural"? What is the relation of God and Nature?

(2) Does the rise of our moral standards "just happen"? If not, how does it come to pass? Give some illustrations for your answer.

(3) My friend said to me, "I will follow the guidance of the man of authority in science or in literature, but he is out of place in religion. There I am my own authority." Discuss this.

(4) Give some reasons for accepting Jesus as the final authority on God. What moral right does he have to require us to believe in his testimony?

(5) What was the attitude of Jesus toward the question of the existence of God? What suggestions are there here for us?

(6) This chapter suggests that there is an important difference between belief about a person and belief in a person. Discuss this difference so as to make it clear.

(7) Men of every race have believed in God, even though their ideas of God have varied. Is this sufficient reason for us to believe? If not, what bearing should it have on our belief?

(8) Your agnostic friend is interested in your reasons for belief in God. Where will your arguments for the existence of God be most likely to fail to convince him? Why? What can you do to cause him to share your faith?

It is quite legitimate to "fel after God," for "the heart has reasons which the mind does not know." Reason, also, has a legitimate place in checking our faith, but we must be particularly careful to wait until the evidence is all in before discarding a faith which has proved socially beneficial but for which we cannot at the moment give full intellectual justification.

We must refuse to be disturbed by lesser doubts, and must be particularly careful not to permit doubt regarding part of God's word to prevent us from doing what he clearly wants us to do and what we clearly ought to do.

Lesson Three

II—GOD IS OUR FATHER

MERE SIZE OR POWER IS NO INDICATION of true greatness. Many of us know men whose work is admirable but who are not admirable in themselves, skillful men who are dominated by their own passions. Deep down in our hearts the most cynical of us knows that goodness is infinitely precious, that character is the greatest achievement of mankind, and that self-sacrifice born of love is the finest evidence of character.

Jesus tells us that God is our Father, and this conforms to our highest conception of Divinity. There is no more worthy concept. To know that God is our Father is much more than to know him as our Maker. It means that his own life is inextricably involved in ours. When Jesus shows us God as the Father of man, with a heart big enough to concern himself with the destiny of each one of us, we see the highest possible revelation of Divinity. Our remaining task is to see what this guarantee of divine Fatherhood means to us.

Fatherhood means impartial love. We differ from each other in many ways. One appears to have every advantage, and another every drawback in life. One is born in a saintly home and another never knows the meaning of home. Yet in spite of such differences, Jesus assures us that behind all our apparent inequalities is the love of God guaranteeing to every man an equal chance to realize his full possibilities. And the more we act as if this message of Jesus was true, the more we feel within ourselves that it really is true.

It is not unusual for children in good homes to feel that their parents have discriminated against them; and that other members of the family are given better clothes or more food or greater privileges. There are two possible attitudes in such a situation: to explain every action to such children and assure them that there is no partiality, or to help them to realize that their parents love them far too much to be partial. The first solution has to be applied over and over again. The second is permanent; and this is the solution for our discontents which is offered by Jesus.

To our complaint that others are better treated than we, Jesus answered, "God is our Father." At first this seems like begging the question, but after a time we realize that it is the only answer which will finally satisfy our questioning. If he is our Father, we can trust him to be fair to us and to all his children.

We must remember, also, that not all those who appear to hold enviable positions are really to be envied. It is said that Emil Ludwig, the world famous biographer, was asked which was the greater man, William Gladstone or Abraham Lincoln. We may disagree with the answer given, but the reason for this answer is illuminating. Herr Ludwig said: "Gladstone was the greater man. Lincoln only had to fight poverty and homeliness and the frontiers, but Gladstone had to fight riches and social graces and too-easy opportunities. It takes a greater man to withstand the temptations of riches than it does to overcome the handicaps of poverty." It may well be that, in spite of appearances, our burdens are not so unequal after all.

Another aspect of divine fatherhood which we accept as true on the testimony of Jesus and on the verdict of our own best experience is that he is personally concerned about every one of us as an individual. At times some of us are disturbed by thought of the majesty and power of God, and this makes it difficult for us to believe that he is actually concerned about us as persons. Yet, once again, a glance at modern life will help us to understand. The greatest teacher is the one who knows most about his topic and about the art of teaching, and who applies his knowledge in accordance with the individual needs of his pupils. The greatest surgeon is the one who knows most about the human body and its ailments and the remedy for these ills, and who applies this knowledge with due regard for the physical individuality of every patient. The greatest leader is the one who knows the common needs of humanity, and yet who understands the individual needs of the members of his group. Similarly, the testimony of Jesus regarding our Father, and our own distinctive feeling that this is essentially right, combine to assure us that God cares for us personally, as a father should, and that the greatness which we ascribe to him is not complete except as it includes the power and the disposition to single us out for his individual care and guidance.

In the best homes that we know, affection and discipline go hand in hand. When a child in such a home becomes wayward and rebellious, the discipline of the home becomes operative for his reclamation. So, also, is our Heavenly Father's home. He "chasteneth every son whom he receiveth." This individual correction, rooted in love, is one of the evidences of his true greatness, and one of the tests of our love for him is that we accept his chastisement without complaining and seek to learn the lesson which he thus seeks to impress.

Yet again, *fatherhood involves eagerness to forgive us*. As Isaiah said in the Heavenly Father's name long ago, "I, even I, am he that blotteth out thy transgressions for mine own sake" (Isa. 43:25). So long as we are willing to turn to him, we find him eager to receive us. We can test this in experience whenever we care to do so. No matter what our mistakes or what our deliberate sins may be, if we repent truly and searchingly, we find him running to meet us with open arms. There are some, as we know, who have stayed away from their Father so far, and have lived for so long with persons who are totally unlike the Father, that they no longer have any interest in the Father's home and are quite unmoved by evidences of his love. If we ever get into such a condition, it will be because we have chosen to go and live in that state, and have repeated this choice over a long, long time, so as to become hardened in our resentment and rejection of the love which searches after us. But one of the evidences that God is our Father is that it is so hard to escape him. It is very, very difficult to find a completely bad man. No man is completely bad as long as there is in him some faint spark of goodness which the love of God might yet fan into flame.

Study Outlines

God Is Our Father

Lesson Purpose

To indicate the significance of the fatherhood of God and to create hunger for active participation in the life of his family.

High Points of the Lesson

Realization that God is our Father should give us confidence that he has wisely determined our place in life.

It is impossible to love a person without wishing for his love in return. God is concerned about our response to his love.

There is no greater incentive toward clean and intelligent and forward-looking life than a deep-seated conviction that we are called to partnership with God.

Questions and Discussion Topics

(1) Discuss the statement that "character is the greatest achievement of mankind." Do you agree? Why?

(2) One man is bitterly resentful regarding his lack of opportunities in life. Another, who comes from the same environment, accepts what he has as a steppingstone to something better. Which of these two has the best claim on divine help? Why?

(3) Is it possible that God is too great to be concerned with us individually? Should our discovery of the vastness of the universe cause us to expect him to be concerned about us, or should we expect him to forget us in the mass of his creation? Why?

(4) In what sense is God jealous? What is the effect of his jealousy in our lives?

(5) Paul says, "We know that all things work together for good to them that love God." Does this mean that God makes life easier for his Saints or that he strengthens us to meet life, or both? Illustrate your answer.

(6) A specialist in child training suggests that "only those who love us have the right to discipline us." Is this true? What does this mean in relation to the love of God for us?

(7) Is it possible to love without cost? What does God's love for us cost him?

(8) What evidences cause you to believe that God loves you? What does this belief mean in your life? How may it be strengthened?

What the Lesson Means Today

It is most difficult to believe in God when we are in the company of persons of small spiritual stature. If we are to have a vital faith, we must, therefore, learn to cultivate the fellowship of the faithful.

If we have grown to maturity but have failed to find any purpose in life and have no settled convictions about God, we have somehow missed the way and need help.

It is not enough to say that we are not interested in our relation to God. Such an important question cannot go by default. Matters affecting our eternal destiny demand serious consideration, and consideration involving all that we are at our best.

Lesson Four

III—GOD, THE FATHER, IS ALMIGHTY

A SURPRISING NUMBER OF PEOPLE find difficulty in believing in God because of the disorder and pain which they see on every side. They feel that if there is a God, he ought to do something about these things.

It is not long since many people were asking, "Can't God stop the war?" Following this came a whole series of questions: "If he can, why does he not do so?" "If he cannot, where is his power?" Such questions are typical, and they lead to a final question which is important to all of us: "Granted that there is a God, and that he loves us, is he powerful enough to make that love count in our lives?"

The believer's answer to these questions comes in a ringing affirmative of faith, "I believe in God, the Father, Almighty." This answer and affirmation has echoed and reechoed down the years because it meets the facts of experience squarely but sanely. It does not mean that God can do two mutually exclusive things. He cannot make a thirty-year-old man in a moment. He cannot convey experience to us without permitting that experience to develop over a period of time. He cannot force us to be good and still permit us to be free. But he can and does work out his righteous purpose by the use of means which are under his control: love, wisdom, patience, skill, courage. This is the testimony of history. It has been the sober experience of thousands of godly men and women.

Let us go back to the questions about the war and examine them. If our Heavenly Father had stopped the recent war by some great demonstration of his power, what, in fact, would he have done? All the colossal sinning, the organized selfishness, the mad scramble for profits, the oblivion to the higher values of life, which lay behind that conflict, would have been denied their natural fruition. We would have sown the wind, but would not have reaped the whirlwind. After having sown the seeds of war, to have avoided war would have confirmed us in our national and international wickedness. This God would not do.

We frequently pray, "Deliver us from evil," when what we really mean is, "Deliver us from the ill effects of our evil doing." This is not what the Lord's Prayer means. It means what it says—"Deliver us from evil." The punishment which descends on the evildoer is like the toothache, a danger signal calling attention to an unhealthy condition. If God should remove the painful results of our evil-doings, without some other factors being brought into play, the greater ills behind them would continue unchecked. It is only when war tears the mask from the sins of society, and we see social sin in its true guise that we come to hate our common sins as we should.

God will not do that which will defeat his own purpose. He will not forever wink at our shortcomings. He will not forego the discipline that the development of our character requires. He will not listen to the fearful cries of those cowards who wish to be saved from the results of their transgressions, but who will sin again tomorrow if they think they can get away with it. He will forgive those who are truly repentant, but he will not forgive those who are merely scared. His attitude in these matters arises out of his strength and not from weakness. To do otherwise would be a denial of his true divinity.

Let us go back now to our larger question: "Can we believe that God is Almighty in view of the facts of life as we know them?" As we have already stated, our best thinking and our deepest feeling convince us that there is a purpose behind the universe, and that this purpose is God's purpose. As we read the pages of history, we see this purpose being wrought and note the gradual liberation of mankind from the bondage of ignorance and sin and political slavery which held them in the yesterdays. We see the emergence of a public opinion which condemns slavery, graft, organized vice, and the like; and we feel assured that these facts prophesy that these and other ills shall in time be overcome. We see the barriers of time, distance, and isolation broken down by the advancing arts of civilization. We see the dawn of real hope for the kingdom of God, and the shaping of the tools which could make the kingdom possible if they were used wisely by good men. And as we look, we realize that humanity is growing up, and the way of the kingdom is being prepared.

Slowly the significance of history dawns on our minds. The creation of mankind is not yet completed but is still going forward; history is only the second chapter in the story. There is only one way in which we can be made into the image of God. We must willingly consent to the process. We must grow in passionate eagerness to become Godlike. And we must be willing to pay the price for this, even though the price is as great as history has revealed it to be. There is no other way.

No external compulsion can build character. When we were children, we were disciplined by our parents until we learned enough to discipline ourselves. As we grew up, much of that discipline was removed. One of the signs of our growing maturity was that we became capable of exercising independent judgment. So, also, are the larger issues of life. We are ultimately successful only as we develop the powers which belong to mature personalities and are persuaded to enter into life at its richest and best.

Herein lies the almighty power *of God*. It is power to achieve his highest purpose through infinite understanding wedded to perfect self-control. Nothing could make men in the image of God save unerring insight and unfailing patience. Somehow we must be stirred to use the only tools out of which greatness can be fashioned—intelligent love for God and for our fellow men. Our Heavenly Father is powerful enough to restrain himself from the temptation to coerce us because he knows that for his purposes he must win our hearts. He therefore goes with us every step of the way as we learn the lessons of life, enduring with us and for us.

Our Heavenly Father has identified himself with our needs. Although he seems to stand aloof at times while we learn our lessons, it is not because he is indifferent but because for our sake he must not interfere. He is Almighty not because of what he can do *for* us, but because of what he can do *in* us. When we are suffering, he can ease our pain; and he does so whenever this is consistent with his greater purpose. He knows how to answer our prayers, and does so whenever it is for our good and for the good of humanity. The riches of the earth are his, and he shares them gladly with his people, but only when this sharing means also the sharing of eternal riches.

If we are to believe in God at all, we must believe in him as being almighty in this sense. It is not wisdom alone which makes him great, but power controlled by wisdom and dedicated to the salvation of men. Such power, we must believe, is available in God. If we do not believe this, then the kind of power that we need to draw upon to live our best is not available, at all, and we are left without hope. Our confidence in God who is our Supreme Friend gives us assurance.

If we believe that God, who is our Father, and who is almighty, adjusts himself to the requirements of our larger life, and shows his power by using the laws which he has set in motion rather than by flouting them, then our greatest virtue will lie in intelligent obedience to these same laws. This means that instead of expecting God to do great things for us, we will expect him to do great things in us as we learn to follow him in seeking a finer and more enduring righteousness.

Study Outlines

God, the Father, Is Almighty

Lesson Purpose

To show what is meant by the power of God and to lead to faith and patience and co-operation with him.

High Points of the Lesson

God counts in the struggle of life.

The best evidence of a man's power is not in his ability to do what he wants to do, but in his determination to do the best he knows. The first shows strength, but the second shows self-mastery. Our Heavenly Father is almighty in the sense that his great power is directed without deviation to the best possible ends.

Our Heavenly Father achieves his purposes by setting in motion the causes which produce the desired results.

Questions and Discussion Topics

(1) Why did most people want God to stop the war? Can anything justify his failure to do so? What?

(2) Is our Heavenly Father trying to stop other evils? How?

(3) What would we lose if God should force us to be good? Why is this important?

(4) Which is the greater deliverance, that evil shall be removed, or that we shall be strong enough to withstand it? Discuss this briefly.

(5) What is the relation between the love and power of God?

(6) It has been said that the greatest evidence that God is almighty is that he is never deflected from his purpose. Discuss this. Is it true?

(7) A certain king was a great warrior, and he loved his son. How could he best prove his own power, by winning a battle himself or by winning through his son? Why?

(8) What is the relation between law and power? Discuss this briefly.

What the Lesson Means Today

Our Heavenly Father helps us when he can do so without defeating his larger purpose, and suffers with us when suffering is unavoidable.

Mature manhood and womanhood come through acceptance of responsibility.

God lets us work out our own salvation, but his happiness is involved in the struggle.

The way to greatness is through intelligent obedience.

We must acknowledge the love of God with our hearts as well as with our minds.

We long to be at home in direct proportion to the affection we find there. We shall be at home in God's world when we really believe that God loves us and fashioned this earth for our dwelling place because of this love.

Assurance that God loves us ought to school us to patience and good will, even under adversity. It will be a profitable exercise to examine ourselves and see whether we act as though we believe that our Heavenly Father really does love us.

Lesson Five

IV—GOD CREATED THE WORLD THROUGH HIS SON

CHRISTIANITY AFFIRMS that the universe is friendly because Jesus is at the heart of it. Today, when modern telescopes are revealing myriads of worlds occupying utmost parts of space, each obeying the laws of its creation and all of them keeping their ancient places, it is more important than ever that we shall be reminded of this truth. It is the inspiration of many men who serve science in faith and may well aid all of us in finding our places in a world made beautiful by the presence of God.

It is not long since scientists believed they could sort out this vast immensity of space into ninety-two basic elements. Everything was conceived as being governed by laws which are predetermined and unalterable and which even living things obey. But the scientists of this century have explored beyond the atom to find the electron; and they now affirm that the basis of all things is to be found in the behavior of tiny electrical charges, and that the laws which these electrons obey include something very much like free choice. Sir James Jeans described the change as follows: "To my mind the laws which nature obeys are less suggestive of those which a machine obeys in its motion than of those which a musician obeys in writing a fugue or a poet in composing a sonnet" *(The Mysterious Universe,* page 136). This changed point of view meets a need deep within us, for it helps us feel that while the universe obeys the laws of its being, these laws are not mechanical and impersonal but are an expression of the directing will of Divinity. Listen, again, to Professor Jeans:

> Mind no longer appears as an accidental intruder into the realm of matter; we are beginning to suspect that we ought rather to hail it as the creator and governor of the realm of matter—not, of course, our individual minds, but the mind in which the atoms

out of which our individual minds have grown exists as thoughts.
—*Ibid.*, page 148.

Two points of view are thus possible as we stand in awe before the immensity of space. A young astrologer expresses one of these points of view in Thomas Hardy's novel, *Two on a Tower:*

> The imaginary picture of the sky as the concavity of a dome whose base extends from horizon to horizon of our earth is grand, simply grand, and I wish I had never got beyond looking at it in that way. But the actual sky is a horror. There is a size at which dignity begins; further on there is a size at which grandeur begins; further on there is a size at which solemnity begins; further on a size at which ghastliness begins. That size faintly approaches the size of the stellar universe.

In contrast with this is the point of view of Sir Francis Younghusband. This president of the Royal Geographic Society stated, after returning from a journey in Tibet and Northern India, where he often seemed to be nearer the stars than the plains below:

> What stirred me was the presence, subtly felt, of some mighty all pervading influences which ordered the courses of the heavenly hosts and permeated every particle . . . . At the back of everything we realize there is a Power constant and dependable in whom we can absolutely put our trust. . . . We seem in the very midst of the great Presence. We are immersed in it. It is pervading us on every side. We do not expect it to alter the whole course of nature for our private good. But we feel confident that the course of nature is for good—that nature is a beneficent and not callous power, and has good at heart. Because the foundations are so sure and good, we can each pursue our way in confidence.

The Inspired Version of the Holy Scriptures records a revelation to Moses regarding the creation which is not found in other versions. It says: "I am the beginning and the end; the Almighty God. By my only Begotten, I created these things" (Gen. 1: 2). This truth was confirmed in the experience of John, who was perhaps nearest to the Master of any of the apostolic circle, and who probably achieved a more mature understanding of Jesus than any of his compeers. John tells us: "All things were made by him; and without him was not anything made that was made" (John 1: 3). Paul, too, had this same testimony and wrote to the Colossian saints: "By him were all things created that are in heaven, and that are in earth, visible and invisible, whether they be thrones or dominions, or principalities or powers; all things were created by him and for him: and he is before all things, and by him all things consist."—Col. 1: 16, 17.

The inspiration of Joseph Smith confirms the testimony of these other men of vision. One hundred years ago he added his testimony that the light of Christ "is in all things" and "giveth life to all things" and "is the law by which all things are governed" (Doctrine and Covenants 85: 2, 3).

The testimony of these inspired men therefore places Christ at the center of the living universe and confirms the testimony of the scientists that the creation of the world was not a purely mechanical process, like making a tool or building a house, but was more like the planting of a beautiful garden for the enjoyment of loved ones. The Gardener was an expert who knew well the laws of effective horticulture, but who worked for the joy of creation and brought to each task a vision of our need and of our satisfaction in his work. This Gardener, we verily believe, is still cultivating his garden. Its laws are such as will best advance the eternal happiness and dominion of those who live in this garden for a time, and in an ever-finer garden for eternity.

Study Outlines

God Created the World Through His Son

Lesson Purpose

To show that the universe is friendly, and that the laws of life are means through which God blesses us.

High Points of the Lesson

Jesus loved us both when he was creating our world and also when he was suffering for our sake. We may therefore expect to find the universe friendly to the activities of good people.

He who created the universe is still at work in it.

God seeks to speak to us through Nature, which derives her life from him.

Questions and Discussion Topics

(1) What is the teaching of the Scriptures regarding the origin of the earth? Regarding its destiny?

(2) Do you ever take time to listen to the voice of God in Nature? What thoughts or feelings come to you at such times? Discuss them briefly and their significance.

(3) What is the Christian faith regarding the relation of Christ to the universe? Is this confirmed in modern insight or have we grown beyond it?

(4) Do you think of creation as a finished process, or is it still going forward? Does the life of Nature still depend on God, or was Nature set at work and then left to itself? Is God still involved in Nature?

(5) How does God feel about the work of Burbank and other men who specialize in improving the types and qualities of fruit, vegetables, etc.? Is it possible that the world is incomplete just so that we can help to improve it, and to grow thereby? Discuss this briefly.

(6) Wordsworth and other great poets have felt that all living things should be dear to men because they are dear to God. What value does this thought have for us today?

(7) The universe functions in harmony with certain laws which await our discovery. Does the reign of law limit our freedom? Discuss this briefly.

(8) Does it sound reasonable to think of the earth as the "habitation of the righteous"? Why?

What the Lesson Means Today

We can co-operate with God in developing new fruits and flowers, and in creating a new manhood. The basic necessities are already available.

There is no essential conflict between the biologist, the zoologist, etc., and the theologian.

That which is governed by law is also preserved by law. (Doctrine and Covenants 85:8.)

Chapter III

GOD SEEKS TO MAKE HIMSELF KNOWN

In nature—In history—In humanity—In Jesus Christ his Son.

Lesson Six

I—REVELATION IN NATURE AND HISTORY

IF WE ARE TO THINK OF GOD AS OUR FATHER, it is inevitable that we shall also think of him as seeking to reveal himself to us, for fatherhood at its best necessarily includes communion between the father and his children. No matter how great we may become, or how far we may wander, our Heavenly Father is personally concerned about us. He wants us to love him and to keep in touch with him and, most of all, he is eager that we shall carry on the best that is in himself. All his plans and self-sacrifice are directed to this end. If, then, we are to think of God as our Father, we must also think of him as seeking us out, and as desiring that we shall know him and reach up toward his greatness.

There is a sense in which it is impossible for any living person to avoid revealing himself. All that we do betrays us. Those skilled in music recognize the artistry of Beethoven or Bach or Handel; those versed in literature know the literary characteristics of Shakespeare, Gray, Wordsworth, and Tennyson; the students of paintings can tell the work of Raphael, Burne-Jones, Sargent, and Millet. At the other end of the scale, the burglar reveals himself not only by his fingerprints, but by the manner in which he commits his crime. And between these extremes, the remainder of us are constantly identifying ourselves in a thousand ways. If we are persistently careless, unskillful, or undiscriminating, our work shows it. If we have a passion for doing things well, our work shows this also. In the same way it is inevitable that our Heavenly Father shall reveal himself in his work. For those who have eyes to see, every created thing reveals something of his nature and purpose.

As we come to know our Heavenly Father, we feel that not only is he revealed in his work, but that he wants us to find him there. He planned life that way. Blame for our failure to know him does not lie with him but with us, that we are so "slow of understanding." Either we pass by the evidences of God at work and give no heed to them, or we become so engrossed in the thing created that we give no heed to the Creator. If we do not exert ourselves to see the truth that lies behind the appearance of things, we miss our chance to learn the great lessons of life, lessons which have to do with Truth, Beauty, Goodness, and with the nature of God himself.

What has already been written may have helped to clarify this fundamentally important fact: divine revelation to man involves both divine disclosure and human understanding. No matter to what pains our Heavenly Father may go in order to make himself known to his children, there is no true revelation until his self-disclosure is matched by sufficient insight on the part of those who see him at work for them to know something about who he is and what is going on.

Moreover, since whatever our Father does is permeated at every stage by the love which is the very essence of his being, we never truly understand any situation in which he is involved except as we sense this overflowing affection. To believe other than this is to believe that we can know the glory that is motherhood by watching mothers at work without looking into their hearts and knowing what makes them eager to serve without thought of reward.

And again, since "love" is just a word and has no meaning except among those who have known love in experience, there can be no true revelation except to those whose own lives point the way to understanding. The more we are like God, the more readily he can make himself known to us. The less we are like him, the more difficult it is for him to really communicate with us.

Here is the crux of the problem of divine revelation. If he is to make himself known to us, so that we can see and feel and understand, our Heavenly Father must work in us as well as around us. He must give us ears to hear and eyes to see and hearts to share.

One of the pathways along which God leads us to himself is the pathway of nature. The beauty, order, and creative artistry evident in the world around us leads those of us who are alert to an increased appreciation and understanding of him who created such wonders. The poets often express this thought in their work:

> To me the meanest flower that blows can give
> Thoughts that do often lie too deep for tears.

And:

No flowing mountain curve, no sound of wood or water, no delicately tinted cloud, no march of stars nor order of the seasons which does not speak of him.

The inanimate world is alive with movement co-ordinated in marvelous design and obedient to exact mathematical laws, and this beauty and symmetry is copied and elaborated in flower and tree and brought to still higher perfection in animal life. It is impossible to believe that all this has happened by chance, or that we are deceived when this combined beauty and order stirs us both to admiration and to awe. To believe that nature can thus organize itself without the aid of some guiding intelligence is about as reasonable as to believe that a table of printers' type, scattered on the floor, could set itself by accident into the lines

[40]

of Shakespeare's *Macbeth* or Francis Thompson's *Hound of Heaven,* or that a tray of multi-colored paints upset on a clean canvas would run together to form the inscrutable smile of the *Mona Lisa.* No, the most reasonable explanation of the beauty and order of the animate and inanimate world, in which things answer the end of their creation and grow according to the laws of their being, is that these are directed by both intelligence and love.

Wise men of the past have been deeply conscious of God when in the presence of Nature, and have left us many inspiring records of the influence of Nature in turning their thoughts to God. But this word of Jesus is even more illuminating:

Why take ye thought for raiment? Consider the lilies of the field, how they grow; they toil not, neither do they spin: And yet I say unto you, That even Solomon in all his glory was not arrayed like one of these. Wherefore, if God so clothe the grass of the field, which today is, and tomorrow is cast into the oven, shall he not much more clothe you, O ye of little faith?—Matt. 6: 28-30.

The outburst of flowers in the spring of Palestine is uncertain and short-lived. The poppies, daisies, and anemones, and the fresh green of the grass have disappeared before the end of May; so that their transient season might well suggest the obvious parallel of the brevity of human life. Yet Jesus draws a far truer parallel than this. The flowers cover the face of the arid desert every year and are very soon withered, yet God thinks it worth-while to make them beautiful and to set in operation laws which make for their continued preservation. Will he do less for us? Does not their existence reveal his creative genius, and does not his care for them justify us in anticipating an even greater care for us?

The revelation of God in nature is not forced on us, but is available to all who look beyond its beauty and order to its cause and meaning. The Hebrews have sung for generations, "The heavens declare the glory of God and the firmament showeth his handiwork." But it has remained for men in comparatively recent times to discover how fully the creative love of God has been preparing for our happiness and progress. Long before we were born, our Heavenly Father laid down the forests wherein he stored light and heat for our present use. He has left his mark on the rocks and the hills, in the starry heavens and in the waters of the deep, that we, following after, might come to know him.

Our Heavenly Father is also seeking to draw us to him by revealing himself in the lessons of history. The Jews saw this very clearly. The inspiration of the Book of Judges, and of the history of the kings of Israel and Judah, does not consist in the dates and facts recorded, but in their vivid portrayal of the way of God with the people of Israel—how he challenged them with a great task, judged them for their many disloyalties, rebuked and punished them for their sins and so prepared them to become his messengers to the nations.

Among the New Testament writers, the same sense of God at work in history is clearly apparent. Matthew makes this very clear in his Gospel, and the same conviction is apparent both in Luke's Gospel and in his story of the Acts of the Apostles. Paul had an even broader understanding than his fellow ministers; he reminded the Athenians that God "is not far from any one of us," and that when properly understood, their own history would bear testimony of God even as did the history of Israel.

Today, there is for men of discernment a revelation of the nature of God in the life story of every nation. If some modern historian should express this for us as the Biblical writers did for their day, we would be amazed at the similarity between our record and theirs. And the coming of such an inspired genius is not impossible; for we have already begun to return to the Hebrew point of view, that the great men of history are not the warriors or the kings, but the prophets. Such men as Wesley, Luther, and Joseph Smith have been greater factors in shaping our destinies than a dozen Napoleons.

This, after all, was to be expected. We see in the Bible a constant breaking down of old barriers as the prophets enlarge the thought of the people, and the people respond to the vision and teaching of the prophets. Even though no one has yet written our story, we cannot believe that this movement of God among men stopped when the last of the ancient prophets died. There is a connection between the hatred of injustice which they inspired and our own resentment of current inequalities between man and man. The stirrings of our social consciences are akin to theirs.

If a progressive movement in the curriculum of a high school indicates intelligent and affectionate guidance for our young people, then does not the progessive movement of history and the gradual unfolding of man's understanding, indicate love that would not be denied, patience that could wait through all the years, intelligence to plan, and those other personal characteristics which Nature and Revelation join to tell us belong to God?

Study Outlines

Revelation in Nature and History

Lesson Purpose

To show that God is constantly seeking to make himself known in nature and in history.

High Points of the Lesson

To deny that God seeks to make himself known to us is to deny either his power or his love or both.

Our Heavenly Father uses the appeal of beauty as well as the appeals of truth and of goodness.

The revelation of God in nature is all around us, but is not forced on us. It is available, but we must be of a mind and heart to receive it.

The history of Israel discloses the unfolding of the purpose of God through many generations. The explanation of such growth does not lie in chance, or even in the character of the Hebrew people; but in the character of God, who made them and who inspired their prophets.

Questions and Discussion Topics

(1) What are the characteristics of a good father? From consideration of these characteristics do you think it is like God to reveal himself to his children? Discuss this briefly.

(2) "The works of God reveal him." What does this mean? Is it true?

(3) What lessons does Nature teach us about God?

(4) What may the poet and the painter and the musician each do to help us understand and know God?

(5) What is the spiritual significance of the historical books of the Old Testament and of the Book of Mormon? Discuss this briefly.

(6) What lesson is God seeking to teach humanity through the American people? Through the Russians? Through men of science? Can we learn any spiritual lessons from ungodly people?

(7) What lessons does history teach about God?

(8) Looking at history from the point of view of God, who are the great men and women of the ages? Why? Name some modern men and women, not members of this church, who are being used by God.

What the Lesson Means Today

The unobservant man is shutting his eyes to the glory of God and his ears to the voice of God.

The Saints should be a cultured and grateful people. To fail to praise God for beauty is to miss half its value.

Our Father is seeking to reveal himself in the life of his kingdom. We may aid or impede that revelation.

Lesson Seven

II—REVELATION IN THE PROPHETS AND IN JESUS

WHILE OUR HEAVENLY FATHER has been eager to reveal himself in nature and in history, he has been even more fully made known in the lives of men. How much of the Bible would be left if we should take out the names and the deeds of the great adventurers who sought God and found him—Abraham, Moses, Daniel, Amos, John, Paul, and Jesus the Master of them all. All through history, it has been men and women who, having found God in their own lives, have been the means in his hands of spreading his story to their fellow men. These people have felt a sense of commission, an inner compulsion, which was part of their best selves. Both their words and their lives conveyed their message. So Paul said: "It pleased God . . . . to reveal his Son *in* me."—Gal. 1: 15, 16.

This revelation through human personality is very helpful indeed, but it is never complete. Always it points to something greater. The story of Hosea gives us a touching illustration of this. Hosea was a younger contemporary of Amos. He was deeply devoted to his wife, Gomer, but the happiness of their home was "as a morning cloud, as the dew that passes early away," for Gomer was not true to him. Yet he could not put her away, tear her out of his heart, and start life anew with someone else. His love went too deep for any such cheap solution. Then, in the midst of his pain, Hosea began to understand the quality of the love of God for Israel, a love that would not let Israel go in spite of all her wandering. Presently Hosea's home broke up altogether, but his love for Gomer did not die. She was sold in the market, but he redeemed her at great cost and sought to so change her life that they might yet be all that he had hoped to one another. "This," he then told his countrymen, "is what God is doing for Israel. He loves us.

He will chasten us according to our needs. He will seek to make us fit to occupy a place at his side. He will not let us go."

Through joy and sorrow, through achievement and disillusionment, and through the interpretation of these experiences under the guidance of the Holy Spirit, men have thus come to realize more and more clearly what God must be like. And the finer the man, the surer he is that God must be infinitely greater than he. No concept of God that does not exceed our own personalities will satisfy us, not even the dream of our best selves cleansed of all impurities will do. The God that true men will worship must be all that our best leaders have been, plus something more.

It is the glory of the Hebrew prophets that even before the coming of Jesus they realized that any adequate revelation of the nature and purpose of God must be expressed in life. Under the inspiration of the Holy Spirit, these men of old prophesied the time when the Son of God should stand forth unmarred by sin and unhampered by willfulness, to make known the loving purpose of his Father. As the significance of the prophecies became more clear, expectation grew, and the Jewish people looked forward eagerly to the coming of a Messiah who would love righteousness and hate iniquity, who would embody in his own person what words cannot say about God himself.

It is Christian belief that the expectations of the great prophets of Israel have been fully realized, and that in the person of Jesus Christ, God has lived among men and disclosed himself to us. It is our faith, moreover, that this revelation was planned before the foundation of the world. It was no afterthought; but is the very heart of the movement of God for our redemption, and was his intention from the beginning (John 1: 1ff.).

The life of Jesus was not an argument but a demonstration; it forever lifted Christianity above the plane of mere philosophizing and brought it into the realm of demonstrable facts. His life and message have revealed God to us in terms that all who love him can understand.

Jesus came into the world in order to make his Father known to men. He could do this better than anyone else, for he was his Father's Son. But it would have been useless for him to attempt this task unless he had been akin to us, as well as to his Father, for such a revelation as this searches the very soul of a man. Here, as elsewhere, the teacher and the learner must have a great deal in common. For these reasons and for many others, he who was the Son of God accepted the limitations of our humanity and became one of us.

For morally earnest men, Jesus stands as the living answer to all questions about God. We would not have dreamed that God could be so kind, so generous, and so completely devoted to our welfare if we had not come to know him in the person of his Son. But now that Jesus has made his Father known, we can progressively verify the truth of this revelation by living as if we knew it to be true and finding confirmation in our experience. Certainty of God which is won in this fashion is superior to every doubt. When once our eyes have been opened, the knowledge of God which we have achieved in Jesus Christ becomes the most precious fact of our experience.

The revelation of God in Christ is infinitely greater than we are able to apprehend. This should not discourage us. We are constantly discovering that we do not know even our best friends as well as we thought we did, but what we do know of them makes us eager to know more. In like manner we do not yet understand God as he is disclosed to us in the person of Jesus Christ. But what we already know promises that the further stages of our journey will lead us into new continents of experience with God, where we shall find delights we never knew before.

The word of God which came to us by the voice of the

prophets is made luminous and clear in the life of Jesus Christ. We thank God that his word was thus "made flesh and dwelt among us." Christ was in the world from the beginning. He constantly revealed more of his nature and his love in nature and history and in the lives of good men until, in the meridian of time, the process culminated in the highest revelation that we can receive, and the Son of God took on himself the tabernacle of humanity so that his life might become the light of all mankind.

Study Outlines

Revelation in the Prophets and in Jesus

Lesson Purpose

To show that the greatest revelation of good is not in words, but in life. To set forth Jesus as the final answer to all our questions about God.

High Points of the Lesson

To know God is infinitely more than to know something about him. Our Heavenly Father can therefore reveal himself more fully in the lives of men than in Nature, in good men than in bad men, and in Jesus than in the prophets.

Through his freedom from sin and his perfect obedience, Jesus has become the perfect channel of divine revelation.

There is no need to debate the distinction between God and Christ. Those who truly see the Master see the Father.

Questions and Discussion Topics

(1) What is the difference between revelation and the record of revelation?

(2) In what ways did God make himself known to the prophets? What handicaps confronted our Heavenly Father in revealing himself through them?

(3) What was the central message of the prophets of Israel? In what way was their message of the nature of God related to the needs of their times?

(4) Why could no one but Jesus show us what God is truly like? Discuss this briefly.

(5) What persons are best qualified to understand the revelation of God in Jesus Christ? Why?

(6) What did Jesus mean when he said, "I am the Way, the Truth, and the Life: no man cometh unto the Father but by me"? Is this still true? Will it ever cease to be true? Why?

(7) How do we come to know our friends most intimately? What light does this throw on the best way to get to know Jesus?

(8) What has the life of Jesus taught you about God? What are the characteristics of the Father which you believe because you know the Son?

What the Lesson Means Today

We can learn much about God from studying the Scriptures, but we must read the Scriptures in the light of our knowledge of people, so as to learn to apply their lessons in daily life.

Our richest understanding of God will come from personal communion with him through Jesus Christ, his Son. This communion can be achieved through meditation and prayer, but these must be augmented by activity along lines which he approves.

Our enriched understanding of Divinity must be checked repeatedly with the life of Jesus.

Chapter IV

JESUS CHRIST OUR LORD

Revealed God in the flesh—He ministered among men —He rose from the dead—He will come again.

Lesson Eight

I—THE INCARNATION

THE MORE WE KNOW of God the less likely we are to believe that he waited for a good man to come along so that this man could be adopted as his Son. Such a procedure is not like him. Our salvation was not an afterthought, it was in the mind and heart of God from the beginning. At the very center of the plan of salvation stands One who is close enough to God to be his special messenger, revealing him to humanity in word and in deed, saving men from their sins and leading them back from their many wanderings and into the presence of God. None but the Son of God could do this.

The Christian faith is that in the meridian of time the Son of God became also a man and lived among men, subject to all the limitations of humanity except sin. He had a body of flesh, blood, and bones as we have. He became hungry and needed to eat; he became tired and needed rest. He felt the same emotional strains and uplifts that we feel, and he sympathized with those in sorrow and rejoiced with those who were happy. He cultivated friendships and in the crucial moments of his life depended on his friends just as we do. He grew in understanding, and "learned by the things he suffered," continuing from strength to strength until he received the fullness of the glory of God. When the end came, he shrank from the pain of death, even as other men do, and endured it only because he was resolved to do the will of his Father.

There is a sense in which we may say that Jesus lived the only normal human life ever lived. What is it to be a real man or a real woman? We look around us and within and see a most confusing mixture of goodness and badness, of strength and weakness, of purity and uncleanness, of justice and of partiality. Shall we take Moses or Socrates or Cæsar or Bacon or Newton or Lincoln as our standard? No! Great as these men were, not one of them will do. What we need is a Supreme example. By living among us, and in our life, Jesus has raised just such a perfect standard. It is so pure and so challenging that it forces comparisons between what we are and what we might be. No thoughtful man who is seeking to meet the demands of life in his own personality can ignore this challenge; and when we face it, we see that sin is not truly part of life, but is life beset by corruption.

In spite of the lovable qualities of many good men whom we know, we must admit that their goodness is not vigorous enough to guarantee real brotherhood and peace. Only goodness like that of Jesus can do this. If we were like him, then the problems of human relationships would be solved. But this is just another way of saying that if God lived in us, as he did in Jesus, we would live together in righteousness. So it is that we join with the apostle in his prophecy and his hope, "Beloved, now are we the sons of God: and it doth not yet appear what we shall be: but we know that when he shall appear we shall be like him."—I John 3: 2.

Jesus became man in order that he might teach us about God. If we are to acquire any knowledge of God, it must be in our own ways of thinking and acting. We can only learn a language by finding out what the words of that language mean in our own tongue. We keep a dictionary near us and look up word after word until our expertness grows and our references become less and less frequent.

By this time we have become our own dictionaries, for we have a knowledge of the language within ourselves. In seeking to teach us of himself, our Heavenly Father makes a great effort to induce us to follow a course similar to this. He has given us a great reference to whom we can turn whenever we lack understanding. Jesus Christ is this great reference. As Jesus becomes part of our lives, the mind of Christ dwells in us, and we see life more and more truly; we grow steadily in understanding of the divine purposes. In time, this knowledge becomes a part of us and is incorporated into our very selves.

In Jesus Christ, therefore, we see God in terms of our own experience. There is also a sense in which we may say that in Jesus Christ God sees us in terms of his experience. We should say this reverently, but I think that we should also say it with great joy. Here, from within the life of the man Jesus, God looks out on human life as a man does, and sees and knows this life as one in the process of living it. He can no more be regarded as a distant king who has commanded our obedience, but is to be known as one who is involved in the very process of things. It seems to me that this is of fundamental importance to our faith. Since Jesus has lived the life of man, he has removed the only barrier that made it difficult for us to realize that God knows life as we know it.

Every parent who has been told, "You do not understand us, we are young," knows what a barrier this feeling can create between parents and children. No true disciple ever feels this way about God. Our Heavenly Father does understand. His own life is directly and intimately bound up in that of his Son. This Son, his only Son, once lived among us, bruised by men and circumstances, and betrayed as we are sometimes betrayed. Yet this Son of God lived among men as God wants men to live among each other. God, therefore, knows through his Son both our temptations and our possibilities.

The Incarnation, then, is a fact of tremendous significance to everyone of us. By it God has come near to every man and has shown every man something of his own best possibilities. For example, since the time of Jesus, no man has had to falter at the idea of his own body becoming the temple of God. No Christian can regard his body as something to be whipped and punished in order to "mortify the flesh." It was in such a body that God made himself most fully known to humanity.

Study Outlines

The Incarnation

Lesson Purpose

To discuss the significance of the incarnation of Jesus for today.

High Points of the Lesson

Jesus is the Son of God. He took on himself a human body in order that he might thereby teach us what God is like, and, particularly, how much God loves us.

Jesus became a man, but lived like God. He has shown us that it is possible to live without sin, to love in spite of hate, to be great in spite of poverty, to conquer the world through faith.

Questions and Discussion Topics

(1) What reasons can you give for our belief that Jesus existed with his Father from eternity?

(2) Why were holy men of old eager for the coming of Jesus?

(3) What difference does it make whether Jesus was a good man whom God chose to deliver his message, or whether he is in fact the Son of God?

(4) Why could not God be revealed completely in the lives of the prophets?

(5) State in your own words what we mean when we say that Jesus is God in the flesh? Why was it necessary for him to live among us and with a body like ours?

(6) What is the best picture we have of real manhood? Name some of the highest characteristics of genuine manhood. What leadership has Jesus given us in developing these characteristics?

(7) You have a friend who is the victim of a bad habit. He is trying to give it up, but says that it is too much for him, and that he does not believe it is possible for a man really to be like God. What would you say to him?

(8) What assurance does the Incarnation give us that God understands our point of view?

What the Lesson Means Today

Since Jesus lived on earth, God knows how it feels to be a man. We could not possibly have more sympathetic understanding than this involves.

Every one of us is tempted to think too much or too little of his body. Jesus achieved a perfect balance between body and spirit. Effective Christianity consists in achieving a similar balance.

God is seeking to become incarnate in us, to dwell in our lives so that we shall become more truly his children. The major difference between what we are and what he desires us to be lies in the spirit that dwells in us.

Lesson Nine

II—THE EARTHLY MINISTRY OF JESUS

WE CANNOT PAINT here a picture of the childhood, youth, and early manhood of Jesus. Nor could we do such a theme full justice from the meager materials supplied in the Gospels. But it is certain that in spite of the preoccupation of the gospel writers with other things, and their consequent failure to include so much that we wish we knew, these years of preparation were very significant indeed. When Jesus began his ministry, he did so after rich and full years of growth in wisdom and stature through the joys and disciplines of daily life.

The Jesus who entered upon his public work near the end of the ministry of John the Baptist was known to many of those with whom he must labor. For example, two of his friends were about to be married, and invited him to be an honored guest at the wedding feast (John 2: 2). It is quite possible that they knew a great deal about Jesus and liked him, and that so long as he was regarded as one of themselves he was popularly accepted. But when the very qualities which had made them admire him led Jesus beyond the limitations of their understanding, these erstwhile friends were forced to recognize his greatness or to deny him as a blasphemer. With a human contrariness which we can readily understand, they turned their backs on all that they had previously known of Jesus. We can almost hear them talking among themselves, "Can any good come from this man? He is just one of us. He built our house and worked for us like any other carpenter; yet he comes to us now and pretends that he is a prophet; that he is the Messiah that shall come."

If Jesus had been content to minister to his contemporaries as a local spiritual leader, or even as a successor to the prophets, he might have been accepted. But from the beginning his ministry sounded a note of authority and of challenge which caused men to react sharply for or against his message. It was impossible to be neutral where Jesus was involved. Without a very great stretch of the imagination, one can see why the Pharisees and Sadducees resented what they regarded as extreme positions taken by the young radical. Yet the fact that his ministry was exercised in kindly gentleness, that it was accompanied by many manifestations of healing power, and that Jesus made such a strong appeal to the scriptures and to their own good sense, gradually broke down the wall of amazed bewilderment and prepared many of the common people to accept his message. His ministry began with men asking, "Can any good come out of Nazareth?" It ended with Thomas, the doubter, on his knees crying, "My Lord, and my God!"

Even the men who recognized that the message of Jesus was a threat to their entrenched interests, both theological and material, were aware of his ability. From time to time they tried to trap him when he was teaching the people; always he was more than a match for them. The disciples, however, soon became conscious that he possessed more than mere ability. They found spiritual depth far greater than they had ever known before. His words were not just ideas, they sounded unfathomed riches of understanding and devotion. He was in touch with inexhaustible resources of spiritual energy. They talked among themselves about him and questioned him personally. They brought their successes and failures to him. The more completely they were devoted to him, the more satisfying was the life that they lived with him. Sometimes it was difficult, and they were harassed by doubts; still he held them. As Peter put it, "Lord, to whom shall we go? Thou hast the words of eternal life. And we believe and are sure that thou art the Christ, the Son of the living God."—John 6: 68, 69.

Jesus was truly and fully human. But Jesus was also more than man. He spoke to the men of his time and to all succeeding times with unique authority. In the first three Gospels there are more than thirty references to his unique relationship to God. Jesus believed and stated that he shared the work of the Father during the ages of creation, that he was for men the Way, the Truth, and the Life; and that for his life to dwell in them is the only means of salvation for humanity. John reports him as saying, "He that hath seen me hath seen the Father," "I am the bread of life . . . . he that eateth this bread shall live forever," "I am the light of the world," and "I am the resurrection and the life, he that believeth in me, though he were dead, yet shall he live."

Such claims as these would be the worst possible egotism if they were not supported by a quality of life which was in some way entirely different from the life of the rest of humanity. But the Master's claims were supported by just such a fullness of life. He was different in that he went beyond anything that men have achieved. No man convicted him of sin at any time, and his teachings have never been surpassed in beauty or in spiritual challenge. But his true distinctiveness lies in the matching of precept and example. When prophets and apostles have shared their vision and delivered their message, they must still point beyond themselves. They are witnesses and recorders; but their work is always minimized by the shortcomings of their own lives. This is not so with Jesus Christ. God was revealed in what he was, as well as in what he did, in what he suffered, as well as in what he taught.

The truly divine authority of Jesus is illustrated in his clear perception of truth. Other men might fuss about ceremonial cleansing and about details of Sabbath observance, forgetting the larger principles at issue, but Jesus never did. Smaller men might be blinded by tradition, so as to be unable to see realities, but the Master never was. Commonplace men might be diverted from the joy of living by a too great concern for the minutæ of the law, or from understanding a friend's motives because of too great preoccupation with his acts, but in such vital matters the wisdom of the Lord Jesus never faltered. It was consideration of such facts as these that inspired Robert Browning to write:

> All the world's coarse thumb
> And finger failed to plumb,
> So passed in making up the main account;
> All instinct immature,
> All purposes unsure,
> That weighed not as his work, yet swelled the man's amount:
> Thought hardly to be packed
> Into a narrow act,
> Fancies that broke through language and escaped,
> All I could ever be,
> All men ignored in me,
> This, I was worth to God, whose wheel the pitcher shaped.
> —Rabbi Ben Ezra.

The unique spiritual stature of Jesus is further indicated by his habit of appealing to the best possibilities of humanity. He dealt in maximums, not in minimums, declaring that the righteousness of his disciples must exceed that of the scribes and Pharisees. Those who follow him must go the second mile whenever necessary; they must keep not only the law but they must do so in a spirit of good sportsman ship. Grace must be added to truth, and Christians must do right graciously and not awkwardly. Jesus had no patience with those who wanted to "get by." He set before his followers difficult tasks which would require moral and spiritual excellence to perform. He lived the abundant life, and called for his followers to give good measure, pressed down, shaken together, and running over. He was two thousand years ahead of modern businessmen in emphasizing the importance of good will, mutual helpfulness, brotherhood.

The superlative moral excellence of Jesus is demonstrated

in his reiterated appeal from external rewards to the consequences involved in right doing. He showed how our Heavenly Father blesses both the just and the unjust, and helped those near to him to see that what a man gets for following the prescribed course of action is not so important as what he becomes in following that course of action. He told the parable of the talents and impressed on his disciples the thought that the reward of faithful service is a further opportunity to serve. So, the great reward of the kingdom-builder is the kingdom itself. Similarly, the persistent question of the true disciple is not, "What shall I get?" but "What shall I become?" The Master was concerned about personality and its growth, both individually and within the kingdom.

We are suffering today from ills which are strangely akin to those which beset the world which Jesus knew as a man. We are confronted by a wholesale disregard of law and order, an alarming uncertainty regarding the principles of right doing, a terrifying abandonment of long-held beliefs and conventions in the field of common morality, a careless contempt for yesterday's institutions, unaccompanied by any sure word of truth on which new institutions can be built. In such a world as this we are in desperate need of just such a leader as Jesus. And it is not impossible to have such leadership today. All that we need to do today is to accept him and become his loyal followers.

In the desperate business of fighting through to a world safe for democracy and worthy for heroes to live in, we shall find that Jesus is still a dependable factor. There is no figure in human history which signifies more than Jesus. If the snap judgment of his contemporaries had been adequate, Jesus would have been a figure of antiquity by this time. If the restricted understanding of his early followers had been any measure of the lordship and power of Jesus, the march of time would have passed him by. If he had come with merely intellectual brilliance to recommend him, he would have been numbered with the great philosophers of the world, and nothing more. But because Jesus is the Son of God, who through his perfect life gave new meaning to home, life, work, friendship, and pain, Jesus lives and reigns with an authority which grows stronger as men come to know him better.

Study Outlines

The Earthly Ministry of Jesus

Lesson Purpose

To present a picture of Jesus at work among men; to show the relation between his life and his ministry; and to emphasize his right to lead us.

High Points of the Lesson

Jesus spoke directly to the hearts of men because he knew men and loved them and they felt it.

Jesus considered all the common appeals of his time: the appeal of tradition, of law, of reputation, of caution, of cupidity. He lifted them all to a higher plane.

Jesus is still a dependable factor in the business of building a better world.

Questions and Discussion Topics

(1) Discuss, briefly, the childhood of Jesus. What bearing did his childhood have on his ministry?

(2) What do you think was the outstanding characteristic of the work of Jesus the carpenter? What effect did his years as a carpenter have on his subsequent ministry?

(3) Why did the people of his home town reject the ministry of Jesus? Was it not a perfectly natural thing to do? How do we compare with them in this respect? What do you suggest we might do so as to avoid blindness like theirs?

(4) What do we mean by authority? In what sense was Jesus an authority?

(5) What is the value of tradition? What is its weakness? What attitude should we adopt toward tradition?

(6) Why is it so very important that our hearts shall be right with God, and our thoughts clean and kind? What may we do to raise the tone of our inner life?.

(7) A man was found doing something rather questionable. In self-defense he stated, "If I never do any worse than that I shall be all right." Discuss this attitude briefly. What are its dangers?

(8) What would happen if Jesus came to your town? What would he resent most bitterly? What is your attitude toward these things?

What the Lesson Means Today

We never have to wait to grow up in order to live. Each age has its own joys and opportunities, and fullness of life at any one stage of life is the best possible preparation for fullness of life at a later stage.

Jesus brought to bear on commonplace things and commonplace ways of living a new spirit, a new power, and a new point of view. He has thereby shown us how we may live so that life need never be commonplace again.

We learn to be stable and yet progressive, to find peace in the midst of disaster, as we put the first value on first things. We can best learn to do this by living with Jesus.

Lesson Ten

III—JESUS ROSE FROM THE DEAD

Jesus Christ Our Lord

LIFE HOLDS NO MORE BITTER EXPERIENCE than that which was shared by the disciples at Calvary. Some of their expectations were worthy of them and of their great leader—all their fine ambitions for learning the truth, for telling the message, and for healing the nations. Some of their other expectations were totally unworthy. Among the latter were their personal ambitions for prominent places in the kingdom, for dominance over their enemies, and for accomplishing their spiritual ends by fearsome displays of power. All of these high hopes, the good and bad alike, died with Jesus. It is no wonder that Peter resigned himself and said, "I go a fishing," and that the others replied, "We also go with thee."

To men in such dire straits, the news of the Resurrection seemed almost too good to be true. Then, as they became sure, their whole perspective shifted. Pain, suffering, and death, which before had loomed so large in their experience, became incidental; and so also did worldly fame and honors, because Jesus Christ had triumphed over all of these. The timidity and fear which had hampered the disciples until now seemed inexplicable. Once it had happened, the Resurrection seemed the only thing that could have happened. Once they had been reunited with Jesus in his glorious victory over his enemies and death it seemed that this was what the whole world had waited for.

Once they knew it was true, moreover, the Resurrection seemed to his followers to be an experience for which Christ was peculiarly fitted. It was not just the mark of a victory over death, but also the seal of the victory over life which had already been won. As they looked back with newly-opened eyes, they felt that the Resurrection was really guaranteed at Calvary, for every creative act of righteousness and every triumph over temptation had served to make sure that this would ultimately come to pass. Resurrection is the natural result of the way of living demonstrated by Christ.

The evidence of the Resurrection is overwhelming. In the Gospels we made the acquaintance of men who were to become the leaders of the church after the Ascension of Jesus. But when we met these leaders in the Acts of the Apostles, they were not the same men. They had been transformed in temper, in faith, and in spirit. At Calvary they had all the facts of the Christian message except the central fact of the Resurrection, and yet they deserted their Master. After Easter they followed him to the ends of the earth. The explanation lies in the Resurrection. No other explanation which will adequately explain the miraculous change in these men has ever been offered.

The ministry of Paul began after the death of his Master, yet he received divine assurance of the Resurrection and made it the very heart of his message. To him this was the major evidence that the Son of God had indeed dwelt among men as a man. Without hesitation, and yet with an unfailing sense of wonder, he bore testimony everywhere that Jesus had indeed risen from the dead. As Lord Lyttleton has stated, "Nothing else and nothing less than the real Resurrection of Jesus supplies an adequate cause for such a psychological phenomenon as the facts of his case present." Paul was a man of deep convictions, eager to know the truth and willing to follow wherever it might lead. His conversion to Christianity cost him everything which he had previously held dear. It meant denunciation of the law of which he had been such an able exponent. It meant proclaiming his own blindness publicly. It meant admitting his guilt in the death of Stephen. But he counted all these as nothing beside the one outstanding fact: Jesus, who was dead, has set the seal upon his divinity by his victory over death.

The gospel of the Resurrection was first preached in Jerusalem, in the very place where the Crucifixion had taken place. At once, and on the spot, the very men who so recently had been bewildered, fearful, brokenhearted, and hopeless now stood clear-minded and of good courage, setting forth the fact of the Resurrection in such a way as to confound the leaders of their nation. This does not sound like fraud. When men who have lost hope are suddenly transformed and stand up together with such power of conviction that their adversaries are confounded and they themselves are committed to a life of witnessing from which they never turn away, some explanation must be found. The New Testament narrative gives this explanation: It is the transforming effect of the Resurrection.

The apostolic campaign of testimony spread like fire. There were two major reasons for this. The first of these is that so many people knew the facts and the second is that they *acted* as though they knew. The witnesses included "all the disciples" (Acts 9: 4, 5), several of the women, five hundred of the brethren who saw Jesus at the same time, and last, but not least, the Apostle Paul (I Cor. 15: 3-8). Their influence was so deeply felt that when Paul wrote to the saints in Thessalonica, Galatia, and Rome, he is able to assume in each of these letters that the Resurrection of Jesus is accepted as true. This, once again, does not sound like fraud. It is the kind of appeal made by a man who is sure of his ground. Many of the people whom he called on as witnesses were still living. Their testimony was available, and the fact that Paul relied on it so confidently is the strongest presumptive evidence that it was favorable.

There has been a disposition in some quarters to discredit the testimony of the New Testament writers on the ground that they were not skilled in observation and were victims of the superstitions current in their time. This objection will not stand in view of the available facts. But, as if to still any possible doubt, Latter Day Saints have the testimony of an experience received jointly by Joseph Smith and Sidney Rigdon during a period of remarkable spiritual insight. In recording this experience, they say:

> And, now, after the many testimonies which have been given of him, this is the testimony, last of all, which we give of him, that he lives; for we saw him, even on the right hand of God; and we heard the voice bearing record that he is the Only Begotten of the Father.—Doctrine and Covenants 76: 3.

When we declare that Jesus Christ rose from the dead, we are not advancing a theory or a philosophy, we are stating a fact. It is part of the record of history and as such requires explanation. The evidence is too strong to be overcome by a simple denial or by our indifference or unbelief. In a day when we are proud of our ability to face facts and to discover their meanings, it is foolish to refuse to face this stupendous fact. As we do face it and seek to explain it, we find that the Christian explanation is, after all, the most reasonable. The sudden transformation of the disciples from cowards into men of courage, the quickening of the Christian movement when everyone expected it to collapse, and the testimony of many hundreds who have received personal evidence of the Resurrection, all combine to show that the Christian explanation of the Resurrection is the true one. Once we accept this conclusion, it turns a flood of light on all that we have believed.

We are concerned in this chapter with the fact of the Resurrection of Jesus. With the principle of the Resurrection we shall deal later. What, then, is the significance of this fact? The Apostle Paul, the greatest Christian statesman of all times, regarded the Resurrection of Jesus as the final evidence of his divinity and of the supreme importance of the Christian message and movement. In line with this conviction, Paul wrote to the saints in Rome that Jesus is "declared to be the Son of God with power, according to the spirit of holiness, by the resurrection from the dead" (Rom. 1:4). And Paul's insight has been abundantly vindicated. In the Resurrection God and man came through a crucial test victoriously. Wicked men did their worst when they killed Jesus; but God moved, and the wickedness of men was set to one side. Nor was it the physical life only of Jesus that had been preserved; the Resurrection showed clearly that the wrath of his enemies cannot affect the spiritual standing of a good man. Christ Jesus survived in body and in spirit the worst that wicked men could do to him; and with his resurrection other men have the promise of victory.

Throughout history men have been "subject to bondage through fear of death" (Heb. 2:15). Jesus has shown us that there is no room for this fear. Death is an event and not an end, a gateway and not a blank wall. We may therefore reasonably begin tasks here which will require eternity to fulfill, and may love our dear ones, knowing that there is no fear of eternal separation. Death awaits all of us; but the resurrection also awaits us, and if we live worthily, we shall yet be reunited in bodily fellowship with the great company of good men and good women who have lived in the light of God from the dawn of history.

Study Outlines

Jesus Rose From the Dead

Lesson Purpose

To present the Resurrection as a fact of history and to show its significance.

High Points of the Lesson

The evidence for the Resurrection is overwhelming and has been augmented in our own time.

What men want in religion is power. The Resurrection is a demonstration of power great enough to overcome death itself.

The fact that Jesus, who loves us, has passed through the gateway of death has robbed the grave of its terror for all who put their trust in him.

Questions and Discussion Topics

(1) How did the disciples react to the news of the Resurrection?

(2) Enumerate the evidences indicating that the Resurrection of Jesus actually took place.

(3) What evidence confirming the New Testament story of the Resurrection is especially available to Latter Day Saints?

(4) An inquirer who has been discussing religion with you states that he finds religion too impractical. How does the Resurrection of Jesus help you to meet this objection?

(5) A friend objects that he cannot believe in the Resurrection "because it is so improbable." As you think about the kind of person Jesus was, and the power of God, do you think that the Resurrection is improbable? Give reasons for your answer.

(6) What difference does belief in immortality make in your way of living? What does this indicate about your faith?

(7) What have the death and Resurrection of Jesus done to enable men to die with courage and hope?

(8) What difference would elimination of faith in the Resurrection make in the appeal and power of the gospel?

Lesson Eleven

IV—JESUS WILL COME AGAIN

THE MOSQUE OF SAINT SOPHIA in Constantinople is a transformed Christian church. Many years ago all the Christian inscriptions and symbols were painted out, and Moslem inscriptions and symbols were put in their places. But E. Stanley Jones says that as he and a party of friends recently stood under the great dome, they could see the figure of Christ with hands outstretched in blessing, showing through the paint which had so long obscured it. Doctor Jones turned to a friend and said: "He is coming back. You cannot block him out. Through the obscurity and darkness of the centuries, he is coming back again. He shall yet reign. The future belongs to him."

There is a sense in which Jesus is constantly coming into his own, for as the gospel is preached more and more widely, more and more hearts are opened to receive him. The early Christians were vividly aware of the possibility of such a return as this. Paul, for example, tells us that the Lord came and stood by him when he was on trial. But in addition to such individual experiences, the early disciples eagerly expected their Master to return and reign over the righteous in a visible demonstration of his power.

The scriptural statements indicating the nature of the second coming have an impressive authority which commends them to our attention. They clearly indicate that the return of our Master will be personal and visible. Thus the disciples who watched the Ascension were told: "This same Jesus which is taken up from you into heaven, shall so come in like manner as ye see him going into heaven" (Acts 1: 11). This is readily believable when we remember that the return of Christ is part of the great movement in which he shall "make all things new" (Rev. 21: 5), and in which he will be hailed by those who have long waited for the redemption of their bodies (Rom. 8: 21, 23).

We do not know when Jesus will return, but the principle of being ready for his coming is nevertheless of evident importance. When the Hanoverian kings first sat on the throne of Great Britain, the Jacobites never ceased to labor and to sacrifice for the return of the glamorous Stuarts. They never tasted their wine without passing their glasses over the water bottle, in silent toast to "the King across the water." They never joined in song without renewing their oath of allegiance; and they pledged themselves to Bonnie Prince Charlie repeatedly. So, at last, he came. A similar longing, a similar eagerness, a similar pledging of ourselves to his cause, supported by the evidences of our sincerity, will prepare the way for the return of our King.

While the specific time for the coming of our Master is wisely hidden, reason and revelation combine to indicate that it is near at hand. We shall not look for his coming until the gospel is preached among all nations (Matt. 24: 14). But we shall look for his coming then. This great preaching task, which once looked so stupendous, is daily becoming more possible. The facilities for preaching the gospel are being multiplied. The radio, the air liner, the motion picture, the wire-photo, and similar devices are eliminating the physical handicaps of time and distance. Today "one man is as a thousand" if, with intelligent consecration, he uses the means which the new age gives for preaching the gospel and promoting the kingdom.

Simultaneously, with the extension of the gospel, we are witnessing an increase in the wickedness of the wicked. Around us the cleavage between good and evil becomes increasingly more apparent as modern knowledge and modern instruments enable wicked men to flaunt their wickedness in new and more varied fashion. In spite of our best brains and our most adroit diplomacy, the threats of war are again multiplying, and graft and licensed vice are rampant. Labor troubles are plaguing the nations, governments rise and fall over night, and these social and political convulsions are paralleled by an unprecedented increase of physical disasters—storms, earthquakes, tidal waves, drouths, and the like.

Amid these national and international upheavals, one of the most striking phenomena is the return of the Jews to their national homeland. This is no longer a dream. As all the world knows, the regathering of the Jews has taken on a new and practical urgency because of the horrible persecutions of World War II; and the work done before the war is now being hastened and enlarged with a passion which is only paralleled by the determination of their enemies that it shall not succeed. Indeed, the pressure being exerted toward the re-establishment of a Jewish homeland has forced this problem on the attention of the world and, despite all opposition, there is a growing conviction that the national aspirations of the Jews can and must be met.

These three things—the preaching of the gospel in all the world, the time of great upheaval, and the regathering of the Jews—have long been associated in prophecy with the culmination of the present age and the return of our Lord. This is an outstanding testimony to the practical significance of prophetic insight, for the convergence of the major forces of our times is in the nature of things. The inventive genius of modern men inevitably leads to chaos unless it is dominated by good will. To this our present turmoil bears striking testimony. If the Jews, with their remarkable potentialities in both practical and spiritual concerns, should ever become a people with a national homeland, this will become even more apparent. By right of their own progress, therefore, both Jew and Gentile are rapidly coming to the place where they must choose between closer co-operation with God and the organization of society apart from him. This will be the end of the age, the great occasion for the demonstration of God's power, the unique setting for the return of the King in power and great glory to rule over his Saints. For such a coming, we confidently look forward.

There are many who profess to believe in the return of Jesus, but who see little practical significance in this teaching of the church. This is in marked contrast with the Christian attitude in apostolic times. In those days, no motive was appealed to more frequently than the promise of our Lord's return. This is explained in part by the fact that many who were yet alive knew him and others had heard every detail of his life so frequently and so lovingly discussed that they felt an intimate acquaintance with him. That sense of intimate association with the Master which they had and which we lack, is what robs our religious life of much of its power.

If we were closer to the Master, it is altogether likely that we would do more for him, receive more from him, and be more sure of his return when our growth and our necessity combined to demand this return. We have made some progress since the early years of the Christian era; but loss of the sense of the personal presence of Jesus is not a sign of that progress, nor is the widespread indifference to the prophecies of his return.

Before our Lord made his first appearance among men, the way was prepared by John the Baptist, who declared that the prophecies of the Messiah were about to be fulfilled, and called on all men everywhere to repent. It is not unlike our Lord to give us similar specific guidance concerning his return. Indeed, it is part of our faith that Joseph Smith, a modern John the Baptist, came to this generation to prepare the way before the coming of the Lord. The church carries forward his work by preaching the "baptism of repentance for the remission of sins" and by calling all men to his standard. Our work is urgent. The issues involved are of universal significance. The hope of our Lord's early return must spur us to active and devoted service in preparation for his coming.

Study Outlines

Jesus Will Come Again

Lesson Purpose

To state the teaching of the church regarding the second coming and to present reasons why we should live in anticipation of the return of our Lord.

High Points of the Lesson

We confidently expect the visible return of our Lord.

The world-wide preaching of the gospel, the gathering of the Saints, the increase of knowledge and skill—all join to indicate that the day of the return of Jesus is near at hand.

Joseph Smith, like John the Baptist, was called to prepare the way for the Master. We are committed to the same task. Eagerness to prepare the way before him will prove a major incentive to righteousness.

Questions and Discussion Topics

(1) Does it seem reasonable to believe that Jesus will return to the earth? Discuss this briefly.

(2) What do the Scriptures say about how Jesus will return?

(3) What events will precede the return of our Lord? Why?

(4) In what sense is Jesus already coming again? In what similar sense are we preventing his return?

(5) Why is it better that we do not know the exact time of the second coming? Discuss this briefly.

(6) Why were the saints of apostolic times so deeply concerned regarding the return of the Lord? How might our interest in his coming be stimulated?

(7) In what way can Joseph Smith be likened to John the Baptist? In what way should the church share in the work of preparation?

(8) What is the practical result of belief in the second coming? What difference does it make to you?

What the Lesson Means Today

Jesus comes into our lives by the power of his Spirit as we learn to do his will. He thus assures us of his more permanent return when more of us do his will.

It is hard to imagine the Master's returning to share our modern life. Surely the hope of the second coming should be an incentive to build a social order wherein we may entertain our Lord without shame.

The fact of the Resurrection still stands. No philosophy which ignores this fact is true or well-balanced.

The Resurrection assures us that Christianity is much more than a philosophy. It is essentially a life of power—power stronger than evil. We are called to live in the strength of this power.

The Resurrection is the best guarantee we could possibly have of life beyond the grave, and life beyond the grave begins here.

Chapter V

THE HOLY SPIRIT

The Holy Spirit—The bestowal of the Spirit.

Lesson Twelve

I—THE HOLY SPIRIT

BEFORE JESUS DIED, he promised his disciples that a special Comforter would be sent in his place and would be to them in a spiritual sense all that he had ever been while visibly present among them. The experience of the church was that this promise was abundantly fulfilled. The disciples no longer had to seek out Jesus, and to wait their turn until he could be free to attend to their needs; instead they found the Helper and Comforter available to instruct and enlighten them according to their several needs. They were so sure of this that they felt that God himself had stooped to enter into their hearts and dwell with them, as an ever-present friend. Harriet Auber has expressed this belief in a hymn which all of us should know:

> Our blest Redeemer, ere he breathed
>   His tender, last farewell,
> A Guide, a Comforter, bequeathed
>   With us to dwell.

The promised Guide and Comforter, the Holy Spirit, is divine and shares in the work of redemption. The primary task of Jesus Christ is to reveal God to man. This revelation is, in a sense, objective. The primary task of the Holy Spirit also is to reveal God to man. But the revelation of the Holy Spirit is subjective. Just as God seeks after us in the life and ministry of his Son, so also he seeks after us in the persuasive inner ministry of his Holy Spirit, which teaches and warns and strengthens and reminds and guides. The Holy Spirit is God at work from within. Moreover, just as the incarnation of the Son of God indicates how truly God and man can be knit together, so that no one can draw a clear line of distinction between Divinity and humanity, so also the indwelling of the Holy Spirit in the inner life of a man is such that no one can say what inner propulsion is divine and what is human. At his very best man thinks and feels and acts like God. He is at his best when the Spirit of God has untrammeled sway within him. By the miracle of the divine indwelling, the birth of the Spirit, the influence of Divinity can be as strongly felt in the life of a man as the influence of that man's own father. This does not mean that the personality of the twice-born man is stultified, but that it is enriched. There is no violation of his agency because he rejoices in his sonship.

A great amount of time and thought have been spent in attempts to discriminate between the Father, the Son, and the Holy Spirit. No sincere and earnest study of the mystery of Divinity should ever be disparaged; but it is unfortunate when logic is given a place which rightfully belongs to experience. Our logic is so tragically earth-bound, and deals so exclusively in terms of things which we can encompass and measure. Experience, on the other hand, actually establishes contact with the unseen. The righteous man knows more than he can fully explain. His experience tells him that the Redeemer who works without and the Comforter who works within are in such perfect harmony that each constantly penetrates the domain of the other, and that the full and divine ministry thus afforded is necessary in every part to our full life in God.

The reborn man is a son of God, and has within him the Spirit which bears witness of his sonship. With this in mind, Jesus said, "That which is born of flesh, is flesh; and that which is born of the Spirit, is spirit" (John 3:6).

Paul had the same central thought in mind when he wrote to the saints in Rome:

> For they that are after flesh do mind the things of the flesh; but they that are after the Spirit the things of the Spirit. For to be carnally minded is death; but to be spiritually minded is life and peace. . . . But ye are not in the flesh, but in the Spirit, if so be that the Spirit of God dwell in you. Now if any man have not the Spirit of Christ, he is none of .his.—Rom. 8:5, 6, 9.

The quality of life thus achieved is so different from the life of the natural man that Paul continues:

> If the Spirit of him that raised up Jesus from the dead dwell in you, he that raised up Christ from the dead shall also quicken your mortal bodies by his Spirit that dwelleth in you . . . . For if ye live after the flesh, ye shall die; but if ye through the Spirit do mortify the deeds of the body, ye shall live. For as many as are led by the Spirit of God, they are the sons of God.—Rom. 8:11, 13, 14.

The Holy Spirit did not wait until the day of Pentecost to begin working in the lives of men. In the morning of creation, the Spirit of God moved upon the face of the waters, and from that time forward it has been constantly active among men. It was by the inspiration of the Holy Spirit that the prophets and psalmists led ancient Israel (Acts 1:16). This same Spirit was most fully active in the life of Jesus (Acts 10:38), so that here, in a perfect human personality, God was fully revealed. During the years of his earthly ministry, the power of Jesus reached out most wonderfully to those who saw him. One woman just touched the hem of his garment and was healed; and on another occasion Jesus had but to say the word, and it was enough. When the time for his departure was at hand, Jesus comforted his disciples with the promise that the light of the Spirit, which had been focused for this brief season in his own life, would continue with them just as truly and just as unmistakably as when he was here on earth.

The belief of the church, then, is that God still works with us, and that Jesus is still present with us, by the power of the Holy Spirit. This was the faith of the early church, and it is our faith today. When the early disciples were perplexed by such problems as whether or not Gentile converts must be obedient to the law of Moses, they relied on the Spirit for guidance, and their verdict was, "It seemed good to the Holy Ghost and to us" (Acts 15:28). So today, the Spirit of God is leading us onward to understand what he would have us do, and our question as we confront the problems of religious life is, "What will be pleasing to the Holy Spirit?" It is this Spirit which modern revelation urges us to trust and to follow (Doctrine and Covenants 10:6).

What difference will it make if we believe these things? The answer is: To truly believe in the Holy Spirit is to be assured of power adequate to our need, of progress that shall satisfy our deepest nature, and of cleansing that shall fit us for communion with the highest. As we read the record of the work of God with men, and note the ministry of the Spirit of God with men and with nations, we become aware that in spite of the different ways in which the Spirit has functioned in the lives of different men, the Spirit has done one thing for all men; it has brought them power. More than anything else the church of today needs people who will look at the tasks and opportunities of our time, small or great, with the assurance that the Spirit of God can make us adequate to these challenges. It was in such a spirit that Paul said, "I can do all things through Christ which strengtheneth me."—Phil. 4:13.

To believe in the Holy Spirit is to place emphasis on the importance of our inner, spiritual life. It is to respond to those forces which build the soul. It is to learn the lesson of Elijah in the wilderness, that although the Lord may not be seen in the thunder and the earthquake and the storm, he shall be found in the still, small voice which whispers peace.

STUDY OUTLINES

THE HOLY SPIRIT

LESSON PURPOSE

To prepare the way for greater co-operation in the work of the Holy Spirit.

HIGH POINTS OF THE LESSON

The Holy Spirit is the invisible presence of God, which bears testimony of the truth and leads us Godward.

The Spirit seeks to persuade us to "live in the light of our own proper character," to choose to live rightly and abundantly. To this end we are cleansed, enlightened, and strengthened.

The function of the Spirit is to lead and to guide, but never to compel. The Spirit works with us and for us, but it cannot work in us except with our full consent.

QUESTIONS AND DISCUSSION TOPICS

(1) What is the relation between the work of the Spirit and the work of Jesus? In what way does the Spirit do for us what the Master did for the disciples who were with him in Palestine?

(2) When was the Holy Spirit most fully active among men? Why? What lesson is there for us here?

(3) Is the ministry of the Holy Spirit restricted to members of the church, or does it reach out to all men? Give reasons for your answer.

(4) What is the work of the Spirit?

(5) What conditions are most favorable to the work of the Spirit?

(6) How is the work of the Spirit impeded?

(7) Recall some examples of the power of the Holy Spirit in the life of the early church. What were the gifts of the Spirit? What are the major fruits of the Spirit?

(8) What does the ministry of the Spirit of God mean in your life? How might it mean more? How might the church cause it to mean more?

What the Lesson Means Today

The Master is available now. All that his disciples learned in conversation with him we can learn through the ministry of the Holy Spirit.

We can prepare for the blessings of the Spirit by becoming aware of our needs, eager for guidance, ready to receive guidance when it comes, and prepared to devote the gifts of the Spirit to the tasks of the kingdom.

Since the task of today is a joint task, we shall do well to seek enlightenment together. When we have learned to worship together we shall be better prepared to work together, and as we work together we shall lay the foundation for constantly greater enlightenment.

Lesson Thirteen

II—THE LAYING ON OF HANDS

Everyone who would serve God acceptably must be completely cleansed and dedicated. This is symbolized and registered in the baptism of water. But every disciple must also be newly empowered, and this is symbolized in the laying on of hands and achieved in the baptism of the Spirit. In this chapter we are concerned with the laying on of hands and its intimate relation to the baptism of the Spirit.

There are certain occasions in the life of every man when he needs a particular endowment of the Spirit of God, and when it is important that this need be satisfied in a significant act wherein he recognizes that God is committed and his need is supplied. Our Heavenly Father has recognized this fundamental need of his children, and has provided the ordinance of the laying on of hands as a means through which the Spirit of God is especially imparted in times of crucial need. We do not believe that our Heavenly Father is restricted to this one means of bestowing his Spirit; yet the teaching of Scripture and the experience of the church combine to indicate that the ordinance of the laying on of hands brings our need into focus in a moment toward which our spiritual energies can be directed, for which we can make special preparation, and in which we can come acceptably into the divine presence for a blessing.

On one occasion when Jesus had been harassed by the questioning of the scribes and Pharisees, he told them the story of a man from whom an unclean spirit had been cast out. This spirit, the story said, sought rest elsewhere, but found none. It then came back to the place from which it had been cast out and, finding it "empty, swept, and garnished," brought in other evil spirits so that the last state of the man was worse than the first (Matt. 12: 43-45). After the baptism of water, important though it is, our lives are clean but empty, merely "swept and garnished." We still need the spiritual protection which comes from being filled with zeal for the cause of Christ. Without such zeal, we are an easy prey to old habits and old desires. It is quite natural, therefore, that the baptism of water should be followed shortly afterward by the laying on of hands for the reception of the Holy Spirit, which is sometimes referred to as the "baptism of fire."

POWER IN THE HANDS

The ordinance of laying on of hands is peculiarly suited to its purpose, for the hand is our most intimate and available means of power and is therefore the natural symbol of our progressive achievement. None of our dreams is embodied in reality except as we add to it the skill and strength of our hands. In the words of William Patterson, "From the crude drawings on the walls of cave and canyon to the masterpieces of a Rembrandt; from the unshapely models of clay to the inimitable works of Michelangelo; from the awkward writing on parchment and clay to the mighty and tireless printing press; from the unlovely arts of primitive people to the matchless work of Grecian architecture, the skill of the hand is at all times significant. It is the hand which erects cities, constructs ships and planes, bridges time and space, supports nations, and saves man from extermination. Therein is the hiding of his power."

Our need of the blessing of the Almighty becomes acute in several typical and often recurring situations: when we have been baptized for the remission of sins and need the endowment of the Spirit to start us forth into new life; when we are physically, mentally, or spiritually sick and need rejuvenation; when we are called to some special work, especially the work of the ministry—where the cares of life require that we shall be stabilized by the consciousness of a father's blessing; or when, as children, we are not yet ready for the responsibility of church membership but nevertheless need the guidance and protection which shall lead us in the way of truth. Let us consider these in the order in which they are named here.

BIRTH OF THE SPIRIT

First is the laying on of hands for the gift of the Holy Ghost; or, more briefly, "confirmation." For this ordinance there is abundant authority both in reason and in Scripture. The beginning of the work of the Christian church in Samaria, for example, emphasizes this close relation between baptism and the bestowal of the Holy Spirit. Philip had preached Christ in Samaria and had baptized a number of men and women, including Simon the sorcerer. Philip reported his success to the apostles at Jerusalem, and they sent Peter and John,

> Who, when they were come down, prayed for them that they might receive the Holy Ghost; for as yet he was fallen upon none of them; only they were baptized in the name of the Lord Jesus. Then laid they their hands on them, and they received the Holy Ghost—Acts 8:15-17.

An almost parallel incident occurred later when Paul met twelve men at Ephesus who had been baptized "unto John's baptism," probably by Apollos. After Paul had explained the way of life to them more fully, these men were rebaptized "and when Paul had laid his hands upon them, the Holy Ghost came on them; and they spake with tongues, and prophesied" (Acts 19:1-6). It was to this and similar experiences that Paul referred when he wrote to Titus:

> Not by works of righteousness which we have done, but according to his mercy he saved us, by the washing of regeneration, and renewing of the Holy Ghost; which he shed on us abundantly through Jesus Christ our Saviour.—Titus 3:5, 6.

Administration

Next is the laying on of hands for the healing of the sick or "administration." This is in line with modern trends, for during recent years there has been a widespread revival of interest in the relation between religion and physical healing. This relation was not always admitted. For many years the idea of spiritual healing was frowned upon, on the supposition that there was no relation between spiritual well-being and physical health. But experience has forced doctors to recognize this relationship and has drawn popular attention back to the clear teaching of the New Testament.

One of the last things which Jesus said to his disciples was that certain blessings should follow those who believe in him. Among these blessings he states specifically, "They shall lay hands on the sick, and they shall recover"—Mark 16: 18. This promise of Jesus was reinforced by his example. Although he could do no other "mighty works" among his own people, Jesus "laid his hands upon a few sick folks, and healed them" (Mark 6: 5), and the fame of his healing ministry spread so far abroad that:

> When the sun was setting, all they that had any sick with divers diseases brought them unto him; and he laid his hands on every one of them, and healed them.—Luke 4: 40.

Again, when Jairus came to Jesus, to tell him that his daughter lay at the point of death, Jairus must already have known of the means used in blessing, for he said, "Come and lay hands on her that she may be healed; and she shall live" (Mark 5: 22, 23). And it was out of a similar background of experience and understanding that James later wrote:

> Is any sick among you? Let him call for the elders of the church; and let them pray over him, anointing him with oil in the name of the Lord: and the prayer of faith shall save the sick, and the Lord shall raise him up; and if he have committed sins, they shall be forgiven him.—James 5: 14, 15.

Ordination

Coming now to the third of these occasions of special need for spiritual blessings, it is particularly important that the spiritual leaders of our time shall be distinguished by the power of the Holy Spirit working through them. It is desirable that the men of ministry shall be wise and able, but it is imperative that their wisdom and grace shall be born of the Spirit of God and shall be matured in experience under the direction of the Spirit. We are not surprised therefore to find that where the New Testament tells of setting men apart to the ministry, it invariably associates this setting apart with the ordinance of the laying on of hands. Mark tells us that Jesus:

> Ordained twelve, that they should be with him, and that he might send them forth to preach and to have power to heal sickness, and to cast out devils.—Mark 3: 14, 15.

John also says that Jesus told his disciples:

> Ye have not chosen me, but I have chosen you, and ordained you, that ye should go and bring forth fruit, and that your fruit should remain: that whatsoever ye shall ask of the Father in my name, he may give it you.—John 15: 16.

Here Jesus was evidently concerned that the work of the ministry should be stable. He wanted the apostles to be fruitful and was anxious that the fruit of their labor be conserved. The reference brings a reminder of the basic law of the church given in this dispensation:

> It shall not be given to anyone to go forth to preach my gospel, or to build up my church, except he be ordained by someone who has authority, and it is known to the church that he has authority, and has been regularly ordained by the heads of the church.—Doctrine and Covenants 42: 4.

The means of ordination in all these cases was through the imposition, or "laying on," of hands. It was thus that

Barnabas and Paul were "separated" for the work whereunto they had been called by the Spirit (Acts 13: 2, 3); it was after this fashion that the seven deacons were set apart by the apostles (Acts 6: 5, 6); and it was in this manner that Timothy was set apart for his ministry (I Tim. 5: 14). The ministry of today are set apart after the same pattern (Doctrine and Covenants 17: 12).

Patriarchal Blessing

And yet again there are times of crisis in the life of every man when he needs a reservoir of spiritual strength upon which to draw. On many occasions in the past it has pleased God to bless his children so that in these times of crisis they might look back to the day when their course was clearly marked before them, and they could return to their tasks with added courage and renewed strength. Not infrequently the blessings given for this purpose have been both clear-sighted and prophetic, revealing to the recipient the innermost thoughts of his own heart and the problems and duties lying ahead of him. Thus we read with interest of the blessing of Jacob on the heads of his children and grandchildren (Gen. 48, 49). The use of the ordinance of the laying on of hands for such blessings has been authorized and commanded in modern revelation. One of the functions of the evangelical ministry of the church is: "To lay on hands for the conferment of spiritual blessings" (Doctrine and Covenants 125: 3). Many people have testified that through this means they have been blessed in ways which they did not at first understand but which became more richly significant with the passing of the years.

Blessing Children

Another illustration of this principle of laying on of hands in situations of special need is the blessing of little children. It is the nature of the Christian enterprise that it shall be shared by people of mature wisdom and judgment; yet, as we well know, infancy and childhood are important formative periods. During these years the twig is bent in the direction in which it is likely to grow thereafter. It is a beautiful tradition, therefore, that the heads of families in the church carry forward the instinctive gesture of the fathers and mothers who loved Jesus and bring their children to the Master for his blessing.

Such children as these are not ready for baptism, but they do need the guidance of the Spirit of God. We do not believe that children who do not receive such a blessing will be damned. There is nevertheless abundant precedent for the blessing of children and observance of this rite brings a moment of insight and devotion and power to parents and to older children and to the church. Such an ordinance cannot fail to be fruitful when it is shared in the right spirit. This blessing not only brings something into the life of the child, but it emphasizes a group responsibility before God which can only be fully discharged as the child is divinely guided, both directly and through the spiritual life of the community.

These are not the only occasions on which we need a special endowment of the Holy Spirit, but they are typical and they are recurrent. Our Heavenly Father is eager to supply our need, and he has set the ordinance of the laying on of hands in the church so that we might know through his promise and our own experience that here is a means of grace and power. When the elders live so that they can truly minister in God's name, and the people make adequate spiritual preparation, both the people and the church are greatly blessed through this channel.

Study Outlines

The Laying On of Hands

Lesson Purpose

To indicate the purpose of the laying on of hands and to prepare the way for effective use of this ordinance.

High Points of the Lesson

The ordinance of the laying on of hands emphasizes the fact that we need power from above in order to accomplish heavenly tasks.

The baptism of water is not complete until it has been followed by baptism of the Spirit.

To the child this ordinance brings divine guidance; to the convert, strength for the new task; to the sick person, forgiveness and healing; to the minister, authority and power.

Questions and Discussion Topics

(1) What is the relation between the baptism of water and the baptism of the Spirit? Why does confirmation follow shortly after baptism?

(2) Discuss the symbolism involved in the laying on of hands. In what ways does it express the inner spiritual reality which completes the ordinance?

(3) What happens when a new convert is confirmed? Why is this ordinance called "confirmation"? What accompanying conditions contribute to the spiritual effectiveness of confirmation?

(4) What are the purposes of administration? What Biblical evidence is there supporting this practice?

(5) Why should the ordinance of laying on of hands be used for setting apart the ministry? Recall some scriptural support for this practice. What is the advantage of a specific ordinance in this connection?

(6) In what way are children benefited by the laying on of hands of the elders? What are the social values of this practice?

(7) What do we mean by a "patriarchal blessing"? What is the value of such a blessing? What are its dangers?

(8) Relate some examples of the laying on of hands which have been followed by pronounced blessings. What factors contribute to these blessings? In what way can we make this ordinance a greater source of power in the church?

What the Lesson Means Today

Every member of the church needs a sense of having been set apart for the service of God. Such a conviction can be received through the laying on of hands when proper preparation has been made.

Power from above is available to meet the needs of all who are engaged in the work of the kingdom.

There is no magic in this ordinance. It is effective when it is practiced under proper conditions if it is related to the other aspects of the Christian life.

Chapter VI

THE ANTIQUITY OF THE GOSPEL

Christ from the beginning—Adam received spiritual law—God tries to reveal himself to men.

Lesson Fourteen

I—THE CHRIST FROM THE BEGINNING

IN ANY FAMILY some things are possible later in the family life which were not possible at an earlier period. We shall expect this, too, in the family of God. There are some things which our Heavenly Father can do for us now which he could not do for the people of past generations. That is what we mean by saying that this is the "dispensation of the fullness of times" (Eph. 1: 10). Our Heavenly Father is gathering together all the hopes and ambitions which failed of fruition in earlier years because the time was not then ripe, and is now bringing them to pass.

While we shall expect that the progress of history, and our consequent maturity, will give our Heavenly Father constantly increasing opportunities to speak to us in terms which we can understand, we must also believe—if we are to believe in God as our Father—that from the beginning he has sought every opportunity to make himself known to men and to bind us together in the fellowship of believers.

We cannot believe that God would let men grow up in a rude and barbarian state, deeply entangled in sin and error and idolatry, without giving them some knowledge of himself. The more we know of our Heavenly Father, as revealed to us by Jesus Christ, the more we shall expect to find that he sought to enter into moral relations with his children from the first, giving them the greatest possible light for their guidance. It is the clear teaching of the

Scriptures that there was no period in the history of the world when men were without some degree of enlightenment from God. From the dawn of history, the piety of good men was not merely an instinctive groping after the right. It had revelation as its basis and was their response to the light with which God had blessed them. God has always taken the initiative in bringing men to him.

Order is the essence of effective teaching. The experiment which enlightens the student at the end of his second or third year of study would merely have bewildered him at the beginning of his course; and he must go further yet before he can appreciate a more advanced demonstration. For this reason it was impossible for our Heavenly Father to share the great experience of the incarnation of his Son with humanity as a whole before they were ready for the experience. Therefore, although Jesus was "the lamb slain before the foundation of the world" (Rev. 13: 8), it was ordained for the good of man that his actual incarnation and earth ministry should take place in the "meridian of time." In preparation for this revelation, we find God at work with humanity in general and with the Hebrew people in particular, preparing the way for our Master to come at the time when he could most fully influence the children of men, both individually and collectively.

In the Name of Jesus Christ

The conditions of eternal life are necessarily the same in every age. Even God himself cannot give us eternal life except by inducing us to be obedient to the conditions which produce that life. This was true from the beginning. In every age the way to be righteous is to be righteous; and no exercise of mercy or of clemency can guarantee to men what is won only in obedience to the laws of life. The Bible states clearly that no salvation is available through any name except the name of Jesus (Acts 4: 12), and we have the Master's own voice assuring that he is the Way, the Truth, and the Life, and no man can be reconciled to the Father except by him (John 14:6). This applies to Adam and to all who have lived since his day.

Early in the history of the Restoration, the church was assured that the gospel is the power of God unto salvation, through Christ.

> Not only to those who believed after he came in the meridian of time in the flesh, but also to all those from the beginning, even as many as were before he came, who believed in the words of the holy prophets, who spake as they were inspired by the Holy Ghost, who truly testified of him in all things.—Doctrine and Covenants 17:5.

From this we understand that righteous men who lived before the coming of Jesus looked forward to the days of the Messiah in faith. They knew that they were not living on the strength of "cunningly devised fables"; but that the Son of God would actually take on the limitations of the flesh and live and die for the salvation of mankind. Their hope centered in him, as does ours; and they were blessed, as we are, through the enlightening ministry of the Holy Spirit which bears testimony of him. In harmony with this, the Book of Mormon tells us:

> The prophets and the priests and the teachers did labor diligently, exhorting with all long suffering, the people to diligence; teaching the law of Moses, and the intent for which it was given; persuading them to look forward unto the Messiah, and believe in him to come as though he already was.—Jarom 1:24, 25; Alma 19:24-27, etc.

THE GOSPEL TO ADAM

The Inspired Version of the Holy Scriptures states that after Adam transgressed and was cast out of the Garden of Eden, he was commanded to worship and to offer sacrifices. The purpose behind this was explained to him:

This thing is a similitude of the sacrifice of the Only Begotten of the Father, which is full of grace and truth; Wherefore, thou shalt do all that thou doest, in the name of the Son. And thou shalt repent, and call upon God, in the name of the Son for evermore. And in that day, the Holy Ghost fell upon Adam, which beareth record of the Father and the Son, saying, I am the Only Begotten of the Father from the beginning, henceforth and forever; that, as thou hast fallen, thou mayest be redeemed, and all mankind, even as many as will. . . . And thus the gospel began to be preached from the beginning, being declared by holy angels, sent forth from the presence of God; and by his own voice, and by the gift of the Holy Ghost. And thus all things were confirmed unto Adam by an holy ordinance; and the gospel preached; and a decree sent forth that it should be in the world until the end thereof; and thus it was. Amen.—Genesis 4: 7-9; 5: 44, 45.

The work which was begun with Adam was continued down the stream of time. There was persistent effort on the part of Divinity to bring men to a state of stable goodness, but this was constantly counteracted by the gravitation of sin; and each new revelation was succeeded by a falling away from that which had been revealed. Nevertheless these successive apostasies, gross as they were, each left some residuum of enlightenment as the common possession of humanity. Thus the progressive movement toward the meridian of time went forward, and the testimony of history was added to revelation through the prophets.

We catch glimpses in the Scriptures of some of the spiritual heroes of these early dispensations. Thus Enoch, the seventh from Adam, "walked with God" (Gen. 5: 24). This communion with Divinity was so intimate that he saw the works of God to the end of time and prophesied of that which shall come to pass even in the day of judgment (Jude 14, 15). He was "translated that he should not see death, and was not found, because God had translated him, but before he translated him he had this testimony that he pleased God" (Heb. 11: 5).

The Gospel to Noah and Abraham

Noah, also, "walked with God" (Gen. 6:9), and was a preacher of righteousness. Many years later Paul told the saints in Rome that righteousness is revealed in the gospel (Rom. 1:16, 17); so that we are not surprised to learn through the Apostle Peter that Noah's preaching was sufficiently important that those who refused to heed it were punished for their disobedience (I Pet. 3:18-20).

The Apostle Paul seems to have been deeply aware of the unity of the gospel in every age. When writing to the saints in Galatia, he reminded them of the importance of obedience (Gal. 1:7-12), and also that the gospel which he was preaching had already been delivered to Abraham (Gal. 3:8). On another occasion Paul wrote to the saints in Corinth:

> Moreover, brethren, I would not that ye should be ignorant, how that all our fathers were under the cloud, and all passed through the sea; and were all baptized unto Moses in the cloud and in the sea; and did all eat the same spiritual meat: and did all drink the same spiritual drink; for they drank of that spiritual Rock that followed them: and that rock was Christ.—I Cor. 10:1-4.

That the gospel referred to is the same gospel is quite clear from a parallel reference in the epistle to the Hebrews, where we are assured that the same gospel was preached to their ancestors, but did not profit them, "not being mixed with faith in them that heard it" (Hebrews 4:2). Of Moses himself it is stated that he chose to rather "suffer affliction with the people of God, than to enjoy the pleasures of sin for a season; esteeming the reproach of Christ greater riches than the treasures in Egypt" (Heb. 11:25, 26).

Our Heavenly Father, who has loved men from the beginning, has made repeated attempts to reveal himself to them. Some prophetic souls who have received this revelation have sought to communicate it to their fellows, but the people were not yet ready for the fullness of his trust. Every such dispensation was a prelude to the coming of Christ in the meridian of time, and every one built upon the remnants of what had gone before; just as the best English roads are built on the foundations laid by the Romans centuries ago but lost in the intervening years. When the appointed time came and history converged in Palestine, the harvest of the years was gathered. Our Lord lived among men, and so changed the course of history that things were never the same again. Though there came another falling away after the time of the apostles, a richer leaven was at work, and by the time of the Restoration, men had grown so as to be ready for the recommitment of the gospel in its fullness, and for the establishment of the kingdom of God "never to be thrown down or left to another people."—Dan. 2: 44, I. V.

Study Outlines

The Antiquity of the Gospel

Lesson Purpose

To show that the gospel was revealed in the beginning and to impress the fact of our Heavenly Father's impartial love for his children.

High Points of the Lesson

The gospel was revealed to the ancients as the means of their salvation, and in order to affirmatively influence the moral development of the race.

The conditions of salvation are always the same. They cannot be changed to suit the times, but are rooted in necessity.

Many of the ancient spiritual heroes looked forward to the coming of the Messiah and lived in that confident faith.

Questions and Discussion Topics

(1) What is the meaning of the phrase, "The dispensation of the fullness of time"? Why do we consider that we are living in this dispensation?

(2) In what notable ways did our Heavenly Father prepare humanity for the coming of his Son? Why did Jesus come "in the meridian of time"?

(3) Is it true that the conditions of eternal life are the same in every age? Discuss this briefly.

(4) Enumerate some of the evidences causing us to believe that the gospel was known to men anciently.

(5) In what way did revelation received in past ages prepare for the revelation of God in this dispensation? Did the spiritual leaders of yesterday realize that they were building for the future as well as for their own time? Are we?

(6) Name some of the men who were close to God in past ages. Were there just a few such men, or were these the leaders of groups of believers?

(7) How fully were the Book of Mormon prophets aware of the coming of the Messiah?

(8) What difference does it make to your view of the importance of the gospel to realize that it has been available to men at the highest point of their spiritual development from the beginning of time?

What the Lesson Means Today

Each of us is important for his own sake, and also because of his place in the stream of history. If I fail, I fall short of my own possibilities, and I also rob those who come after me.

The church has a dual function in every age: to bear witness to its own day and to provide the link between the yesterdays and the tomorrows.

The men of antiquity saw the fulfillment of their hopes in our salvation. Today good men in many lands are without the gospel. Their needs call to us, just as our needs called to the ancients.

Chapter VII

PRIESTHOOD

The idea of priesthood—Priesthood before Christ—Priesthood in the early Christian Church.

Lesson Fifteen

I—THE IDEA OF PRIESTHOOD

GOD TAKES THE INITIATIVE in winning men back to him. There has been nothing haphazard about our Heavenly Father's approach to this self-appointed task. Our plight was anticipated before the beginning of time; and the means of rescuing us was clearly known and approved. Jesus Christ was the "Lamb slain from before the foundation of the world."—Rev. 13:8.

The plan of redemption takes into account the basic needs of humanity. We cannot find our way back to God without his guidance, but he uses us as fully as possible. From the beginning, therefore, he selected men of suitable natural endowment who were willing to serve him; and commissioned them to represent him among their fellows.

Our Heavenly Father wills that everyone of us shall stand as his brother's keeper, that we shall achieve true manhood only as we concern ourselves with the welfare of all men, and that we shall partake of the divine nature as we share in the work God is doing for the world of today and of tomorrow. This is at the very heart of the work of God in every age. To understand this is the key to understanding the selection of those special representatives of God who form his ministry.

In order to win us, our Heavenly Father seeks to lead us through certain experiences with himself. He does not merely tell us to be good, honest, just, and devoted, but he also grants us experiences which epitomize his will and way of life for us. These brief but tremendously important dramatizations of the spiritual life are known as the sacraments or ordinances of religion. When we submit to such rites as baptism or the laying on of hands, or partake of the sacrament of the Lord's Supper, it is of paramount importance that we shall feel that our Heavenly Father truly participates in what is taking place, and that he is fully committed thereby. One of the means he has designed to give us this assurance is to set apart such men as he chooses to be his authorized representatives, and then to give in their ministry the evidences of their calling. These ministers have delegated authority only. They do not function in their own name, but in the name of God; yet when they do so function and match their calling with their practice, the evidences of their divine appointment follow them continually.

Worldly ways of life are organized with regard to the wishes of men rather than for the purposes of God. We have grown up in this environment, and have become so accustomed to it that only a miracle can enable us to see clearly. Our vision is impeded by the cataracts of sin. Our Heavenly Father therefore encounters great difficulty in discovering men who can represent him fittingly. Indeed, only one man in all the history of humanity ever represented the Lord of Life perfectly. In the absence of better material, however, he selects the most suitable men available, and uses them as pioneers to lead the way in spiritual understanding. These trail blazers for God and the truth seek to bring their friends to the Master, and as they succeed, a constantly growing company is enlisted in his cause. When we realize that the major qualifications for this kind of ministry include not only character and intelligence, but also a peculiar ability to understand the will of God, we shall see how important it is that God shall choose his own ministry, and not that they shall be chosen by someone else for him.

The central idea of the priesthood is well illustrated in an experience of Moses with a group of priests who sought to depose him from the leadership of ancient Israel. These men complained that since all the people were holy, Moses was taking to himself an authority as leader which he did not rightfully possess. They were not quarreling with the idea that men should be in touch with God and receive divine direction in the conduct of their lives. The objection was against one person having pre-eminence over others in spiritual things and daring to claim prior authority to represent Divinity among his fellows. Moses' answer indicated that they took too much upon themselves in thus seeking to dictate the means that God should use in leading his people. He told them the test by which those whom the Lord had chosen should be known. Continuing, he epitomized the central idea of their own ministry, and pointed out that they did not need to seek the chief place, because they already had important places in the divine scheme of things. He said:

Seemeth it but a small thing unto you, that the God of Israel hath separated you from the congregation of Israel, to bring you near to himself to do the service of the tabernacle of the Lord, and to stand before the congregation to minister unto them?—Numbers 16:9.

Ministers are set apart to their several tasks by the rite of ordination. Such a ceremonial induction is obviously necessary in order to indicate both the call of the minister and the nature of his duties. If there was no specific act initiating members of the priesthood into their ministry, we would not know when or in what degree they were commissioned. Furthermore, ordination by the laying on of hands is not only sanctioned by ancient practice and by the word of God, but is also beautifully adapted to symbolize the inner significance of the investiture of which it is part. These two principles which underlie ordinations are recognized and applied in many parallel fields. For example, no matter what the native ability of a president of the United States may be, nor how large a majority he may have secured in the election, he cannot function until he has been inaugurated. Moreover, at the inauguration, the procedure is specially designed to indicate and solemnize the nature of the duties which he is about to undertake.

Those who have been properly instructed regarding the lines of procedure followed by our Heavenly Father in days past are well aware of the place of priesthood in the divine economy. It is apparent both from the ancient Scriptures and from modern revelation that he is eager for us to share, as fully as possible, in the responsibility of commissioning those whom he selects to represent him in the priesthood. For this reason no one is ordained as a member of the priesthood except as his call is indicated through those already holding priesthood and as this call is validated by the free consent of the body. This does not mean that we elect the ministry, as a city elects a mayor or the Masonic order selects a worshipful master, but it does mean that we should consent with our full faculties to be directed by the men whom God chooses, and that we should indicate this consent at the beginning of their ministry by joining in authorizing their ordination.

The work of God among men is so great that it cannot be fully appreciated or accomplished in any one generation. It is necessary, as Malachi reminds us, that "the hearts of the fathers shall be turned to the children and the hearts of the children to the fathers" (Mal. 4: 6), which we understand to mean that the generations shall all be knit together in one great endeavor. In such a great work, it is the divine intention that there shall be continuity of spiritual direction. For this reason, each minister receives his commission by ordination under the hands of another minister so that the priesthood of every man is joined to that of his predecessors and his successors, while the work of all is rooted in the revelations of God. Priesthood is therefore, "without father, without mother, without descent having neither beginning of days or end of life" (Heb. 7: 3, I. V.) It is as eternal as our need of God. Wherever the ordinances of the gospel are ministered, there is priesthood.

II—PRIESTHOOD BEFORE CHRIST

According to the Old Testament, priesthood fulfilled a threefold function. They presented the sacrifices of the people to God, they inquired his will, and they were the guardians and teachers of his law (Schaff-Herzog Encyclopedia, "Priests and Priesthood"). There are indications that from the very beginning of time our Heavenly Father selected righteous men to perform these functions. We are informed in the Inspired Version of the Holy Scriptures that "Adam taught his children and administered in the holy ordinances" (Gen. 5: 45, I. V.), and we read that "this same priesthood which was in the beginning, shall be in the end of the world also" (Gen. 6: 7, I. V.). Noah, a "preacher of righteousness," was the father of all who lived after the flood.

It is not surprising, therefore, that the idea of priesthood was well understood among the ancients even though many of their religious practices were only distantly related to those of the true representatives of God. The Egyptians, the Babylonians, the Phoenicians, and others all had their orders of priesthood, and something akin to the prophetic office was of major importance among them.

One of the earliest and most distinguished ministers of ancient days of whom we have any record was Melchisedec, king of Salem, whose spiritual authority was recognized by Abraham. Through him Abraham paid tithes (Heb. 7: 1, 2). The Tel-el-amarna tablets which were discovered in Egypt in 1888 indicate that Melchisedec united in himself both the kingly and the priestly offices, and was not the only occupant of that dignity, but was one in a succession of priest-kings which continued for a considerable period.

The Bible gives us little light regarding those who officiated in this priesthood from the time of Adam to that of Melchisedec, although we have brief glimpses of Enoch and Noah. Modern revelation, however, tells in considerable detail of the ministry of the ancient patriarchs (Doctrine and Covenants 83: 4), and traces the spiritual lineage of Moses, who received the priesthood under the hands of Jethro, his father-in-law.

Under instruction received by revelation, Moses shared something of his priestly authority with seventy of the elders of Israel, who were thus associated in the government of the people for many years. Later, because of their transgression this priesthood was taken out of their midst. The right to represent God in the higher ministries of his word and power was withheld, while the people continued under the tutelage of the law of Moses administered by the descendants of Levi. These men held what is known as the lesser or "Aaronic" priesthood (Doctrine and Covenants 83: 4).

This Aaronic priesthood did not originate with Aaron, nor in his day (Exod. 28: 1). The office was already extant, and Aaron and his sons were appointed to function therein (Lev. 8:30). Those who ministered in this office offered sacrifices and in other ways sought to prepare the children of Israel for the ministry of the greater law (Heb. 10: 1). This lesser priesthood therefore ministered a preparatory gospel which taught repentance and baptism and the remission of sins, and sought to bring men near to God through obedience to the "law of carnal commandments" (Doctrine and Covenants 83: 4). The members of the Aaronic priesthood had authority to administer in the lesser ordinances and in temporal affairs, but not in the higher and more spiritual concerns of the kingdom of God. Nevertheless this ministry was an important one; and its functions could not be usurped with impunity. The priests of this order conducted the worship of the children of Israel for many years, and although they lost much of their spiritual power, they kept the idea of priesthood alive and did much to preserve the worship of Jehovah.

From the references here presented, and from other sources, it is apparent that in his dealings with men both before the time of Moses and subsequent thereto, our Heavenly Father appointed and blessed men to serve in a priestly order, some of whose members exercised more authority than others, but each of whom was authorized to represent God along the lines of his commission. There was therefore constantly presented to the righteous a living picture of their dependence on God for guidance. This does not mean that they were unable to approach him and to receive direct guidance and blessing; but it does mean that, in the affairs of the kingdom, Divinity was properly represented by the officers of the kingdom, and that the people of God were knit together by a ministry so appointed as to recognize the right of Divinity to call and empower, and also the fact that men are inseparably joined together, and are dependent on each other for the full riches of salvation.

Study Outlines

The Idea of Priesthood

Lesson Purpose

To indicate the central idea of priesthood and to show the major characteristics of priesthood before Christ.

High Points of the Lesson

The first task of any minister is to represent God, and the basic necessity for effective ministry is godlike character.

The priesthood are called to administer the ordinances of the gospel in such ways that these ordinances become living experiences with Divinity.

The priesthood forms a chain of faith and of ministry which joins the ages together from the beginning to the end of time.

The children of Israel were not willing to live by the higher law of the gospel, and were therefore given the law of Moses which was administered by the Aaronic priesthood. The members of this priesthood ministered the law of "carnal commandments" and the "preparatory gospel."

Questions and Discussion Topics

(1) What do we mean by the "ordinances of the gospel"? What is their purpose? Why is it important that they shall be administered by divinely authorized priesthood?

(2) Why is it important that a minister shall be a good man? Are not the ordinances just as effectively administered whether the minister is good or not?

(3) Why is ordination important in connection with priesthood? What does ordination accomplish?

(4) What reasons have we for supposing that it is a wicked and dangerous thing to minister in the name of God without authority from him? Discuss briefly the principle involved.

(5) In what way does the group participate in the selection of ministry? Why?

(6) When was the priesthood first bestowed? How widely was the idea of priesthood understood? What were the functions of the priesthood in Old Testament times?

(7) What priesthood was taken away after Moses? What priesthood continued?

(8) What is the function of the Aaronic priesthood? What did the Aaronic priesthood do for the children of Israel?

Lesson Sixteen

III—PRIESTHOOD IN THE EARLY CHRISTIAN CHURCH

When Jesus began his earthly ministry, he had behind him the religious traditions of the Jews. Some of these traditions were a marked hindrance to his work, but some were very helpful. This was to be expected, since some traditions were in faithful continuance of an earlier revelation and others were corruptions or distortions of what had once been just and true.

Like his predecessor, John, who had been sent from God (John 1: 6), Jesus received divine appointment and authority for his mission among men. He told his disciples, "I came down from heaven, not to do my own will, but the will of him that sent me" (John 6: 38); and again, "I have not spoken of myself; but the Father who sent me, he gave me a commandment, what I should say, and what I should speak" (John 12: 49). But the authority which Jesus exercised was greater than any the Jews had known throughout their lifetime. It reached back beyond Aaron and Levi, and recalled Moses and Melchisedec; it was the priesthood of Melchisedec, or more correctly, the priesthood which is after the order of the Son of God (Doctrine and Covenants 104: 1).

Many of the more devout Jews recognized that the difference between the ministry of Jesus and that of their own leaders was essentially one of authority (Matt. 7: 29). They were accustomed to a ministry rooted in tradition. The authority of the scribes and Pharisees was borrowed, and their teachings consisted largely of quotations. Jesus, on the other hand, had an original authority which gave his words a ring of truth such as had not been heard for many years. It remained for the writer of the letter to the Hebrews to express what many of them felt, that here was a new order of priesthood (Heb. 5: 6), or rather an old one revealed again. This higher priesthood was not primarily concerned with "the law of carnal commandments," but with the "power of an endless life" (Heb. 7: 16).

Jesus was anxious that this life-giving ministry should continue with the church and kingdom. He was the great "Apostle and High Priest of our profession" (Heb. 3: 1), and he chose other apostles and high priests who would carry forward his work in his Spirit and by his authority. The importance which he placed upon the selection of these men is indicated in the preparation which he made:

> And it came to pass in those days, that he went out into a mountain to pray, and continued all night in prayer to God. And when it was day, he called unto him his disciples; and of them he chose twelve, whom also he named apostles.—Luke 6: 12, 13.

The commission held by Jesus Christ was thus passed on by him to his disciples, and was made effective during their three years of intimate association with him. There was need to remind them, "Ye have not chosen me, but I have chosen you and ordained you (John 15: 16); nevertheless they grew under his tutelage so that after his Resurrection he was able to commission them: "as my Father hath sent me, even so send I you. . . . . Whose soever sins ye remit, they are remitted unto them; and whose soever sins ye retain, they are retained." —John 20: 21-23.

After the close of the earthly ministry of the Master, the work of the church was left in the care of these apostles, among whom Peter, James, and John evidently exercised leadership (Gal. 2: 9). Under their ministry, and by the guidance of the Holy Spirit, the church was wisely and rapidly extended. They continued the orders of ministry already set in the church in the days of Christ, such as the seventy (Luke 10: 1) and the elders. Then, as the church grew, and as they were directed by the Spirit, they chose the deacons (Acts 6: 3-6) and other ministers, as these were needed. What was done at Jerusalem was copied elsewhere. For example, Paul ordained Timothy, who had been pointed out by the spirit of prophecy, and Titus who had probably been indicated by similar inspiration. Later these were sent to Ephesus and to Crete, respectively; and were instructed to organize and set the work in order after the pattern laid down.

As the apostles looked forward and anticipated their own deaths or the curtailment of their ministry through imprisonment, they were particularly careful to see that the church was provided with ministers who would carry on their work. Thus the presiding elders, called by the Holy Ghost, were made overseers over the church in Asia Minor, and were charged to concern themselves with the flock under their direction.

All these ministers—apostles, prophets, evangelists, pastors, teachers, and deacons—exercised a ministry which is not clearly outlined in the New Testament, but which has been clarified by the light of modern revelation. Although there were wide differences in the individual duties of these ministers, the work of all of them centered in teaching sound doctrine, creating spiritual health, and proclaiming eternal life. Their commission was more than a delegation of authority to function in the rituals of the church. They were ambassadors for Christ.

Under the direction of the Master and of the Holy Spirit which guided the apostles, the church took on such life that it became evident a new day had dawned. Divested of power, the old order ceased. It could not have been otherwise; but the Aaronic priesthood was continued and was revitalized through the endowment of the Spirit and association with the Melchisedec priesthood. Paul wrote, "If that which was done away was glorious, much more that which remaineth is glorious" (II Cor. 3: 11), and again, "He also hath made us able ministers of the New Testament;

not of the letter, but of the spirit; for the letter killeth, but the spirit giveth life."—II Cor. 3:6.

Under the new covenant the work of the Aaronic priesthood was still a work of preparation. Hitherto the priests of the Aaronic order had functioned under the law, in preparation for the time when this "schoolmaster" would be done away and the gospel would be preached in its fullness. When the anticipated day of power had come, although the Aaronic priesthood continued to minister the "law of carnal commandments," their ministry was a prelude to the richer ministry of the Spirit exercised through the Melchisedec priesthood and carrying their work forward to a far greater glory.

An interesting illustration of the distinction between the work of these two priesthoods is found in the story of Philip and his work among the Samaritans. Philip went to Samaria and there made many converts and baptized them in accordance with the authority which belongs to the Aaronic priesthood. Then, when the word of his missionary success was received at Jerusalem, Peter and John went to Samaria and by the imposition of hands conferred the gift of the Holy Ghost upon the new converts. Philip could administer baptism, but it required the priesthood which is after the power of an endless life, the Melchisedec priesthood, to fill with the Holy Spirit the lives of those who had been baptized.

The men holding the Melchisedec priesthood could of course minister in the rites and duties of the Aaronic order, and at the point where obedience to the lesser law merged into spiritual responsiveness, the two priesthoods came together. It was in this manner that Christianity saved the Aaronic priesthood. Before the coming of Christ, the devout had offered sacrifices in obedience to the law. Now they presented their own bodies as living sacrifices, and counted this a reasonable service. Life was filled with new spiritual significance, and this was augmented as men of the Aaronic and Melchisedec orders joined in showing how spiritual achievement demands that material things shall be dedicated to spiritual ends.

We may thus say that there was a divinely appointed ministry in the apostolic church consisting of men set apart to two major orders of priesthood. The men of these ministries were ordained to their respective callings by the laying on of hands by men who already held priesthood. Thus Barnabas and Saul were separated unto the work to which they had been called (Acts 13: 2, 3), and in like manner, men were appointed in the various local churches (Titus 1: 5). Of course many of these early ministers died, but the ministry continued. It was with this fact in mind that the Apostle Paul wrote to the saints in Ephesus.

He gave some, apostles; and some, prophets; and some, evangelists; and some, pastors and teachers; For the perfecting of the saints, for the work of the ministry, for the edifying of the body of Christ. Till we all come in the unity of the faith, and of the knowledge of the Son of God, unto a perfect man, unto the measure of the stature of the fulness of Christ: That we henceforth be no more children, tossed to and fro, and carried about with every wind of doctrine, by the sleight of men, and cunning craftiness; whereby they lie in wait to deceive; but, speaking the truth in love, may grow up unto him in all things, which is the head, even Christ.—Eph. 4: 11-15.

Study Outlines

Priesthood in the Early Christian Church

Lesson Purpose

To indicate place and function of priesthood in the early Christian church and to note change in work of the Aaronic priesthood under the new covenant.

High Points of the Lesson

The Jews were accustomed to the idea of priesthood, knew the importance of authority, and had to be convinced that Jesus had the right to represent God.

The priesthood were set in the church to teach the truth, to administer the ordinances, and to build the kingdom. They were not great in their own right, but were honored as the representatives of Divinity.

The Aaronic priesthood continued the ministry of preparation in the new dispensation, but their work was directly associated with the ministry of the Melchisedec order and was adjusted to the new dispensation.

Questions and Discussion Topics

(1) What was the essential difference between the authority of Jesus and that of the scribes and Pharisees?

(2) How did the early ministry receive their authority? What were the conditions of their effectiveness?

(3) By what right did the apostles pass on their authority to others? How did they do this? What part did the saints play in calling the ministry? Give examples.

(4) Illustrate the serious nature of a call to the ministry.

(5) Name some of the offices held by the ministry of the early church. What was the duty of these offices?

(6) What functions were discharged by the Aaronic priesthood in New Testament times? What was the difference between Aaronic ministry then and under Moses?

(7) How long were the various orders of the priesthood intended to continue? Give reasons for your answer.

(8) What ordinances were administered by the Melchisedec priesthood? What were administered by the Aaronic?

What the Lesson Means Today

In the early Christian church many obscure men achieved greatness by their devotion to the Christian task. Today men can be similarly blessed.

Now, as then, a major factor in the effectiveness of the priesthood is the support of the people.

Both Mosaic and Aaronic priesthoods are available to us. Yet many of us live below the Aaronic plane. Those who have not rendered full and glad obedience to this ministry of preparation are unready for the richer blessings of the Melchisedec order.

The priesthood has been continued among us because we need to be taught what God wants us to do and to be.

The presence among us of a ministry called by God and to whose appointment we are morally bound, should be a constant reminder of our relation to Divinity.

Authority in the priesthood is derived from three sources: the call of God, the quality of the minister, and the needs of the people.

Chapter VIII

SIN AND FORGIVENESS

Sin—The forgiveness of sin—Atonement—The principle of repentance—Baptism in water.

Lesson Seventeen

I—SIN

EVERY THOUGHTFUL MAN recognizes within himself the tendency to do wrong. Only a fool ignores this tendency and tries to forget it. The bridgebuilder who ignores the steady downward pull of gravitation, or shuts his eyes to the destructive power of the flood beneath his structure, cannot hope to succeed. Nor can the builder of a life succeed unless he is wide awake to the downward pull of evil and to the persistent strength of the tide of wrongdoing which seeks to engulf him. The wise man recognizes this. He knows that sin constitutes a major threat against his happiness and well-being, and so he builds strong defenses against it.

The deeply religious Jews faced this downward pull of evil and considered the problem of sin one of the problems of religion. That is why many of them were so indignant when Jesus claimed to forgive sin (Matt. 9: 2-10; Luke 7: 48-50). They thought that only God could forgive sin and that the claims which Jesus made in this connection were blasphemous. On the other hand, some of the Jews welcomed Jesus just because they felt that the Master could touch the need of humanity at this point. Among these was John the Baptist, who introduced Jesus to his followers with the words: "Behold the Lamb of God, which taketh away the sin of the world" (John 1: 29). Jesus fulfilled John's insight into his work, and before his death, the Master told the disciples that his blood was to be "shed for the remission of sins" (Matt. 26: 28). After his resurrection, when he walked with his two disciples on the way to Emmaus, he opened their minds that they might understand the scriptures, and said to them, "Thus it is written, and thus it behooves Christ to suffer, and to rise from the dead the third day; and that repentance and remission of sins should be preached in his name."—Luke 24: 45-47.

The apostles caught from Jesus something of his deep concern over the sin which separates men from God. In his first sermon to the Gentiles, Peter announced that "whosoever believeth in him shall receive the remission of sins" (Acts 10: 43), and Paul bore his testimony to the Corinthian saints that "God was in Christ reconciling the world unto himself" (II Cor. 5: 19). He announced that the central purpose of his own ministry was that the Gentiles "might receive the forgiveness of sin" (Acts 26: 18). Perhaps John made the most significant statement of all, "If any man sin, we have an advocate with the Father, Jesus Christ, the rightous; and he is the propitiation for our sins, and not for ours only, but also for the sins of the whole world."—I John 2: 1, 2.

"What is sin?" One answer which is quite popular at the present time is, "Nothing." According to this theory evil is just the absence of good, as darkness is but the absence of light. The difficulty with this explanation, however, is the demonstrable fact that evil is just as real, just as tangible, and just as apparent as good. If evil is nothing, "it is a strangely active, positive, and potent nothing, with all the qualities of a something. The theories which attempt to account for sin by tracing it to a mere negation or the absence of good raise a harder question than that which they attempt to answer."—*The Sin of the World,* by Henry Van Dyke.

Sin is a fact, not a theory. It is both an act and an attitude of rebellion against God. As an act, sin involves transgression of the law. But this legal definition does not go to the heart of the matter. It is when we believe that God is our loving Father that sin is revealed to us in its true light. A discourtesy offered to a stranger is but a discourtesy—bad enough, but not vital. But a discourtesy offered to one who loves us and who treasures every act by which we indicate our response to that love, we will regard as mean and despicable. So, also, unkindness toward a chance acquaintance is bad enough of itself. But when we realize that our best friend died for this very person, then unkindness takes on new proportions. It is because Christianity adds this vital element to human relationships that it is our most powerful ally, as we struggle upward from selfishness to nobility.

Sin is the major tragedy of the soul. Adam lost Paradise when his sin separated him from God; the prodigal son lived in tragedy even though he fared sumptuously and lived riotously. The evil in which they had trusted turned against them and betrayed them; and we are sons of Adam and kin to the prodigal. If we trust in sin, it will betray us as it betrayed them. No compromises are possible. We must conquer sin or sin will kill us. We must fight; and as we fight, we must remember that victory involves correcting our distorted vision as well as strengthening our weak will. It necessitates eradicating habits which have become parts of us as well as resisting specific temptations. It means shutting out ungodly environment and responding wholly to the influences of godliness.

As an attitude of rebellion against God, sin involves the whole background of evil tendencies out of which specific sins arise. All of us share this background to a greater or a lesser degree. It was this that Paul had in mind when he wrote to the Romans, "Who shall deliver me from the body of this death?" and "When I would do good, evil is present with me." When he wished to do the will of God, the evil habits of bygone days were still present with him, clouding his vision, stealing his courage, and sapping his strength.

This state of sin involves our whole social structure. Our modern life has given opportunity for sins which did not afflict earlier generations. Dr. Shailer Matthews has written:

> The more refined sin becomes, the greater may be its danger. The world abounds in thieves, liars, and adulterers, but it is not clear that they are the worst sort of sinners. As civilization develops, sin grows corporate. We sin socially by violating social rather than individualistic personal relations. Individually a sinner may be kindly and pure and honest. There is many a theater manager growing rich by pandering to sexual excitement who is a faithful husband. There is many a gambler who is never charged with cheating. There are many directors and stockholders of corporations who are exemplary in their individual relations, but who in their corporate capacity do not hesitate to connive at efforts to bribe legislatures, adulterate foods, unscrupulously crush out competitors, destroy family life by subsidizing saloons, corrupt public opinion by distorting news, induce unsuspecting investors to buy worthless stock, crush out the lives of children in factories, and underpay women employees in their stores. Such men—and some women—are tempted to protect themselves by retreating behind the theory that such matters belong to the realm of business rather than that of ethics. But they cannot thereby escape. The God who is working in human society will not be deceived by charters, or bought off by dividends.—*The Gospel and the Modern Man,* pages 168, 169.

In view of the foregoing we may now distinguish between sin and sins. Sin is the fundamentally wicked attitude of self-will, and of rebellion against the will of God; while sins are the specific and particular manifestations of this fundamental attitude. At first this distinction may appear to be merely technical, but in experience it goes much deeper than that. One can abandon specific sins, and yet continue to be a sinner. He can stop being a drunkard; but can still be self-centered and self-willed and self-indulgent. For this reason, no inducement to abandon our specific sins penetrates to the heart of our deep need as sinners. No redemption is full and sound which does not change our underlying attitudes from rebellion to discipleship.

Study Outlines

Sin

Lesson Purpose

To portray sin as active enmity against God which excludes the sinner from His family circle.

High Points of the Lesson

We may disguise sin under the cloak of respectability, but it is still sin.

The closer we are to God the clearer we see our own sinfulness.

Neither Jesus nor his disciples made any attempt to minimize the problem of sin. Both he and they gave their lives to kill it.

We are in a "state of sin" where we live in enmity against God. Sin is also the specific act of rebellion. Every such act confirms us in our sinfulness.

Questions and Discussion Topics

(1) Why do we regard sin as the central problem of religion?

(2) What did Jesus and the apostles mean by forgiveness of sins?

(3) What is sin? Is it just the absence of good? Why does God concern himself about it?

(4) What do we mean by a "state of sin"? What is the relation between our environment and our desire to do right?

(5) What did Paul mean when he cried out, "Who shall deliver me from the body of this death!"

(6) Why does the love of God make sin more terrible? Illustrate your answer.

(7) Enumerate some deadly modern sins. How may these be overcome?

(8) How may we best achieve such a sense of the true awfulness of sin as to sustain us in our fight against it?

What the Lesson Means Today

There is no need to be morbid about it, but there is great need to be serious about it: all of us are sinners. We live in a state of sin, in the sense that we are habitually selfish, inconsiderate, and unkind.

We must be shaken free from complacency due to familiarity with sin. Only God can do this for us. We must seek him in worship and prayer to this end.

Lesson Eighteen

II—THE FORGIVENESS OF SIN

The sinner is at enmity against God. He has separated himself from the family circle of our Heavenly Father. The problem created by his sinning must therefore be solved, if it is solved at all, on two levels. The sinner must abandon his sinning and the attitude of rebellion which induced that sinning, and he must be received back into the family circle. This means that he must repent and that he must be forgiven; and until both of these adjustments have taken place, the solution is incomplete.

Repentance is not easy for us; and forgiveness is not easy for God. Repentance is not easy because so few of us really believe that we are sinners, or that our sinning is really important. And forgiveness is not easy because it is immoral when it is not accompanied by repentance. Many of us think that all that our Heavenly Father has to do in order to forgive us is just to "say the word." Actually, the first thing to be done is to pierce the shell of our complacency and to cause us to see ourselves as we truly are. Like the prodigal son, we must "come to ourselves" and realize where we are, before we are ready to start home from the far country into which we have strayed. Our Heavenly Father cannot take us back until we have done this. Forgiveness is thus more than willingness to "let bygones be bygones" or to "wipe the slate clean." Forgiveness which goes no farther than this would be just blind sentimentalism, and would permit the sinner to retain a low concern for the seriousness of his wrongdoing. Our Heavenly Father will never consent to such an arrangement.

Perhaps we can illustrate the situation in the interest of clarity. Let us suppose that a father discovers that his son is a drunkard. If that father passes by his son's drunkenness without comment and behaves as though nothing has happened, or if he just washes his hands of the situation, the boy soon comes to feel that his sin is not very serious or that his father has no deep convictions about it. This will never do. Yet to threaten and to harangue are useless, for the son may then become sullen, or defiant, or may offer shallow excuses, while he continues in his sin. Somehow the father must overcome all resentment that his son should betray him in this manner, and must stand by his son in a wise and patient and yet passionate endeavor to change the boy's way of life. Yet he cannot forgive his son, and treat him as he did before, so long as the boy continues to be a drunkard. When the boy comes to hate his drunkenness, and quits drinking, then he can be forgiven. Until he does this he may be loved, but he cannot be fully forgiven for fear that this forgiveness shall appear to be a condoning of his sin.

The problem of forgiveness is made even more difficult because our Father has such scrupulous respect for our right of free choice. He surrounds us with "temptations upward," but he will not *force* us to take the upward way. He does his utmost to persuade us; but when we change our way of living, we must do this of our own volition. In view of this, we may safely say that when we are truly forgiven, something has been done in us as well as for us. The scars left by sin may still be visible, but they speak no longer of the death which once threatened us; they speak instead of the new life into which we have entered with God.

The solution of the problem of sin also becomes more difficult the longer it is postponed. The more steeped in sin a man is, the more he needs forgiveness, and the harder it is to awaken him to a sense of his condition, so that he will play his part manfully in his own rescue. This problem would be insoluble if God waited for sinful men to take the first step. Our salvation is possible only because our Heavenly Father does not stand aloof until we come to ourselves. Instead, he uses all the energies of his great love to make us feel his affection and to cause us to yearn for reconciliation with him and then to attack from our side the barriers that separate us from him.

The conditions of eternal life are fixed by the very nature of things. We cannot journey toward hell and arrive in heaven. Because he knows this, because he loves us, and because he wishes us to enter into life at its best, our Heavenly Father is as inexorable in his demands as he is infinite in his compassion. He loves us too much to wash his hands of us; but neither will he compound our felonies. He prefers to suffer with us until the cost of our sin to him becomes too much for us to bear. Then, and then only, are we truly forgiven.

Study Outlines

The Forgiveness of Sin

Lesson Purpose

To show that the great problem of forgiveness is to make sinners forgivable, and that the great achievement of forgiveness is the readmission of onetime sinners to the family circle of God.

High Points of the Lesson

Our Heavenly Father is pained by our sinning, but does not hold resentment against us.

God cannot ignore our sinfulness, for this would confirm us in wrongdoing. We must change before we can be forgiven. Since many of us do not even realize that we need to change, our first need is to have our eyes opened to our true situation.

God will not force us to give up our sins, but he will use every persuasion to make us abandon them. When we renounce sin, he can forgive us and accept us back into fellowship with him.

Questions and Discussion Topics

(1) Why is our Heavenly Father concerned about the problems of our sinning?

(2) What readjustments are involved in true forgiveness?

(3) If our Heavenly Father desires to forgive us, why does he not do so freely and without obligation on our part?

(4) What is the first thing God must do for us before he can forgive us?

(5) What is sin? What is forgiveness?

(6) What is the immediate effect of sin on our own nature? How can this effect be removed?

(7) If a man does wrong to me, what is my responsibility toward him? Is this responsibility discharged by merely forgetting the matter?

(8) Discuss briefly, the statement that "in the long run the test of religion lies in its capacity to arouse repentance."

What the Lesson Means Today

We do not yet hate our sins as we ought to do, but we know that God hates them. We shall, therefore, do well to cultivate his attitude toward our sins by reviewing them frankly in his presence.

We are hungry for forgiveness in the same proportion as we are hungry for God. There is a direct relation between worship and forgiveness. Before we can be forgiven, we must show God that this forgiveness will not confirm us in our sins.

Lesson Nineteen

III—ATONEMENT

We have seen that the essence of forgiveness is in the restoration of friendly relations between man and God, and that the most difficult part of securing this reconciliation is in persuading a man who has strayed from God to want to come back again. It is not enough to preach at sinners, for talking does not go to the heart of this problem. The only thing that we have yet found powerful enough to turn people away from a life of sin to a life of righteousness is love. Many of us have been kept straight by our love for our mothers, and theirs for us, and when we realize how much that love costs them, we are more likely than ever to be clean and fine for love's sake.

There is a story of a little girl whose mother was a singularly beautiful woman except for her hands, which were badly disfigured. One evening, in an outburst of affection, the little girl said, "Mother, you are beautiful, and I love you very, very dearly." Then, wishing to be honest, she added, "except for your hands." Drawing the girl closely to her, the mother answered, "Daughter, let me tell you a story. Many years ago, when you were just a little girl, my hands were as beautiful as my face. One night, when I came back from visiting some friends, I was horrified to find our house on fire, and the firemen apparently unable to do anything about it. Of course, the first thing that I said was, 'Where is my little girl?' Somehow, everyone had taken it for granted you were safe, but I soon realized that you were still in that blazing building. I am not sure what happened during the next few minutes, although I remember the firemen trying to hold me, and saying that I could not go into the house. But I pulled away from them, and after a few terrible minutes of groping through that blazing furnace, I was back again in the cool night air, and I had you with me. My poor hands were terribly burned, and have never looked the same since; but for some reason I have not minded nearly so much as you might expect." The little girl was quite silent for a moment; then she said, "Mother dear, you are beautiful, and I love you more than I can tell. Your hands are most beautiful of all."

Love is like that. It always reveals itself in readiness to bear burdens and to make sacrifices for the one whom we love. And love is constantly breaking through barriers of pride and indifference to awaken its own echo in the lives of those who are beloved. So, in such a world as ours, where we are constantly falling short of his high purposes for us, his own great love demands that God shall sacrifice to the uttermost in order to win us back again. And because our Heavenly Father knew our need for this sacrifice in the very beginning, and because his Son was one with him in the desire for our salvation, Jesus was the "Lamb slain from the foundation of the world" (Rev. 13:8). This great sacrifice is made meaningful when we come to "love him because he first loved us" (I John 4:19), and when "the love of Christ constraineth us" (II Cor. 5:14) to do what is right.

The sacrifice which God has made in order to win us to himself and to our own best selves is expressed in theological terms in the doctrine of the atonement. Ever since the time of Jesus, thoughtful men have been advancing theories to explain just what the atonement is and what it does for us. None of these explanations has been completely satisfactory, for we are constantly impressed that God has done more for us than it is possible for us to put into words. But the clear verdict of Christian experience is that the death of Jesus on the cross was the inevitable result of the kind of life that he lived. His dying was not something apart from his living. Instead, it throws a flood of light back on all that he was, and forward to all that he now is to humanity. Jesus both lived and died in order to persuade us to do our part in restoring communion between God and man.

Apparently it would have been easy for Jesus to avoid Gethsemane and Calvary. The fact that he did not do so emphasizes that what happened was not an accident. On the contrary, the cross is the outcome of the deepest spiritual life and thought of the Master. It gathers up and expresses his life purpose more than any other single act of his life.

Although his friends had not anticipated the crucifixion of Jesus, it had been written into the scheme of things from the beginning. This is because people who stand squarely for human rights against the entrenched interests of their times must be prepared to pay the full price of their pioneering; if Jesus was to give us an example of this type of courage—which makes insight effective—it was necessary that he should pay this same price. It was therefore in the heart of God from the beginning that Jesus should pay the ultimate penalty for his devotion to the truth. If he had not done so, he could not be our leader. Since he has done so, he stands forever as the foremost pioneer of wise and good and courageous living.

So, when the time came, Jesus went up to Jerusalem to carry on and consummate his work. So long as there was nothing to be gained by facing the final issue, he avoided it (John 8: 59). But after his disciples had received their training, and his enemies were still set in their resolve to murder him, he quietly and steadfastly chose the time and place, and there faced the issue created by his righteousness and their iniquity. This thing was not done secretly or under cover. It was done under such circumstances as to challenge a large number of men to think what it all meant and—what is perhaps more important—to feel what it meant.

Jesus was crucified by ordinary men. The leaders of the Jews who appeared against him were not the monsters of wickedness that we sometimes consider them; but were the respectable men and women of their day.

The motives that are thought good enough for everyday life were potent enough to crucify the Son of God. Ordinary selfishness, ordinary cowardice, ordinary prejudice, willful blindness, and insecurity—these sins, common to all times, were found to be so deeply rooted in human nature, and so at enmity with the will of God, that when they were confronted with the Holy One, full of grace and truth, men were not abashed, but only stung into a blind passion of hate and fear.—*The Meaning of the Cross*, page 5, by W. R. Maltry.

What did Jesus accomplish at Calvary? First, he revealed to men the unfailing love of God which has been round about us from the beginning of time, and which seeks us out at any time. And, second, he revealed the true nature of sin. These two were not separate achievements. Indeed, they belong together. We cannot know the great love of God until we see that love revealed in a death struggle with sin.

At Calvary, Jesus made our sinning his business; and by so doing he did something for us that we could not do for ourselves. We sometimes think that it is easy to know the difference between right and wrong. But, as a matter of fact, this is not true at all. Sin has become such a part of the world in which we live that our familiarity with it has blinded us. Even though we should recognize the more flagrant sins, such as dishonesty and indecency and untruthfulness, we are strangely acquiescent in the presence of successful sinners who sit in high places; and we look down on those who have not been sufficiently adroit in their selfishness to find their way to the chief seats. Now, as then, someone from outside our sinful environment is needed to help us to see things as they truly are. The Son of God has satisfied this need by reaching across our blindness, and taking on himself the sacrifice and the cost, and so showing us the wealth of the love which pursues us and which is so eager to bless us.

Mr. G. A. Studdert Kennedy tells of visiting a man who was imprisoned for forgery and embezzlement. He could not move the man one inch toward repentance; the only sign the man gave of being interested in the visit was when he asked the minister to go and see his mother. Mr. Kennedy went and found the old lady looking so worn and so bitterly ashamed that Mr. Kennedy was moved to paraphrase the statement of Isaiah, "Surely she hath borne his griefs and carried his sorrows; she was wounded for his transgressions; she was bruised for his iniquities; the chastisement of his peace is upon her; and with her stripes he shall be healed. He has gone astray and turned to his own way; and love has laid on her the iniquity of her son" *(The Wicket Gate;* Isaiah 53: 4-6). Her mother heart, which knew little of sin, had been made to feel exceedingly sinful for his sake. Such love as this woman poured out on her son, and which made her so completely at one with him that his sin was her sin, his disgrace was her disgrace, his shame was her shame, is the nearest approach we can find upon earth to the love of God, to what God is. Calvary shows us, in one clear flash of revelation, how deeply Jesus suffers when we sin.

Then, again, at Calvary Jesus revealed the true nature of sin. We are deeply stirred when we contemplate what the men of his time did to Jesus. It is not as though he was a sinner like us, and part of the whole selfish business. He was completely guiltless of anything which merited punishment. So, when he was crucified, the awfulness of the sin which murdered him struck home to the hearts of those who loved him; once for all sin was forced into the light and revealed as the slayer of the innocent. At Calvary Jesus stood up in the midst of history and said, "Look, all of you, and I will show you in my own body what sin is, and what it does to innocent people. If you are determined to be sinners, you shall at least know what sin really means."

Calvary is a frank appeal to the emotions, but it is an emotional appeal at its very best. Here Jesus did for humanity what no amount of logical exposition, or of mere arguing could ever do. The tragedy of Calvary has become the seed of more triumphant life than any other event in history. There was no other way to appeal to men for all time, and to move humanity so deeply and to such worthy ends, because everyone understands the language of sacrifice and pain.

All great work has behind it some suffering. A wise teacher once said to a group of students for the ministry, "If you go out into your work and succeed without suffering, be not unduly elated—someone who preceded you has already suffered. If you suffer without succeeding, be not unduly cast down—someone who follows will yet succeed where you have suffered!" If our predecessors had not died for the good they held dear, we should still be living in worse conditions than we can imagine. We are all the gainers by other people's sacrifices. If we are content to bask in the freedom that other people have fought for, but will do nothing to win larger freedom for those who are coming after, we are traitors to our ancestry and our posterity. The line of progress must be advanced, no matter how difficult. It is this capacity for willing suffering as the price of our contribution to humanity which marks our kinship with God.

We can now consider the question: "How can Christ save us?" This is not a matter for argument, but for experience; the simple fact of experience is that contemplation of Christ —who he is and what he did for our sake—has been the most potent factor of history in inspiring men to do right. It has turned drunken men from the gutter, lifted the fallen and set them on the highway of salvation, and called many a seemingly respectable sinner to a life of genuine godliness. We are not faced with an academic theory, but with the most powerful influence in the experience of the race.

The Sermon on the Mount is an excellent statement of Christian ethics for a man who is already won to Christianity. But no ethical statement has power enough to take hold of men who are degrading themselves below the beasts and transform them into ministers of God to their fellows. Only the love found at Calvary can do this. When we really see what happened there, we echo with glad hearts the words of Paul:

> Therefore if any man be in Christ, he is a new creature: old things are passed away; behold, all things are become new. And all things are of God, who hath reconciled us to himself by Jesus Christ, and hath given to us the ministry of reconciliation; to wit, that God was in Christ, reconciling the world unto himself, not imputing their trespasses unto them; and hath committed unto us the word of reconciliation. Now then we are ambassadors for Christ, as though God did beseech you by us; we pray you in Christ's stead, be ye reconciled to God. For he hath made him to be sin for us, who knew no sin; that we might be made the righteousness of God in him.—II Cor. 5:17-21.

STUDY OUTLINES

THE ATONEMENT

LESSON PURPOSE

To consider the love of God and the awfulness of sin as both are revealed at Calvary, and to face the obligations which rest on us as a result of what God has done for us.

Note: There is no point at which mere argument or exposition is more futile than when we are facing the facts of the atonement. Understanding only comes as we read the record with our hearts. This should be kept well in mind when preparing the worship approach to the study of this lesson.

HIGH POINTS OF THE LESSON

Love always involves readiness to bear burdens and to make sacrifices for those whom we love. Love laid this obligation on Divinity.

We are so steeped in sin that we are blinded to it and cannot help ourselves. No one can help us but someone from outside the vicious circle of sin.

Ever since Calvary, men have seen sin in a new light. At the same time they have been astounded that the love of God would go to such a length to help us see sin so clearly as to hate it.

Questions and Discussion Topics

(1) What is the greatest influence for righteousness in your life: love, fear, hope, etc.?

(2) What part did the life of Jesus have in the atonement? Could any man have saved us by dying for us?

(3) Tell the story of the Crucifixion briefly. What were the major events connected with it?

(4) Why was Jesus crucified? Do you think he deliberately chose the Passover season? Why?

(5) How does Calvary reveal the love of God?

(6) How does Calvary reveal the true nature of sin?

(7) How does the atonement reveal us to ourselves? How does it move us to repentance?

(8) Recapitulate the major facts of the atonement as here set out. What does the atonement mean to you?

What the Lesson Means Today

Jesus died for us as well as for other men. He was extremely anxious that we might know just what sin does to men. No wise man avoids the lesson that Jesus seeks to teach us here, for its significance is beyond measure. Do not try to avoid it. For once let us face the fact of sin and its consequences to us and to others.

Jesus was crucified by ordinary men. It was not extraordinary sin that killed him, but the commonplace blindness and bigotry of daily life. The sins of the Jews were the kind of sins that we commit. The sin that was horrible in the Jews is horrible in us.

Lesson Twenty

IV—THE PRINCIPLE OF REPENTANCE

In our discussion of the nature of sin, we have seen that it involves both the misuse of power entrusted to us by God, and also the worst kind of ingratitude and disloyalty. The most immediate and disastrous result of sin is alienation from God, the breaking of personal relations with him. This does not mean that our Heavenly Father ceases to love us when we sin; but it does mean that we cease to be comfortable in his presence, and his Spirit is withdrawn from us. It also means that society which is organized apart from his purposes, and is selfishly motivated, is at enmity against God and is not hospitable toward his work or his people. This is life's major social tragedy; for, as a result, society continues to be the prey of the warring ambitions of sinful men instead of becoming the kingdom of our God and of his Christ.

We have seen that our Father is eager to forgive us, both individually and collectively. Many years ago he said, "I, even I, am he that blotteth out thy transgression for mine own sake" (Isa. 43:25). For the individual this forgiveness involves restoration of the relationship broken by sin, and for society it means the renewed presence of Divinity. Such restoration is not easy; it is worse than useless unless it is accompanied by an inner change, a spiritual readjustment. Jesus died to teach us the need for this return to God, but even this great sacrifice is unavailing unless we match it with our own eager repentance. We must be sincerely sorry for our sins, anxious to make all the restitution in our power, and hungry for readmission to God's family circle. Our Father never ceases to love us; but he does not forgive us until we are truly forgiveable—until we have repented. Any easier forgiveness would confirm us in our sins without permanently blessing us.

Repentance means utter divorce from our sinning. To repent is to feel a godly sorrow for sin, born of the love of God, and as a result to completely repudiate both the specific sin itself and the sinful way of life from which it springs.

The difficulty with repentance is that our sins are not isolated from the rest of our lives. They are manifestations of our true selves. The drunkard is not a good man who has occasional lapses into drunkenness, he is a man with an overpowering appetite for strong drink, and this appetite is part of him. Down in his nerve cells, the record of the kind of person he is has already been kept. For him repentance means a change of heart and mind, but it means more than that. It means a change of his very self. To be delivered from his sin, he must be delivered from the kind of man he has permitted himself to become.

The first step toward genuine repentance is to recognize ourselves as sinners—people whose life is at enmity against God—and to be truly sorry. At first we shall not be able to see our own sin clearly and will tend to defend it; but the closer our communion with God, the clearer we shall see and feel the true horror of sin. We need the help of God at this point, for sin blinds us. "He that hateth his brother is in darkness and walketh in darkness, and knoweth not whither he goeth, because that darkness hath blinded his eyes."—I John 2: 11.

Some hint of the way in which we come to see our sins as they really are is given in the story of a mother who went unannounced to visit her son at college, and found objectionable pictures on the walls of his room. She made no comment; but, upon returning home, expressed to him a beautifully framed reproduction of Hofmann's *The Boy Christ*. Because his mother had sent the picture, the youth hung it on the wall. Later, a friend came in, noticed the absence of the risqué pictures, and inquired why they had been taken down. The student replied, "I could not let them stay up there by Him."

The second step in repentance is to disassociate ourselves from our sins and to repudiate them utterly. All that is good in us must rise up in revolt against the kind of person we have been and the kind of things that we have done. We must be condemned before our own consciences; and must drop all our alibis and renounce with our whole souls the things in which we once delighted. This is not a matter of words but of deep inner conviction, renunciation, and redirection.

The acts of sin which we commit are not isolated from the rest of our lives; they are usually linked in chains of habit. Sin is embedded in our ways of thinking and acting, and its hold is constantly strengthened. The drunken Rip Van Winkle excused himself for every fresh dereliction by saying, "It won't count this time." But every lapse makes habit stronger, and to be delivered from his sin, a man has to be delivered from what has become part of his very self. We might repudiate specific sins by ourselves, but we shall not deny our whole life pattern except as we become new men and women in Jesus Christ.

A third element in true repentance is recognition of responsibility for our sins and eagerness to make restitution. Some years ago the copper refineries of Montana were releasing great volumes of sulphur dioxide into the air. The fumes killed vegetation over wide areas. Finally law and public opinion forced the industry to end the abuse, and the refinery installed equipment to use the obnoxious gas in making sulphuric acid. This acid has many commercial uses, but after a time the price dropped and manufacture became unprofitable. So the chemical engineers shipped in phosphate rock. With this and the sulphuric acid, they made acid phosphate, which is one of the three essential ingredients in agricultural fertilizers. By this cyclical process, the fumes which formerly destroyed crops are now employed to make them grow more luxuriantly. Something like this must happen in the life of the sinner. His change of heart must be accompanied by acceptance of responsibility for the evil consequences of his past sinning. He who once sinned must not only "go and sin no more," but he must now promote the righteousness which he once despised.

The experience of Jesus with Zacchæus illustrates well the point under consideration. Zacchæus was a taxgatherer for the Romans, and a rich man. It was taken for granted that, like other taxgatherers, he had become rich by extortion. For some reason Zacchæus was attracted to Jesus and went to considerable difficulty to see and hear him; as a result, the Master invited himself to a meal at the rich man's house. The outcome was that this Jew who had grown rich promised to restore fourfold any money which he might have secured by unjust means (Luke 19: 1-8). Here, under the inspiration of goodness personified, he saw how little wealth really matters, and out of this conviction came his willingness to accept responsibility and to make restitution if needed.

What is repentance? Repentance is not mere emotionalism, and it is not just a change of mind. It is an upward change in the direction of a man's life—and it occurs because that man has met God, has felt God's rightful claim on his life, and has given to God the place which is His due. Repentance is a change of mind based on a change of heart and issuing in a changed way of living. Although it may be accompanied by sorrow over past sin and guilt, this sorrow is swallowed up in the joy of a new relationship with God and a new power over self.

Study Outlines

The Principle of Repentance

Lesson Purpose

To sound the call to repentance, to show what repentance means, and what it involves.

High Points of the Lesson

Our Heavenly Father wants to forgive us and has done his part toward making us forgivable. Our response to his pleading is repentance.

Repentance involves a change of heart and mind by which we come to love righteousness and hate iniquity. All of us need such repentance.

Sin has become such a part of our lives that repudiation of sin means repudiation of our own habits and ungodly point of view. No man who excuses himself in his sinfulness is spiritually safe.

Questions and Discussion Topics

(1) List the reasons why we ought to repent. Should we act on them? When should repentance begin?

(2) Why is it not possible for God to forgive us until we repent? What would easy forgiveness do to us?

(3) What is the relation between humility and repentance?

(4) What is the cost of sin to society? Mention the specific costs of such "respectable" sins as pride, conceit, commercial ruthlessness.

(5) What is the first step toward genuine repentance? Name some of the barriers which make this step difficult.

(6) What is the next step? What are some of the difficulties at this point?

(7) What is the third step? What does the practice of excusing himself do to the man who does it habitually? What does the acceptance of responsibility do for the individual?

(8) What does repentance do for society? Does our change of heart undo the wrong that we have done? In what way does it remedy the social effect of our sinning?

An important aspect of repentance is facing the facts. It is better to do this on our knees than anywhere else. Frankly, how does your life look to God?

When we have put aside all pretense, and the love of God has laid on us the obligation to be worth something to him, we shall not have to be reminded to make restitution for the wrong we have done. Nor will we have to be urged to join with those who are attacking evil at its source. True repentance will lead to restitution and discipleship. When we feel this deeply and hate sin as it should be hated, there is no danger that we shall think of sin lightly. God can then forgive us without harming us. He gladly does so.

Lesson Twenty-one

V—BAPTISM IN WATER

As we discussed repentance, it became apparent that to repent effectively we must become different people from what we have been hitherto. Indeed, after careful consideration, we can find no better statement of what must happen than a statement of Jesus to Nicodemus, "Ye must be born again" (John 3: 7). Commenting on this statement, Doctor James Bissett Pratt says: "In the whole history of ethical discussion there is no saying more full of insight into the nature of the moral life than those words of Jesus, 'Ye must be born again.'"

You cannot build a new world without new-world builders. Men whose hearts and minds turn to some other homeland can never succeed as pioneers of a new nation. The United States of America was not truly a nation until the founders and patriots ceased to think of themselves as transplanted Englishmen or Germans or Scandinavians, and learned to think of themselves as Americans. It is similarly impossible to build the kingdom of God with men whose interests and affections turn back to the kingdoms of this world. He who would assist in building the kingdom of God must indeed be born again.

The Scriptures are full of this thought; and we must remember that the Scriptures were born in the vital experience of the church in the days of her most productive life. Jesus said to Nicodemus: "That which is born of the flesh is flesh; and that which is born of the Spirit is spirit" (John 3: 3, 6). Paul was relating this fact to the experience of the saints when he wrote to the saints in Galatia: "In Jesus Christ neither circumcision availeth anything, nor uncircumcision, but a new creature" (Gal. 6: 15). Modern revelation says that the faithful among the priesthood are "sanctified by the spirit unto the renewing of their bodies" (Doctrine and Covenants 83:6). In other words, the Spirit quickens and renews the innate powers of men who truly give themselves to the work of God so that their abilities and tendencies, and even their very natures, are made over for God's sake: they are born again.

The unregenerated man is "dead in trespasses and sin" (Eph. 2:1). The rebirth which we are discussing means that he achieves an entirely new attitude toward sin. He disavows his earlier way of life, which has impressed itself on his physique in the form of undesirable habits as well as on his heart and mind and conscience in the form of undesirable thoughts and purposes. Such a change is not won by merely securing information about Jesus, but by the quickening of the heart in response to him.

In view of the foregoing, we can readily see that the technique of Christianity is in sharp contrast to that of any scheme of ethical culture or moral reform. It is not education that counts, but re-creation; not what a man knows, but the forces which inspire him. Frequently the best that education can do is to remove impediments so that the real man can shine out. Christianity is greatly concerned in the matter of education, but it is even more concerned in the matter of re-creation which pierces all veneer and reaches to the soul of the man himself. "The Christian must himself be the holy land where Christ is born, and where he dwells."
—Henry S. Coffin.

The sinner who has been touched by the finger of God and who recognizes himself to be spiritually blind and helpless, is already well on the way toward healing. Under the guidance of the Spirit of God, he expects great things from God. He does not ask that someone shall take him by the hand and lead him, even though he knows that he needs guidance. What he asks, and what Christianity promises him, is that he shall be born again and shall once more become the kind of man that he was designed to be before sin entered into the world and into his life, and so marred his spiritual possibilities. He asks for God to dwell in him, to open his eyes, that henceforth he may see in his own right and by the power of God that is in him.

The big thing about the conversion experience is that the person who is experiencing this transformation actually feels that God is at work in his life. Through prayer and meditation, through study of the Scriptures and a sincere attempt to practice their precepts, he has prepared the way for the divine indwelling. But when he finds new life stirring within him, he realizes that it is the life of God, given him from above rather than achieved by his own power.

The miracle of rebirth does not lie in the speed of this transformation but in its quality. Rebirth does not mean the attainment of moral character at a stroke any more than physical birth means sudden and mature appearance in the world. It does mean possession of a new spirit and a new power for living; it means new devotion and new passion; it means a redirection of the entire personality from earthly to heavenly purpose. The reborn man still finds many enemies within and around him. But he knows them for enemies which have no right to a place in his life, and he declares war on them as fast as he recognizes them.

At this point the Christian doctrine of baptism by immersion in water, by one recognized as having authority, becomes significant and helpful. True repentance prepares the way for the new birth; it becomes more effective after this rebirth takes place and is particularly effective if that which has taken place within is paralleled by an actual physical experience. What is taking place is death to sin and resurrection to a new life of righteousness. Baptism by immersion symbolizes this, and when rightly explained to the participant, becomes a physical and historical monument to his decision for God. From that day forward, he does not look back to a gradual inner development only, but to a specific experience with God, to a time of definite commitment in which Divinity was represented by a recognized ministry, and when a covenant was made in due form, in the presence of witnesses, and so became binding and immediately effective.

The commission given to the apostles was: "Go ye into all the world and preach the gospel to every creature. He that believeth and is baptized shall be saved; he that believeth not shall be damned" (Mark 16:15, 16). The apostles evidently took this commission seriously, and believed that baptizing believers was an integral part of the work they were to do. While they were probably not greatly interested in the physical act of baptism by itself, they were tremendously concerned about registering the great spiritual change of which baptism is part and symbol. They were concerned in making a dramatic appeal to the best in a man, and in calling for a dramatic response to their appeal. The command to be baptized which was voiced by Peter at Pentecost and by Ananias to Saul was a command to commit themselves decisively to the Christian life and to membership into the Christian community. Baptism was this commitment and this induction.

There hardly seems to be any necessity for extended discussion of the mode of baptism. Baptism by immersion was taught by Jesus, John, Peter, Ananias, and others; and modern revelation confirms the teaching of the Scriptures at this point. Yet it seems to me that demonstration of the importance of baptism by immersion does not lie in argument, but in examination of the nature of what happens in the experience of rebirth. No other rite matches this experience as to symbolism, distinctiveness, authority, and spiritual effectiveness.

At Pentecost those who had consented to the death of Jesus became truly repentant. Peter was tremendously concerned that their repentance should become effective for good both within their own lives and in the life of the community. Under the guidance of inspiration, therefore, he commanded them to be baptized (Acts 2: 37-39). This baptism rescued their repentance from ineffectiveness; for baptism is a dramatic registration of the change which takes place in the life of a converted man, and at the same time it is the rite of initiation into the kingdom.

No sinner is able to undo the results of his sinning by himself; but a body of repentant sinners, knit together in a fellowship of love and motivated by the directing influence of the Spirit of God, can extend the forces of righteousness in the world, and so, in God's good time, can establish his kingdom. The truly repentant man is therefore eager to multiply his spiritual effectiveness by becoming a member of the body of Christ. He who thus enlists as a junior partner in God's work, is saved from pettiness and insecurity and is held by a great devotion to a great task. But he who fails to associate himself with the work of God is damned, for damnation is no mere theological concept. It is the condition of a man or woman who chooses darkness rather than light.

The church must define herself at some point. We must know who is in the church and who is not; who may be regarded as fully committed to the task of Christ, and who have yet to be won to complete submission and surrender. Baptism is this act of definition. It is, of course, true that many who have been baptized have not shown sufficient insight or devotion to enter truly into the baptismal experience. It is also true that there are many who are not formally inducted into the kingdom who are nevertheless truly sympathetic toward the work of the church. But the effective proponents of the kingdom of God are to be found among those who have made covenant with him, and whose decision has been registered in their own lives and in the life of the church by this specific act of dedication

Baptism is a moral virtue and not just a physical act. It is not an outward form, but is the response of a good conscience toward God. We have no need to mumble when we repeat the words of Peter, "The like figure . . . . even baptism doth also now save us" (I Peter 3: 21). Baptism is an act having moral quality rooted in the conscience; back of it is the same divine authority which sanctions any other moral transaction. It is as necessary to spiritual life as paying one's bills is to honesty.

The electrical genius learns something of the laws by which electrical power is generated and controlled; he then builds a machine, patiently and purposefully, and so appropriates these laws to his desires. The patriot immerses himself in the spirit of his country and surrenders himself to the demands of his patriotism; power flows through him, and he is lifted up towards greatness. So also, when the Christian surrenders his life to the supreme will of Christ, and shuts out of his life the things which are at war with the purpose of God, it is not surprising that new power flows through him to the achievement of the divine purpose. Given such a cause to enlist his devotion, the most ordinary human being transcends himself. His instincts are controlled, inconsistencies are straightened out, obstacles are overcome, health is restored, abilities are augmented, and the whole personality is illuminated and directed toward a new freedom.

STUDY OUTLINES

BAPTISM IN WATER

LESSON PURPOSE

To show that repentance is not fully effective until consummated in baptism, and that specific commitment to the work of God is essential to the forgiveness of sin.

HIGH POINTS OF THE LESSON

The man who truly repents is a new man, with new ambitions, new affection, and new hopes. There are still many enemies within, but now he is ready to fight sin wherever it is.

It is imperative that the converted sinner shall understand clearly what is happening and by whose grace he is reborn to a new life. Baptism is the most succinct and dramatic statement of these facts that we know.

The church is the fellowship of baptized believers. Its members hate sin and their connection with it. Individually sinners cannot do much to overcome sin, but we can make an affirmative collective approach by building the kingdom of God.

QUESTIONS AND DISCUSSION TOPICS

(1) Why and how is repentance connected with baptism?

(2) Refer to some of the Scriptures which indicate that baptism is essential to salvation.

(3) Discuss, briefly, what Jesus meant when he told Nicodemus that he must be born again.

(4) What is the value of baptism in commiting the convert to a new way of life? Is it an actual part of the experience of rebirth?

(5) Why is it important that we shall be baptized by a properly commissioned minister?

(6) Why is the mode of baptism important?

(7) In what way does baptism help the repentant sinner undo the results of his past sinning?

(8) The Scriptures tell us that he that believeth and is baptized shall be saved, and that he that believeth not shall be damned. What is salvation? What is damnation?

WHAT THE LESSON MEANS TODAY

Repentance is first of all a change of heart and last of all a dedicated life. When we repent, we forget ourselves in our eagerness for the kingdom where we can get a footing to fight sin most successfully.

Our baptism is intended to commit us both in our own eyes and in the eyes of the world. It has all the solemnity of a contract. It is an undertaking such as an honest man ought not to break. It is like the act of becoming naturalized; after that, sin is treason.

Chapter IX

THE CHURCH

The church—The nature of the church—Characteristics and functions of the church.

Lesson Twenty-two

I—THE CHURCH

IT IS THE MOST NATURAL THING in the world for Christian people to get together to talk of the many things which God has done for them and to plan what they can do together in return for his goodness. It is a good thing that this is so, for personality is very largely dependent upon social environment for its existence and development. We do not grow best by ourselves, but in the process of rubbing shoulders with other men; and the highest type of personality is achieved in association with good people in challenging and worthy tasks.

This consciousness of kind is not a new thing, but is of the very nature of Christianity and goes back to the beginning. Jesus attracted good men to himself and loved to have them with him. At times he seemed to depend on his friends for their sympathy and understanding, and he missed them sorely in the crucial moments when he had to face the demands of his great task alone. The Master therefore had good reason, grounded in his own experience, for trying to safeguard those who followed him against spiritual isolation. He did this by making them the nucleus of the church. The twelve, who were chosen that they might be with him, were also chosen to be with each other, and to strengthen their brethren (Luke 22: 32).

While Jesus was here, he fully understood the purposes of God and lived a life of sinless devotion, so that he became at once the teacher and the example of all who were truly seeking light. But in spite of his splendid instruction and example, the early disciples fell far short of the pattern set for them, and it was only by uniting them in the body of Christ, to which every member could contribute his part, that there was any hope that they would carry forward his message and his example to the people of their own day and to those of succeeding generations.

The experience which men gain as members of a well-integrated body is much more than the total of their individual experiences. The sweetness of fellowship in communion with each other and with God is beyond the reach of any number of individuals, as individuals. It cannot be appreciated from observation, but must be shared by those who are bound together by their joint devotion to the divine purpose, and who thus become one in spite of their many other differences. It was because of this that the hours which Jesus gave to the instruction of the twelve were not spent with twelve individuals, but with twelve members of a group in which each man lost something of himself in becoming part of the whole.

The church was built, then, not merely because of the human tendency for persons with common interests to get together, but for this reason plus other specific and urgent necessities: the necessity for the disciples to share their expanding experience of life with Christ, the necessity for demonstrating the power of Christ to unbelievers, and the necessity for providing continuity between the religious life of one generation and that of the next.

The church which was built for these and other reasons existed before the day of Pentecost. Certainly there was some delegation of authority even in the apostolic group, for we note how frequently Peter, James, and John were given special instructions and responsibilities. There was also a treasurer of the twelve (John 13: 29), and while the first celebration of the Lord's Supper probably occurred at an actual meal, and was somewhat informal, yet all who participated—with the exception of Judas—were bound together by just such ties as ought to unite the members of the body of Christ.

After the Resurrection and Ascension of Jesus had been followed by the endowment of Pentecost, the church was well launched on her work of testimony. The members of the body were equal in spiritual standing in the sight of God but were blessed with a diversity of gifts according to his will and were assigned their several places in harmony with these gifts (I Cor. 12). Peter, James, and John were apparently leaders, but closely associated with them were the other apostles, the seventy, the elders, and the other men of the ministry. The ministering women also had their place, and from the first there was an inspired movement toward unity in diversity, the co-operation of all to the one purpose in accordance with gifts given them of God.

This expansion of the work of the church was not an attempt to improve on what Jesus had done, but to unite the growing body of the disciples under the direction of the Holy Spirit, and in harmony with the pattern given by Jesus (Acts 6: 1-6). Christ was with the church in his lifetime and continued with it afterward through the ministry of the Holy Spirit. Paul was particularly insistent on recognition of this fact; he reminded the Saints in Rome that Christ is the husband of the church (Rom. 7: 4), and gives it His name (Rom. 16: 16), while to the saints in Ephesus he wrote that Christ is the head of the church (Eph. 4: 15), and is her Saviour, and that he loves her and has sanctified her (Eph. 5: 23-26).

Study Outlines

The Church

Lesson Purpose

To present the church as a divine creation, and its members as belonging to each other because they belong to God.

High Points of the Lesson

The church is an essential instrument in the hands of God through which the nature of Christianity is to be demonstrated, the unbelieving converted, and the gospel given continuity.

The church was established by Jesus. Under the apostles it spread throughout the world, but its distinctiveness still lay in its relation to Christ.

The members of the body do not live for themselves but all grow together as the body is united in love under God.

Questions and Discussion Topics

(1) What is the difference between a group of Christians and the church? What is the bond of their union?

(2) Why was it necessary for the disciples to share their expanding experience of the meaning of Christianity?

(3) What missionary strength does the church have which no group of individual Christians can have? Does this constitute a reason for joining the church?

(4) Should one generation of Christians know more about Christianity than the preceding generation? Why? How is the knowledge of each generation conserved?

(5) Is the church essential to salvation? Can we say that a man who refuses to join the church is refusing to exert his full strength for Christ?

(6) What do we mean by saying that we are "members" of the church? Does our membership emphasize our duties or our rights?

(7) What are the major functions of the church? What is our relation to the discharge of these functions?

(8) What is the relation of Christ and the church?

What the Lesson Means Today

The church is a living body, every member of which should rightfully belong to every other member.

The effective ministry of the church depends on the full cooperation of all the members in her life.

In a true marriage the husband and wife should each be concerned with the total marriage situation. Similarly, when we are truly baptized, we should live for the church, suffering in her shortcomings and growing in her growth.

Lesson Twenty-three

II—THE NATURE OF THE CHURCH

The church was formed to continue the work of Jesus Christ in the world under the direction of the Holy Spirit. It was established by Jesus, and is primarily a divine creation rather than a human institution; in this fact lies its distinctiveness. The church bears his name, transmits his life, teaches his laws, interprets his purposes, seeks his children, acts with his authority, and is the promise and precursor of his kingdom.

Because the church is a divine creation rather than a human institution, it enlarges our sympathies, reinforces our powers, multiplies our contacts with good men, and joins us to them with a binding and attractive power not known elsewhere. The living church is an organism rather than an organization. Its members are joined together as the parts of a body, and not just as bricks in a house; they belong to each other because they first of all belong to Christ.

Within the church the various members of the body function according to their several gifts and thus minister to the total good, just as the head, the heart, and the hand all minister to the life and health of the body. And just as the parts of the body do not exist for themselves, so the body of the church as a whole does not exist for itself. Paul has rightly called it the Bride of Christ (Eph. 1: 22, 23), which he loves and seeks after and ministers to, and which in turn loves and lives with him.

When we really grasp the idea that the church is created to be a divine and human organism, in which God and man are inseparably connected, as in the body of Jesus, we realize how urgently we need to be sustained by the life of the church in order that we may fit into our rightful places. The effectiveness of the church in the world centers in our fellowship with each other and with Christ. "If we walk in the light, as he is in the light, we have fellowship one with another" (I John 1:

7). Through the Spirit of God found in this fellowship we are filled with new life, work with new purpose, and are inspired with a new affection.

The living church is designed to stand in every age as "The church of the Living God, the pillar and ground of the truth" (I Tim. 3: 15). As Jesus embodied the truth in his life, so he has called on the church to embody the truth in its life and to proclaim this truth to all mankind. Thus the church continues unchanged as an organism and its purpose continues, even though the individual members of the church may pass away, very much as our own bodies continue even though the specific materials of which they are formed are constantly replaced.

The church which bears testimony to the unchanging purpose of God must also grow into a more and more abundant life in her self and in her members. She will thus fulfill the purpose of Christ who said, "I am come that they might have life and have it more abundantly," (John 10: 10). The "greater works" which the church is designed to make possible, will in no way vitiate the works of the past, but will come from a more faithful presentation of the purpose of Jesus than was ever possible before. Moreover, this abundant purpose is not confined to the present life, but looks toward partnership in the purposes of God himself. This concept is gathered up in the marvelous statement of modern revelation, "This is my work and my glory, to bring to pass the immortality and eternal life of man."—Doctrine and Covenants 22: 23.

Because of the spirit within the church, it is her very nature to become the herald and the prophecy of the kingdom of God. Indeed, so closely are the church and the kingdom related that the two terms are frequently used interchangeably in the Scriptures and in the thought and conversation of the Saints. But this identification of the church and the kingdom is not strictly accurate, for in every age there have been some who have submitted to the ordinance of baptism, but who have not truly been "born of the Spirit" (John 3: 5), and so have not entered into the kingdom of God. Nevertheless, a work of assimilation goes forward steadily within the body of Christ. As we truly become *members* of the body, so can the body itself fulfill its purpose and build the kingdom.

III—CHARACTERISTICS AND FUNCTIONS OF THE CHURCH

The early Christian church was a vital force in the life of her people, and made an amazing contribution to her generation and to those generations which followed after. Because of this, and because of our deep conviction that the church as portrayed in the New Testament ministered to men's deepest and most enduring needs, and not to the superficialities which change with the passions of thought, we have a deep interest in its history and functioning.

We go back to the apostolic age in order to see the church when she was in close contact with her Master, when the memory of his earthly ministry, his resurrection, and glory was still poignant in the hearts and minds of his disciples.

The church of these early days was intensely doctrinal. The first Christians had little time to bandy opinions back and forth on the topics of current interest. They felt that they were faced with two urgent and significant tasks: to make over their own lives and the life of the church in constantly closer harmony with the life of Jesus, and to win as many people as possible to the same spiritual enterprise. We therefore find them proclaiming the facts of Christianity with great earnestness and pleading to all sorts and conditions of men that they rebuild their lives in harmony with those facts. This was doctrinal preaching of the highest order.

In those early days there were many philosophers abroad—Stoics, Cynics, and the like. The Christians let them dispute and argue without hindrance; but the Christians themselves preached a definite and important message which had to do with the actual dealings of God with men. It was no mere exhortation to adopt a new life program. It was no tepid invitation to others to join the Christian church *if they did not already belong to some other church.* Peter began it at Pentecost when he said: "God hath made that same Jesus whom ye have crucified, both Lord and Christ" (Acts 2: 36). Paul preached in the same strain: "Ye turned to God from idols to serve the living and true God; and to wait for his Son from heaven, whom he raised from the dead, even Jesus, which delivered us from the wrath to come" (I Thess. 1: 9, 10). And again: "Christ died for our sins according to the scripture; he was buried; he rose again the third day" (I Cor. 15: 3,4). They preached the facts, and showed that life was founded on these facts; they did not compromise with truth but proclaimed a way of life which is eternally valid and eternally significant. And their experience confirmed their claims. A man could not be both a Christian and a worshiper of strange gods; he could not accept Christianity and at the same time admit that for other people there might be some other way of salvation. He could not undertake to refrain from seeking converts from other faiths, so as to be a "good fellow" with the ministers of these other faiths.

The early saints were not unkind to those with whom they disagreed, but they were terribly in earnest. Their organization was, therefore, highly exclusive. They could not compel anyone to join them, but they set a high standard for those who wanted to join; they would not lower this standard for anyone. The conditions of eternal life which they proclaimed had been set by Divinity; they felt that they had no authority to change them, and consequently did not attempt to do so. And since the new standard of values made clear in the life of Jesus put a premium on character, but not on any purely worldly advantage, the saints were glad to receive people of character, but made no compromise with those who sought to hedge and to bargain concerning the things of the Spirit.

As we read the New Testament, we find that behind all apostolic ministry there was passionate concern for men. Sin was no theological abstraction, but a terrible reality from which men needed to be saved. There was abundant evidence of this on every side; and this evidence stood out in stark relief, as the Christians demonstrated the quality of their faith more and more fully. Some of the arguments of some of these early Christians may have been faulty or far-fetched, but there was no effective argument against their way of living.

Nowadays we take it for granted that Christians must set a high ethical standard, and that religion is not a matter of disputation but of qualitative living, but it was the early Christians who taught us these things. Christianity did not survive because of its exclusive doctrine alone, nor because of its intolerance of competition, nor even because of the heroic lives of its leaders, but because this doctrinal adequacy and assured intolerance and heroic living became the common possessions of Christian people, who set and obeyed standards of morality far in advance of their times.

The elevated morality of the early saints was directly related to their worship. For many years the children of Israel had proclaimed the glory of The One God, and it must have been quite a struggle for strict Jews like Paul to recognize the rightful place of Jesus at the side of God. The Resurrection could be explained in no other way but by recognizing that Jesus is the Son of God; the Holy Spirit confirmed this conviction within them. So they approached their Master with awe, worshiping him with full hearts; and as they did so they were changed into his likeness.

The early church was, of course, a vigorously missionary body. It never seems to have occurred to these disciples that some of them did not have missionary gifts. While there is every evidence that some were called to be "overseers" and were to take charge of strong local organizations of the Saints, this overseeing did not set them apart from missionary responsibility, but instead gave them peculiar opportunities for missionary testimony. In the New Testament, the only approved Christians we meet are avid personal evangelists.

Strangely enough, persecution served only to fan the flame of devotion instead of dampening it; "the blood of the martyrs was the seed of the church." Everywhere they went, disciples were persecuted; and wherever they were persecuted, churches sprang up. They endured thus a grim test of the effectiveness of their faith. The authorities of the Roman Empire were not greatly interested in the official standing of the members of the church; but they were concerned as to who were the most effective members of each local organization; and it became their standard policy to kill off the church by killing off the most effective Christians. The best test of a man's Christianity in those days was, therefore, the opposition he met from outside the church. The final crown of any man's earthly ministry was the crown of martyrdom.

The early church was a center of divine forgiveness. Converts joined the church tremblingly, deeply conscious of the horror of the sin which they sought to leave behind and almost afraid to believe that the promises of the disciples could be true. But in the fellowship of the Saints, hard at work in extending the kingdom, they found peace and forgiveness and acceptance by God, and the abundant blessing of the Holy Spirit. They were new men. During the height of the Wesleyan revival, Charles Wesley wrote a hymn, "O for a thousand tongues to sing my great Redeemer's praise!" Part of that hymn reads: "He breaks the power of canceled sin. He sets the prisoner free." That is what the early Christians found that God had done for them. Their sins had been put behind them when they were baptized. Their remaining problem was to break the power of sinful habits. They actually did this in the church. They were not only pardoned; they were set free. Christ set before them an open door that no man could shut.

The early church was the church of an inspired people. The first and natural result of Pentecost was that the brethren who had great possessions shared their possessions willingly with their less fortunate brethren (Acts 2: 44-46). Paul was telling of a fact of experience when he wrote to the Saints in

Galatia, "Ye are all one in Christ Jesus" (Gal. 3: 28). Their new allegiance overshadowed everything else, and broke down the barriers which had hitherto divided them. Jews and Greeks, men and women, masters and slaves, gathered around the communion table, and in their sense of belonging together was born a sense of mutual responsibility. This might have been a dangerous thing, leading to parasitism, except that membership in the church was likely to cost any man his life, and that is too high a price for parasites to pay. As it was, early saints were glad to count all other things of no importance compared with the excellence of knowing Christ Jesus the Lord (Phil. 3: 8). "So mightily did the message of the Lord grow and prevail."—Acts 19: 20.

Study Outlines

The Nature of the Church

Lesson Purpose

To show the early Christian church as she really was, and to thus pave the way for recapturing the spirit, the seriousness, the enthusiasm, the passion, and the high standards of those early days.

High Points of the Lesson

The early church was essentially doctrinal. The message of the saints was confirmed in their experience. They knew that this was the final test. With such convictions the saints felt that compromise was treason. The attitude of the saints in relation to such matters as personal and public morals, the standards of the home, the relation of slaves and masters, war and peace, was higher than the attitude of the community.

The church was a center of worship and of forgiveness. Here men who had been dead in trespasses and sin found happiness and power in serving God and their fellows.

Questions and Discussion Topics

(1) Why is it important that we shall know something of the life of the early Christian church?

(2) Why were the early saints so concerned about doctrine? Name some of the doctrines which they taught.

(3) Discuss, briefly, the intolerance of the early Christians. Should we emulate their type of intolerance?

(4) Discuss, briefly, the high ethical standards of the Christian church. What was the cause of this elevated morality?

(5) What was the effect of persecution on the missionary spirit of the early saints?

(6) In what sense was the early church a center of divine forgiveness?

(7) Give illustrations of the fellowship of the saints. What caused this fellowship?

(8) What suggestions have you for improving our church life along the lines discussed in the lesson?

What the Lesson Means Today

It is imperative that we recapture some of the zeal and exclusiveness of the early saints who had been swept off their feet by the magnitude of what God had done for them.

We must consider the facts of the Christian message on our knees and so give God a chance to fill us with the Spirit which sets men on fire to build his kingdom.

We must elevate our standards of morality, both individual and social through devotion to Christ.

Chapter X

THE LORD'S DAY

*The old-fashioned Sunday—The Jewish Sabbath—
The new dispensation—The beginning of Sunday
observance.*

Lesson Twenty-four

MANY OF US LOOK BACK with no little regret to the more strict observance of Sunday which was common in our youth. Without question, much of the one-time Sunday observance was formal and uncreative, but this was due to the faulty expansion of an excellent central idea. And it may well be that sooner or later the world will be brought to realize that the old-fashioned Sunday was not a mere survival of Calvinism, but the best device ever evolved for restoring poise and judgment to a fidgety world.

The chief spiritual value of the old-fashioned Sunday lay in its utter difference from the other days of the week. This difference was marked by such outer evidences as clean "Sunday clothes," quiet demeanor, church and Sunday school attendance, the family meal, and dignified social calls. But behind these lay the feeling of obligation and opportunity to cultivate one's soul. Sunday actually looked different and felt different from other days. It brought a message of peace and dignity, and of the importance of spiritual values, such as are sadly lacking in these more hectic times.

The idea of setting apart one day a week for peculiarly spiritual purposes is a very old one. It is not unlikely that this principle was known from the beginning of time, for the earlier inhabitants of the earth were in close touch with Divinity, and were ministered to by a long line of prophets and patriarchs. However, we have no clear evidence of the observance of a special day of memorial and of worship until the time of

Moses. Before that the children of men had been blessed with the fullness of the gospel. (See discussion of the Antiquity of the Gospel.) At this time, however, through their hardness of heart and their unwillingness to remain faithful to the requirements of the gospel law, the Lord found it necessary to give the Jews a lesser law, which was enforced with severe penalties, and was in the nature of a schoolmaster preparing them for their return to the gospel of Christ. As part of this law, the children of Israel were commanded to "remember the Sabbath day to keep it holy."—Exod. 20: 8-11.

The Mosaic covenant was made wholly with Israel. It was not to be sent forth to every creature, as Jesus sent the gospel by the mouths of his disciples, but was for the express purpose of bringing back the rebellious Israelites to the true and enduring worship of God. Thus Moses clearly informed them:

> The Lord our God made a covenant with us in Horeb. The Lord made not this covenant with our fathers, but with us, even us, who are all of us here alive this day.—Deut. 5: 2, 3.

Many years later, Paul wrote to the Galatians:

> Before faith came, we were kept under the law, shut up unto the faith which should afterwards be revealed. Wherefore the law was our schoolmaster to bring us unto Christ, that we might be justified by faith.—Gal. 3: 23, 24.

The Ten Commandments were but a foreshadowing of the higher law of Christ. They prohibited various evil acts, and enjoined certain practices in anticipation of the "perfect law of liberty" which Christ should bring.

The Jewish Sabbath was intended as a day of remembrance. Its purpose was to recall vividly to mind the great things that God had done for his people, and thereby to impress on them the importance of serving him and keeping his commandments (Deut. 5: 15). So important was the observance of this day held to be, that the servants and even the beasts of burden were to cease labor on the Sabbath (Deut. 5: 12-14); violation of this Sabbatarian code was punishable by death. Even the kindling of a fire on the Sabbath day was forbidden (Exod. 35: 3). This law was so strictly observed among the devout Jews during the time of the Maccabees that a group of Jewish soldiers who were attacked on the Sabbath refused to defend themselves and so perished rather than desecrate their holy day.

While the children of Israel were still under the law, their experience matured and the purposes of God ripened toward the day when Jesus could reveal himself and bring the types and shadows of the Mosaic dispensation to an end. The time was coming when his message could be directed to all men, Jew and Gentile, bond and free. The Hebrew prophets recognized this. Thus Jeremiah says:

> Behold, the days come, saith the Lord, that I will make a new covenant with the house of Israel, and with the house of Judah; not according to the covenant that I made with their fathers in the day that I took them by the hand to bring them out of the land of Egypt: which my covenant they brake, although I was an husband unto them, saith the Lord.—Jeremiah 31: 31, 32; see also Isaiah 42: 6, 7.

Accordingly, when Jesus entered on his ministry, he announced that he came not to destroy the law but to fulfill it. This he did in the sense that he taught the full and perfect law of liberty, which embraces all that was good in the old law and fires it with a new spirit and a new passion. The moral precepts of the Mosaic law were restated and were made a part of the gospel covenant. The lesser requirements were discontinued, and many harsh penalties were done away with. The law was fulfilled when Jesus substituted for it one having larger and more truly spiritual significance.

It was difficult for the Jews to adjust themselves to the idea of a new dispensation with a new covenant and a new lawgiver. They especially resented the way that Jesus and his disciples disregarded the Sabbath, and even went so far as to condemn Jesus for healing a man on the Sabbath day (Luke 13: 10-16). On another occasion the Pharisees complained because the disciples plucked corn on the Sabbath while passing through a field, and in taking the kernels from the husk broke the rule against Sabbath work. It was this situation which gave the Master his opportunity to state a principle of great significance which had been overlooked by the Jewish legalizers. He said, "The Sabbath was made for man and not man for the Sabbath" (Mark 2: 27). The Sabbath was not an end in itself, but was a means to an end. It should have been observed with due regard to the wisdom and affection of the Lawgiver and to all the needs of those observing it, and not as a legal requirement having its virtue in the mere fact of being observed.

When the earthly ministry of Jesus came to an end and the gospel of light and peace was proclaimed in all the world, the Mosaic covenant was completely superseded. Many of its moral precepts were carried forward, but it was only operative as it was gathered up and restated in the new covenant. The contrast was so great that Peter referred to the old covenant as a yoke (Acts 15: 10), and John said that "the law was given by Moses, but grace and truth came by Jesus Christ" (John 1: 16, 17). Paul summed up the whole matter in his letter to the Roman saints, to whom he said:

> There is therefore now no condemnation to them which are in Christ Jesus, who walk not after the flesh, but after the Spirit. For the law of the Spirit of life in Christ Jesus hath made me free from the law of sin and death.—Romans 8: 1, 2.

The seventh-day Sabbath commemorated the greatest event in the history of Israel and associated it with the completion of the creative work of God (Gen. 2: 2, 3). In the new dispensation there was every reason for retaining one day a week as a day of worship and of remembrance; but, since God had now done something more for humanity than had ever been done before, there was an excellent reason for changing from the old day of remembrance to a new one. The deliverance of Israel from bondage is secondary to the offering of Christ in Calvary and to the deliverance of all mankind from the fear of sin and death. The early Christians were, therefore, true to the heart of the law of Moses, the "schoolmaster," when they set apart a specific day as a day of memory and of worship; and they were true to the spirit of the new covenant when they chose as the day of memorial for the disciples the day when God did such great things for all mankind.

Very early in the morning, on the first day of the week (Mark 16: 2; Luke 24: 1) the visitors to the empty tomb found that Jesus had risen from the dead. The resurrection set the seal of Divinity on Christianity and by it Jesus was declared to be the Son of God with power (Rom. 1: 4). Such an event demanded commemoration. So we find the saints together on the eighth day after the Resurrection—the first day of the next week—and Christ recognized their gathering by coming into their midst (John 20: 26). Before long, the custom of meeting together on the first day of the week was well established. Thus Paul preached at the regular first-day meeting (Acts 20: 7), and John writes of being in the Spirit on the Lord's day (Revelation 1: 10).

Among Jewish Christians there were some who observed both Saturday and Sunday. This was in deference to their early training and also in respect for the law which had led them toward Christ. But as the world mission of the gospel became more apparent, and it became clear that Christianity was not destined to be a sect of Judaism, but a world movement which would leave Judaism far behind, Sabbathkeeping was discarded, and the observance of the Lord's day became general among the disciples. Indeed, the change from the Sabbath to the Lord's day became one of the outward indications of the change from the old dispensation to the new.

Evidence seems to be clear that the observance of a day of worship every week was sufficiently fundamental to demand recognition in the law of Moses. This law was to prepare men for obedience to the greater law which was yet to be given. When this law was fulfilled at the coming of Jesus, the Mosaic Sabbath was not transferred to the Christian dispensation, but its basic principle was nevertheless carried forward. The weekly day of rest and worship for Christian people therefore stands upon a basic moral need, and not upon the provisions of an imperfect law. Lack of clarity at this point caused our Puritan ancestors to go back to the rigid, legalistic requirements of Sabbathkeeping, which they attempted to enforce without due regard for the spirit of the perfect law of liberty. If we would be in harmony with the Spirit of Christ, we shall avoid this legalism, but we shall nevertheless give to our Sunday observance a richer spiritual devotion than the Jews ever gave to the legal requirements of the Sabbath. We shall not live below the level established by the Jews, but above it, keeping the day of resurrection as a day of remembrance of the great things which God has done for us, and doing this in the spirit of grace and truth.

In the present dispensation, our Heavenly Father has called our attention to the importance of Sunday as a day of rest and prayer (Doctrine and Covenants 59: 2-4; 119: 7), so that the saints are advised by the testimony of three dispensations regarding keeping the Lord's holy day. The Mosaic dispensation emphasized the principle, and because of the willfulness of the people, enforced this principle with dire penalties. The apostolic dispensation freed the saints from the harshness of the earlier dispensation because they could then be trusted to observe the law in spirit and in truth. The dispensation of the fullness of time re-emphasizes the instruction of the apostolic age, and those who wish to observe the law of Christ now set apart the day which commemorates the Resurrection of Jesus as a day different in kind from other days, dedicated to worship and to rest—a day not to be spent in idleness but in spiritual re-creation, that the forces of righteousness may take their place in our lives.

Study Outlines

The Lord's Day

Lesson Purpose

To emphasize the importance of a weekly day of rest and worship, and to show that the change from the Jewish Sabbath to the Christian Sunday was one of the marks of the new covenant.

High Points of the Lesson

The children of Israel were put under the law of Moses when they were unwilling to live the gospel law. Part of the law of Moses had to do with the Sabbath and was designed to reserve one day in seven for worship and rest.

When the Mosaic law was superseded, the Jewish Sabbath was replaced by the Lord's Day of the Christians.

The Lord's Day should not be observed puritanically, but joyfully as a day of worship, quiet companionship, and elevated living.

Questions and Discussion Topics

(1) When was the Jewish Sabbath instituted? Why was it instituted? What was its purpose?

(2) To whom was the Sabbath law given? Was it binding on anyone else but Israel? How long was it in force?

(3) What was the value of the Jewish Sabbath as observed by the strict Jews at the time of Jesus? What were its disadvantages?

(4) What was the attitude of Jesus and his disciples toward the Jewish Sabbath?

(5) When was the change made from the Jewish Sabbath to the Christian Sunday? Why?

(6) What moral values were connected with the Jewish Sabbath? Are these moral values transferred to the Christian dispensation?

(7) What instruction has been received in this dispensation regarding observance of the Lord's Day?

(8) What activities might reasonably fit into a Christian program for Sunday observance?

What the Lesson Means Today

To the Christian every day is holy. Nevertheless, we are aided in maintaining the holiness of the other days if we reserve one definitely for spiritual purposes.

Many of the things which we do on Sunday are not contrary to the commandments, but they are wrong when they rob us of finer spiritual opportunities. Sunday is not intended to be just a day of relaxation, but a day on which to cultivate the soul.

The Christian approach to Sunday is not rigid and harsh, but creative and beautiful. Many of us lack the poise and strength of quietness which could be achieved by a weekly day of rest.

Chapter XI

THE SACRAMENT OF THE LORD'S SUPPER

Its eminence among the sacraments—Its significance—Three prerequisites for participation—The renewal of the covenant.

Lesson Twenty-five

ONE OF THE MAJOR SACRAMENTS of the church is the sacrament of the Lord's Supper. Indeed the social character of this ordinance is so marked, and it recurs so frequently that it is often regarded as the most outstanding of the sacraments, in terms of its unifying and cleansing power. Certainly the Communion, as we call it, has authority among the Saints which has to be experienced to be understood.

Matthew, Mark, Luke, and Paul all tell of the institution of the sacrament. From Paul's account we learn that on the night in which he was betrayed, Jesus took bread and, when he had blessed it, he broke it and said, "Take, eat, this is my body, which is broken for you; this do in remembrance of me. After the same manner also he took the cup, when he had supped, saying, This cup is the new testament in my blood; this do ye, as oft as ye drink it, in remembrance of me" (I Cor. 11: 23-26). Mark adds that the blood of Christ was shed for many, and was the token of the new covenant (Mark 14: 12-26; see also Luke 22: 7-20). Matthew agrees with this, and adds that it was for the remission of sins (Matt. 26: 17-30).

A further glimpse of the Lord's Supper is granted us in the first epistle to the Corinthians, which was written about A. D. 55. From careful reading of this letter, it appears that it had become customary to partake of the Communion in connection with a fellowship meal, and that some abuses had crept in because of this practice. Paul therefore gave instructions that the Communion should be separated from other meals, that those participating must be worthy, and that the sacred meal should constitute a memorial of the sacrifice of the Lord Jesus and a symbol of the unity of his disciples (I Cor. 10: 16-21; 11: 26-30).

The Apostle John gives us the clearest statement of the New Testament on the importance of the Lord's Supper when he preserves for us the words of the Master: "Except ye eat the flesh of the Son of man, and drink his blood, ye have no life in you" (John 6: 53). Then, as if to warn us against valuing the form above the spirit of the Communion, he quotes the further words of Jesus:

"It is the Spirit that quickeneth; the flesh profiteth nothing: the words that I speak unto you they are Spirit, and they are life" (John 6: 63). This sets the Communion in its true light. The form is important, for it has been chosen by God to express a specific idea. And the spirit is important, too, for this carries home the meaning which lies behind the material emblems used. So the bread and wine are important, but only as the service of which they are part is graced with the Spirit of God, as his covenant children remember the sacrifices of the Lord Jesus and keep the commandments which he has given them.

There are, therefore, these three glimpses of the Lord's Supper which we obtain from the New Testament. In the first, we see our Lord instituting the Communion as a memorial of his death. In the second, we see Paul, rescuing it from abuse and seeking to preserve it as a memorial and a symbol of the unity of the body of Christ. And in the third, John shows the pre-eminence of the Communion as a transforming spiritual experience.

Sharing in the sacrament of the Lord's Supper gives us a fuller insight into what God did for us at Calvary than any form of words can possibly express. At the table of the Lord, the truth of God's love comes home to us far more powerfully in our act of affectionate remembrance than it could possibly do through any verbal pronouncement. Thus the Communion brings the fact of the atonement into the forefront of mind and heart and conscience; and, if we will, the Spirit so interprets it as to cleanse and redirect our entire lives.

The table of the Lord, where simple things are shared in the spirit of love and all men are fed, is a standing protest against the extremes of poverty, where men starve for lack of simple food, and the extremes of luxury, where eating is an end instead of a means. At this table the sharing and the mutual concern, which are at the heart of the gospel, are seen to be simple and natural. When we have partaken of the Communion, we have already shared together in the spirit of love. The whole philosophy of stewardship is an unfolding of that which has been begun here.

There are certain requirements which precede participation in the Lord's Supper. The first of these is baptism. We do not give food to those who are "dead in trespasses and sin," but only to those who have been born again. An ancient manuscript, which dates back to the second half of the second century, declares, "let no one eat or drink of your Eucharist [Communion] except those baptized into the name of the Lord; for as regards this also, the Lord has said: 'Give not that which is holy unto the dogs'" (The Didache IX). Even before this time, Justin Martyr had written:

"This food is called among us Eucharist; and no one is allowed to partake of it unless he believes that what we teach is true, and has been washed into the laver for the remission of sins, and for regeneration, and is living as Christ enjoined."

A second prerequisite is that the Communion shall be partaken of worthily. This requirement has given rise to a serious misunderstanding upon the part of some members of the church. These Saints feel, as is right, that they ought not to participate in the Communion service as long as any difference exists between them and their brethren. They therefore refrain from partaking of the Communion until such differences have been healed, and in some instances they refrain for several months on this basis. This is the very reverse of what is intended. The Lord wishes us to partake of the Communion at regular intervals (Doctrine and Covenants 119: 5), and we should hasten to accept this great invitation of our Lord. In preparation for this, and in the spirit of the occasion, we should take special care to see that all hardness of heart is removed. Nothing should interfere with this. No Christian has the right to harbor such enmity against his brother as would prevent his meeting that brother at the table of the Lord. It is our business to forgive each other, and to assist others to forgive us. To postpone participation because we are not worthy is to destroy the very purpose of the ordinance. The frequent repetition of the Communion service is designed to hold before us the need for maintaining fraternity at all times.

It is noteworthy that immediately after Judas had left the upper room to inform the soldiers against Jesus, the Master said, significantly:

A new commandment I give unto you, that ye love one another; even as I have loved you, that ye also love one another. By this shall all men know that ye are my disciples, if ye have love one to another. —John 13: 34, 35.

The new rite was to be a sign and instrument of love among the brethren as well as of love toward Divinity. The Lord's Supper is an ordinance of the family of God. So while it is a means of fellowship with Christ, it is also a means of fellowship with the church of Christ. When people are unworthy of this fellowship we say they are excommunicated, by which we mean that they are cut off from the benefits of communion. The most vivid symbol of this communion is the communion service; and they are therefore excluded from this service.

In partaking of the Lord's Supper we renew our baptismal covenant. As forgiveness of sins follows the first covenant, so it follows the renewal of that covenant. Yet it cannot be said that our Heavenly Father waits until the communion service in order to accept our repentance. He forgives us individually whenever we truly seek him in humble contrition for our sins. But he restores us to the fellowship of the Saints, which is one aspect of forgiveness, when he permits us to feel the spirit of the brotherhood and to share with our associates in the Lord's Supper which unites us at his table.

Members of the Roman Catholic Church believe that, at the moment when the "host" is held up before the congregation at the sacrifice of the Mass, the material elements of the Communion become the actual body of the Lord. To the mind of the average Protestant, this worship of the material elements of the Mass seems very close to idolatry. How much more simple and adequate is the service outlined in the word of God through Joseph Smith. Here the Saints are commanded to kneel while the officiating minister prays that the bread and the wine shall be blessed, so as to become a means of holiness in the lives of those who partake in remembrance of the body and blood of the Son of God, and who witness that they are willing to take upon them the name of Jesus, and do always remember him and keep his commandments so that they may have his Spirit to be with them (Doctrine and Covenants 17: 22, 23). Modern revelation thus retains all the vital significance of the Communion and at the same time avoids the intellectual difficulties inherent in the belief that bread actually becomes the body of Jesus, even though it is in every way identical with what it was before it was consecrated. This simplifies the care of the remaining bread and wine, also. They are no more than bread and wine. Because of the dignity of the service in which they were used, they should be handled with dignity, but they are still just bread and wine. That which was eaten was blessed to the souls of those who partook of it worthily, but that which remained was not specially blessed.

Study Outlines

The Lord's Supper

High Points of the Lesson

This Communion is for the members of the "body of Christ."

If we partake of the Communion thoughtlessly or remember what our Lord did for us without any movement of our hearts toward him, we cannot fail to be condemned. If we partake solemnly, reminding ourselves of his great love for us and recommitting ourselves to his service, we cannot fail to be cleansed and blessed.

Questions and Discussion Topics

(1) In what sense are the material elements of the Communion important? In what sense are they unimportant?

(2) What do we mean by the statement that "in the ordinances of the kingdom the power of godliness is manifest"?

(3) What is the purpose of the sacrament of the Lord's Supper? By whom was it instituted? What does it commemorate?

(4) Do you think that the emblems used in the sacrament of the Lord's Supper are particularly appropriate? Give reasons for your answer.

(5) What is the social significance of the Lord's Supper? Why do you think it is desirable that the "oblation" be connected with it.

(6) Why do we administer the Lord's Supper to members only? Is this practice supported by early church history? Is it supported in any other way? Discuss this briefly.

(7) Is a person under condemnation when he partakes of the Communion while he has a personal difference with another member of the church? Is he under condemnation when he refuses the emblems because he is not reconciled to his brother?

(8) In what ways can the sacrament of the Lord's Supper be made more meaningful?

What the Lesson Means Today

The sacrament of the Lord's Supper means a great deal to the Saints. It can mean infinitely more. This service should be as beautiful as possible, but artistic effects must never detract from the central sacramental purpose.

Contention destroys the central purpose of the service. Principles should therefore be safeguarded carefully, but the spirit of contention should be rigorously excluded.

No member of the church is justified in refusing to partake of the emblems because ill feeling exists. It is his Christian duty to eliminate the ill feeling and partake.

Chapter XII

THE PLACE OF PRAYER

What prayer is—Communion—What it does—An answer to doubts—Co-operation with God—The search for God.

Lesson Twenty-six

IF WE REALIZED THE ultimate significance of Christianity, we would be a better people; and if we understood more readily, we would pray more frequently, and our lives would be richer in spiritual graces. The practice of prayer is absolutely necessary if we are to keep our hearts and minds alive to the world of spiritual realities around us. A man who fails to pray becomes selfish, and his better self dies of atrophy.

Prayer does for the mind, the heart, and the soul what breathing does for the blood and nerves and body as a whole. It has been defined as "the soul's sincere desire, uttered or unexpressed," as "standing tiptoe in earnest expectation born of faith," and in a thousand other ways. All of these definitions embody something of the truth, yet all fall short. Only experience can teach us the true values of prayer. Without this experience, formal definitions are "as sounding brass and as tinkling cymbals."

Prayer is both a means and an end in itself. It is a means, of course, when we expect to achieve something as a result of our praying. It is an end in itself, when we pray just for the sake of praying. Sometimes I talk with my wife in order to get her help. At other times I seek her out for the sheer satisfaction of being with her, and talking over apparently inconsequential things in the atmosphere of mutual affection. Both of these conversations are closely akin to prayer, for, essentially, prayer is communion in which the believer seeks to be at one with God.

Prayer may well be wordless, but yet it is the speech of the spirit. It is a method whereby we seek to give ourselves and our lives, with their joys and their problems, wholly into the hands of God, forgetting all our waywardness and giving him full control.

Many of our prayers are just requests for help. This is to be expected, for we have a right to ask our Father for a share in his bounty so long as we think he will approve what we do with it. Yet, as children of his love, we should not insist on having our own way, since we recognize that our Heavenly Father knows what is for our good better than we know ourselves. The strongest note in genuinely Christian prayer is therefore, "Thy will be done." In the Lord's Prayer, the petition of dedication precedes the petition for bread and for forgiveness and for divine guidance, and makes all our purely personal requests entirely secondary. We will realize how very fundamental it is when we reflect that when Jesus faced the greatest crisis of his life he prayed for deliverance from evil; nevertheless he expressed his willingness to drink the cup if this was demanded by the highest possibilities of the situation.

In this prayer in the Garden we have what is possibly our best illustration of the real meaning of "Thy will be done." The full heart of the man Jesus was behind his plea that if it were possible he might not be required to tread the bloody road to Calvary. Any honest alternative seemed preferable to the way which was opening up before him, so he begged his Father for deliverance. But even as he prayed, he knew that on that night, of all nights, he must be more than merely human. Neither fear nor pain nor humiliation must be allowed to turn him to the right hand or the left. So, before his prayer was completed, he built into it his safeguard against permitting any momentary agony to cause him to lower his standards. "Notwithstanding the agony which makes it so very hard to see beyond this moment," he said in effect, "nevertheless, do no grant me what I now want so desperately, but grant me instead what I would want if I could see as thou seest."

Not all prayer is as deeply agonizing as this. For the most part, prayer is natural and instinctive. Neither education nor eloquence is vital. Some of the most effectual prayers recorded in the Scriptures are among the very briefest: "God be merciful to me a sinner!" and "Lord, what wouldst thou have me to do?" Prayer at its best is nevertheless a high and exacting art; one of the most persistent prayers of the devout is, "Lord, teach us to pray." Speech is common to all men, but the oratory which can move the multitude is the result of years of careful study and practice. The hollow tube through which the boy blows to produce a simple note or two is vastly different from the flute which the finished artist plays in a symphony orchestra. So, also, there is a great gulf between the petitions of a frightened boy and the pleading of a righteous man for the soul of his friend. Prayer is worth-while at every stage of its development, but is most worth-while when it becomes a fine art profoundly enriching the life of a good man or woman.

Sincere and earnest prayer, that "seeketh not her own," helps us to think of life in larger terms and to approach its problems with an illuminated seriousness. Through prayer, which rises to the high point of communion, we gain courage to meet temptation, strength to endure calumny, resolution to oppose wickedness, and love to meet life graciously. It is a fact of experience that facing life from above instead of from below delivers us from pettiness and enables us to see life steadily and to see it whole.

Nothing makes God so real to the soul as the habit of considering the activities of daily life with him.

One of the problems raised afresh by our generation centers in the reasonableness of prayer. The answer is that we do not ask whether it is reasonable to eat, to sleep, or to walk. We do these things because they are the natural responses to our need for food and for rest and for exercise. So also, prayer is a satisfying response to spiritual hunger. He who truly prays is renewed. So many people have found spiritual renewal in this way that it is quite reasonable to recommend the practice of prayer as a satisfying spiritual exercise.

But a troubled young man speaks up after this fashion: "All my life I have been among praying people. I took prayer for granted, and always prayed after a fashion until I became aware of the universe as the scientist knows it. Now I have learned to think of distances so vast that they are measured in terms of light-years, of a universe so large that it staggers thought, of laws which have been in operation through all the yesterdays and which will still be operative through all the tomorrows. How can I believe that prayer avails anything in the midst of such immensities? How can I believe that prayer changes anything in the face of such invariables?"

Such questions as these are not only reasonable; they are inevitable. In answer we observe that before we permit the vastness of our modern world to discourage us from prayer, we should consider the meaning of our Heavenly Father's knowledge of men. When I think of China, knowing very little about it, I imagine a vague multitude of people with faces that all look alike. But when a missionary thinks of China, the vague multitude is shaken loose in one spot, and he remembers individual people with individual abilities and needs. Knowing them even more certainly, when God thinks of China, he must think of them as a whole, yet each separately, as individuals as a librarian thinks of his books, or as an engineer thinks of his turbines. So, also, we each stand forth separate in his thought. He lifts us up from the obscurity of our littleness and picks us out of a multitude of our fellows and gives to our lives the dignity of his individual care. Our Heavenly Father calls us everyone by name. He is not the God of mankind in the mass; he is the God of Abraham and of Isaac and of Jacob. He is your God, and mine.

In further answer to this question, we note that in the realm of things spiritual, as in the field of science, the expert should be permitted to speak with some authority; and on this point the experts are unanimous. There is neither variableness nor shadow of turning in their testimony. Jesus, the greatest of them all, is supported by a great cloud of witnesses, men and women who have made spiritual history. "I can do all things through him which strengtheneth me," says Paul. "My life," says Saint Augustine, "shall be a real life, being wholly full of thee." "Having found God," says a modern Indian poet and saint, "the current of my life flowed on swiftly. I gained fresh strength." Men like the Apostle Paul, Saint Francis, George Fox, John Wesley, Joseph Smith, and General Booth —all blazed trails which could only be cleared by men of vision who were also men of affairs; and they have a right to be heard.

The testimony of such men, it must be admitted, is qualified by the significance which they attach to the word "prayer." For them, as for the Master of them all, prayer was no mere passing on of their problems to someone else, even to God. It involved some effort on their part—much more effort than is involved in letting things slide, and in taking the easy way of life. They found prayer to be reasonable for reasonable and believing men; and the practice of prayer strengthened both their reasonableness and their beliefs. They used prayer as a means of working out the problems of life, but they knew that prayer must be accompanied by other means of grace, such as thought and work and, sometimes, the patience to wait for fulfillment of the divine plan. And all of them knew that prayer holds no abiding promise for spiritually lazy folk who are merely seeking a way of escape from the burdens of our common humanity.

What, then, is prayer, as men of spiritual power have known it? At heart it is a passionate search for God and for the kind of deliverance which he affords. Such prayer is not selfish; it is not indolent; it is not cowardly. It does not ask for deliverance because the one praying is lazy or acquisitive or afraid. It always concerns itself with the best, and seeks to discover and follow the best, even through pain. The man who prays as the heroes have prayed asks for light and food and succor, in order that he may live, and also that he may live to some worthy purpose. Peter says, "Lord, behold their threatenings, and grant that with all boldness I may preach thy word." His only fear was the fear of being afraid. His great deliverance was not from the wrath of the Jews, but from that low regard for the truth which invited him to be afraid. Out of a heart of like faith and courage John Knox, the Scotch patriot and religious leader, pleaded with his Maker, "Give me Scotland, or I die." There was no cry for personal security or power here—only passionate concern for the souls of his countrymen. God is concerned about such prayers. He has always answered them, and he always will.

Let us face the facts clearly at this point. Jesus did not come to abolish pain and sacrifice. He came to proclaim the costly and dangerous but worthy way of the kingdom, to teach men to suffer pain gladly in the cause of right. His way of life therefore has no promise for men whose sole interest in prayer is to avoid pain or danger, or as a means by which they may remain undisturbed in the tranquil possession of what they have, or to thereby gain something for nothing, because the world "owes them a living." But his way of life is full of promise for those who pray from the heart, sincerely, and with a sense of urgency, and who forget themselves in their praying. The prayers of such men and women change their own lives, building therein self-discipline grounded in insight, and their answer is guaranteed in their own nature, whether or not their specific petitions are fulfilled.

When we pray, if we really want to know whether "God is on the other end of the line," the sensible thing for us to do is to take up our end of the line, and to give it an intelligent trial. There is nothing that concerns our lives in which our Father is uninterested; and if we talk to him in the right attitude of heart and mind, he will manifest that interest. The Book of Mormon tells us that the ancient Americans were told to pray over their flocks and herds, and this was good Christian advice.

But let us remember that while our Father is concerned about small things, he is not concerned with trivialities. Do not waste time in praying over petty things or in a petty spirit, for then "the line" is sure to be "dead."

The fundamental consideration in effective prayer is a concern deep enough to require that he who prays shall not stop at praying. When we think of the purpose of God in us, this is reasonable. It is not his purpose to do things for us, but only to aid and protect us as we learn to do worthy things ourselves. In this spirit, Jesus told the seventy to go forth into the world and there to give themselves to the uttermost in the quest for men. Later, when they were weary, but still at work, he said, "Pray the Lord that he will send forth more laborers into the vineyard." If you are concerned enough to work as well as to pray, then the Lord is interested enough to listen and to help. Only by such reserve can he hold the respect and affection of real men and women down the ages.

Study Outlines

The Place of Prayer

Lesson Purpose

To consider the nature of prayer and to lay the foundation for more effective prayer life.

High Points of the Lesson

Prayer is a means of approach to God and of understanding his will. For any person who loves God, prayer is also a satisfying experience which needs no further justification.

We do not have to be eloquent in order to pray effectively. Prayer is, nevertheless, a fine art, yielding its richest values to those who learn how to pray in experience.

To be effective, prayer must have its rise in a deep sense of need, and to be most effective this must be augmented by a deep desire to serve. When these two are joined to courage, our prayers cannot fail to be answered.

Questions and Discussion Topics

(1) Why should genuine prayer include eagerness to do the will of God? Discuss this briefly.

(2) What is meant by "the art of prayer"? How may this art be cultivated?

(3) Enumerate some of the values which accrue from genuine prayer. Is it true that "something always happens when a good man prays"? Explain.

(4) How may prayer become a means of working out the problems of life? What new factors does prayer introduce? To what problems may prayer be applied?

(5) What is the relation between prayer and courage? Prayer and hope? Prayer and work? Prayer and self-discipline?

(6) Quote some definition of prayer. What do you mean by prayer?

(7) List the enemies of effectual prayer. Suggest how they may be overcome.

(8) What are the arguments for regular daily prayer? What are the arguments against it? Is it a good thing or otherwise to form the habit of talking over one's hopes and problems with a wise and dear friend?

What the Lesson Means Today

The experience of men and women who have a right to be heard is that God is eager to help us and that he can be approached through prayer. Our prayers become constantly more worth-while as we inject the notes of earnestness and of dedication.

Prayer is an opportunity for exploring the will of God.

There are few more creative experiences than the habit of praying about what we know God wants us to do, but what we find difficult to do.

Chapter XIII

APOSTASY AND RESTORATION

The apostasy—What was lost by the apostasy—Reformation and Restoration—The background of the Restoration—The Restoration.

Lesson Twenty-seven

I—THE APOSTASY

THE AGE-LONG ENDEAVOR OF GOD toward the redemption of his children and the building of his kingdom has been counteracted by a sort of spiritual gravitation which pulls us downward, or a tide which is set away from the land of promise, and sweeps our feet from under us when we seek to reach the shores of the heavenly country. The strength of these opposing forces has been such that every new revelation of the love of God and every corresponding attempt to build his kingdom has been succeeded by a falling away from the faith and a return to idolatry in one form or another.

The apostles were well aware of the apostasies which had taken place before their day. They knew, also, that although specific events may serve to mark the progress of apostasy, departure from the faith begins in obscure ways and then comes creeping in, like the tide, gaining a little here and a little there and so gradually overwhelming all the outposts of faith and in time flooding even the highlands. Charting the course of apostasy is like charting the course of a river in flood; the wreckage marks its path. So they saw ominous significance in the prophecy of Isaiah:

> The earth also is defiled under the inhabitants thereof; because they have transgressed the laws, changed the ordinance, broken the everlasting covenant.—Isaiah 24: 1-6.

The apostles were terribly in earnest. They looked forward with eagerness to the return of the Son of Man in power and great glory. They wanted to win as many converts as they could so that his triumphant return would find many good people awaiting him. But one of the things which Christianity had done for them was to give them the courage to face facts. Out of their deep concern to know these facts, they were gradually made aware that their dispensation, like the earlier ones, was to be followed by a period of darkness. They were saved from despair by the assurance that while there should come a falling away first, the results of their work should not be entirely lost; and there should come a future "dispensation of the fullness of times" in which God would build out of the spiritual gains of each succeeding age a great citadel of righteousness which should never be overthrown. In spite of immediate victory in the lives of many good people, they faced apparent defeat for the Cause, a defeat which should continue until the foundation was laid for final far-flung triumph.

Paul wrote to the Thessalonian saints, reminding them of their hope of the second coming of the Lord Jesus, and exhorting them to stand fast in the faith that they might share therein. But he reminded them also of the prophecy that the great day of the Lord would not come except there should come a falling away first (II Thess. 2: 3-5). To Timothy, Paul wrote in much the same strain, foretelling that "in the last days perilous times shall come," and describing with remarkable insight the conditions which would prevail in the latter days. As a bulwark against this departure from the truth, Paul required Timothy to "preach the word; be instant in season, out of season; reprove, rebuke, exhort with all long-suffering and doctrine" (II Tim. 4: 1, 2). In the same strain, he charged the elders assembled at Miletus at the conclusion of his third missionary journey:

Take heed, therefore, unto yourselves, and to all the flock, over the which the Holy Ghost hath made you overseers, to feed the church of God which he hath purchased with his own blood. For I know this, that after my departing shall grievous wolves enter in among you, not sparing the flock. Also of your own selves shall men arise, speaking perverse things, to draw away disciples after them. Therefore watch, and remember, that by the space of three years I ceased not to warn every one night and day with tears.—Acts 20: 28-31.

Peter, who rivaled Paul in apostolic ministry, wrote to the saints just prior to his death (II Peter 1: 14) to remind them of their great hope in the gospel, of the coming of the Lord in judgment and great power. But he warned them, too, of the danger of false prophets who should bring in "damnable heresies, even denying the Lord that bought them."—II Peter 2: 1.

By the time that John alone remained of the original apostolic council, the growth of apostasy was already apparent as may be seen by reading the word of inspiration addressed through him to the seven churches of Asia.

John reminded these churches of the coming of Christ (Rev. 1: 7), and then went on to charge the successors of the church leaders whom Paul had warned at Ephesus that they had left their first love (Rev. 2: 4), and were themselves witnesses to the apostasy which Paul had foretold.

It is impossible to draw a line through history and say that prior to a certain date the gospel was known among men and the church was accepted of God, but subsequent to that date the gospel was not known and the church was apostate. But we can note the progress of apostasy and can see clearly that within a few generations the early life and beauty of the church were clouded and thereafter were almost completely lost. This loss came about through the adoption of worldly methods of doing the work of God, through the baptism of many persons who were not truly converted to the truth, and in other ways. Thus there was substituted for the rule of the apostles and prophets and for the blessings and gifts of the gospel, the rule of men of prominence in the empire supported by the resources of their civil offices. In spite of the fact that many of the ministry and people sought earnestly to stem the tide, the gradual and progressive compromise with the truth was too strong for them.

Once started, the course of the apostasy was as strong and implacable as the tide. The Christians of post-apostolic times changed the form and lost the spiritual significance of the ordinances. Being no longer bound to the work of God by ordinances of full and rich validity, they broke their covenants with God. Being no longer allied in the work of God, even though they were enlisted in his name, they set goals which were born of their own pride and which lacked the saving grace of divine rightness.

Latter Day Saints are by no means alone in their belief that this constituted an apostasy from the early truth and power of Christianity. Every Protestant spire that points to heaven is a witness of the protest of those who meet there against the "damnable heresies" which overtook the early church. Even Roman Catholic historians admit the facts. They differ with Protestants regarding the best way to combat these facts; but they do not question their existence. The late Cardinal Gibbons of Baltimore stated:

> It cannot be denied that corruption of morals prevailed in the sixteenth century to such an extent as to call for a sweeping reformation, and that laxity of discipline reached even the sanctuary.

The cardinal, however, affirmed that the apostasy was from the practice and ethical standards of the early church rather than from her doctrine; and that the doctrinal elaborations which had taken place during the centuries were but an unfolding of what was involved in the message given to Peter in the beginning.

As might be expected, the Church of England goes much farther than Cardinal Gibbons in denunciation of the apostate condition of Christendom. In the official declaration of degeneracy as set forth in the *Homily Against the Peril of Idolatry,* the Church of England, says:

> Laity and clergy, learned and unlearned, all ages, sects, and degrees of men, women, and children of Christendom (an horrible and most

dreadful thing to think) have been at once drowned in abominable idolatry, of all other vices most detested of God, and most damnable to men, and that by the space of eight hundred years and more.

This statement is in effect today; it is appointed to be read in the churches "diligently and distinctly" that it may be "understanded of the people."

Among the reformers, John Wesley was particularly impressed by the fact of the apostasy. Preaching on "The Mystery of Iniquity," and reading for his text II Thessalonians 2: 7, he said:

In the very first society at Rome there were divisions and offenses, but how early and how powerfully, did the mystery of iniquity work in the church at Corinth. Not only schisms, heresies, animosities, fierce and bitter contentions, but actual, open sins. We meet with abundant proof, that in all the churches, the tares grow up with the wheat, and that the mystery of iniquity did everywhere work in a thousand forms. That grand pest of Christianity, a faith without works, was spread far and wide. When Saint James wrote his epistle, the tares had produced a plentiful harvest.

This reflects the settled conviction of John Wesley, for the same thought occurs elsewhere in his writings. His position has also been affirmed by many more recent students and writers. Quite recently an author noteworthy for his lack of bias has written:

Somehow or other, as early as the sub-apostolic period, corporate Christianity began to receive a serious twist; it failed to carry out its original pattern and spirit and power. There were great souls and there were great movements. But the original corporate pattern was tampered with. The Reformation, with all its great emphasis upon forgotten truth, did not recover the whole range of the Christian order of things. The Protestant Reformation was a protest. It could not in the nature of the case grasp the entire situation and readjust it. It was a partial movement and the trouble with much of Protestantism since then has been to make a fetish of that partial movement, instead of a starting point for a comprehensive and persistent progressive recovery of the real mind of Christ for the individual and the whole of society.— John Douglas Adam, in *Under the Highest Leadership,* page 31.

Consideration of the apostasy is important to us for many reasons. If the apostasy was not a fact, then the whole Reformation Movement was heretical, and the subsequent Restoration of the gospel was entirely unnecessary. If, on the other hand, the apostasy which we have been considering was an actual fact, then immediately the Restoration Movement has legitimate and urgent claim on our attention. In these days of social unrest many of us have been attracted by the idea of socializing surplus goods. In like manner, if apostasy is a fact of history, and the Restoration is the good news of God for this generation, then we have spiritual wealth which ought to be shared with all mankind.

We stand today and every day at a new parting of the ways. Apostasy is a temptation to individuals as well as to groups. If Paul was fearful lest he who had preached to others might himself become a castaway, then certainly, we also must walk with care. We must realize that although we have assurance that the gospel will never again be taken from the earth, it will be taken from us individually except as we cherish it and live by the light of its provisions. In our own day we have been most terribly reminded of the way in which the damnable heresies of the past can be revived, and can make their way even among the Saints. Eternal vigilance, eternal devotion, and unfailing practice of the requirements of the gospel, both as to ordinances and to the spirit, is required of all who would be faithful.

Study Outlines

The Apostasy

Lesson Purpose

To establish the fact of the apostasy.

High Points of the Lesson

The spiritual heroes of other dispensations anticipated the coming of an apostasy, but looked forward to the ultimate triumph of righteousness.

It is not possible to set a specific date at which the apostasy became complete. It was more like a tide which set in imperceptibly and gradually covered the land.

The fact of the apostasy is widely admitted. Protestantism is built on this fact, and so is the Restoration.

QUESTIONS AND DISCUSSION TOPICS

(1) Refer to some of the Scriptures which indicate New Testament writers anticipated the apostasy.

(2) When did the apostasy begin? How did it begin? How did it become apparent?

(3) Is it possible to draw a line through history to mark the exact date when the church apostatized? Discuss your answer briefly.

(4) What great body of Christians affirms the fact of the apostasy? What is the attitude of the Roman Catholic Church on this question?

(5) Why is the question of the apostasy important to Protestant churches? Why is it important to us?

(6) What are the steps in apostasy? (Doctrine and Covenants 1: 3). Note their sequence and discuss this sequence briefly.

(7) What assurances do we have that the church will not again become apostate? Discuss this briefly.

(8) Discuss apostasy as a personal possibility as well as a group tendency.

WHAT THE LESSON MEANS TODAY

No part of our environment is completely godlike. Both individuals and groups are subject to constant temptations downward; apostasy is an unfailing threat.

The first step toward apostasy is to stray from the ordinances of the gospel. We may do this by changing the form of these ordinances. We are much more likely to do it by neglecting the spiritual meaning of the ordinances. The further steps to complete apostasy are progressive and almost inevitable: breaking our covenant, abandoning kingdom-building, and becoming engrossed in our own affairs.

Lesson Twenty-eight

II—WHAT WAS LOST BY THE APOSTASY

In writing to the Saints at Ephesus, Paul reminded them of their faith in "one Lord, one faith, one baptism, one God and Father of all, who is above all, and through all, and in all." Today such unity is a wistful dream, for nowhere is it yet a reality. The late Reverend Peter Ainslie wrote a popular book on *The Scandal of Christianity*, the divided condition of Christendom being as that scandal. With this most Christians agree. Lack of unity among Christian people is one of the most obvious sources of weakness in combating the evils which beset humanity. Our doctrinal differences arose and are continued because of our lack of communion with Divinity. This in turn is largely due to the lack of divinely chosen and inspired ministry.

The characteristic gifts and graces of the Church of Jesus Christ were lost when men ceased to walk with the Master, and when the church, the bride of Christ, ceased to answer the purpose of her creation.

The first and most distinctive loss occurring through the apostasy was the loss of genuine spiritual authority. This loss of authority was most apparent among the ministry, for the ministerial supervision of the church was changed from the apostolic pattern both in form and spirit. The universal jurisdiction of the apostles gave way to the localized jurisdiction of the bishops, and the guidance of the prophets gave place to the guidance of expediency. Among the early bishops and others who succeeded the apostles were many men of ability and of devotion, but their ability and devotion could not cope with the less than Christian practices which had become accepted and powerful.

The only rightful authority in the Church of Jesus Christ is the authority of her Lord which is shown in love working with discrimination. Without such authority the world became the victim of a coercive system which concerned itself with rituals and penances. There was a form of godliness, but the power of godliness was sadly lacking. The church grew in material strength and her ministers vied with each other for temporal honors; but her moral controls over good men gave way to the dictatorship of force.

Related to the loss of authority was the loss of expectancy of divine revelation. As we have seen elsewhere, it is the clear teaching of the New Testament Scriptures that the function of the Holy Spirit is to guide believers into all truth, and particularly into the truth that Jesus is the Christ, the Son of God. The guidance of the Holy Spirit is so necessary that the Master commanded the apostles to wait for a special endowment before beginning their Pentecostal tasks. Yet it came to be the accepted teaching of Christendom that the occasion of revelation was now past and the canon of Scripture full. "With the building erected, the scaffolding of divine revelation was useless and cumbersome and so was cast away."

In the years under review the church lacked the power of Christ because she had abandoned or recast so many of the ordinances of the gospel. John had seen this peril and had written: "Whosoever transgresseth, and abideth not in the doctrine of Christ, hath not God. He that abideth in the doctrine of Christ he hath both the Father and the Son" (II John 9). And with truly prophetic foresight, Paul had written to Timothy:

> Preach the word; be instant in season, out of season; . . . . for the time will come when they will not endure sound doctrine; but unto their own lusts shall they heap to themselves teachers, having itching ears; and they shall turn away their ears from the truth, and shall be turned unto fables.—II Tim. 4: 2-4.

This prophecy was literally fulfilled, and with the loss of sound doctrine and ordinances, the power and the spiritual authority of the church was lost also.

The various pagan cults which competed with early Christianity for the devotion of the common people were rich in rites and ceremonies. In an attempt to lessen the distance between Christianity and paganism, and thus to make it more easy for converts to bridge the gap, the church adopted certain phases of the pagan mysteries. The practice of exorcism was thus joined to the rite of baptism, and the person to be baptized was supposed to be freed from the bondage of Satan by a preliminary ritual, so that when he was immersed, he could be absorbed into the body of Christ without difficulty. This was the prelude to other changes. Soon sprinkling took the place of baptism by immersion; thereby much of the beauty and fitting symbolism of that divinely given ordinance was sacrificed. Following this, it was not long until baptism began to be administered to children who were not competent to enter into such a covenant, and whose incompetence was recognized in the appointment of godparents to take the vows on their behalf. From this inclusion of infants among those who were to be baptized, it was but a step to the point where the church came to believe that children who died without baptism entered into a horrible state of damnation.

This trend away from the ordinances as practiced in the early church is also illustrated in the transition of the sacrament or communion from a memorial meal into the Sacrifice of the Mass. The original sacramental meal was quite simple, although it was undoubtedly a very solemn and meaningful occasion. Recovery of the spirit of that occasion is important, and such aids as minister to this end may rightly be used; but the elaborate imagery of the mass is completely without justification either in the Scriptures themselves or in the spirit of the original sacramental meal.

The life of the early church was enlightened by the gifts of the Holy Spirit. Without doubt there was considerable abuse of these gifts (I Cor. 14: 1-20), but they were intended to be an integral part of the life of the church (I Cor. 12: 4-11). The gifts had intrinsic value, for through them instruction and encouragement came to individuals and to the church. In addition to this, they also had significance as indicating that spiritual power is available to all believers and is divided among them according to the will of God. These gifts are intended as a testimony of the presence of God and of his willingness to sublimate the natural gifts of his people by the outpouring of his Spirit. When the "mystery of iniquity" spread among the professed followers of the Master, the spiritual gifts were taken away; the people came to rely on magic, and the idolatrous worship of relics of the saints, for the sense of divine nearness which rightfully belongs to the faithful.

The early church was clothed with power and authority in her own field, the realm of righteousness. Such power is the result of following resolutely in the footsteps of Jesus in spite of all temptation to compromise, and is the priceless possession of the "doers of the word" (James 1: 22). When the church began to compromise, it began to apostatize.

Many years ago the Prophet Isaiah called his countrymen to repentance and counseled them to be humble.

> For my thoughts are not your thoughts, neither are your ways my ways, saith the Lord. For as the heavens are higher than the earth, so are my ways higher than your ways, and my thoughts than your thoughts.—Isaiah 55: 8, 9.

The church forgot this admonition of Isaiah's and became lifted up in pride and self-will. Persecution, particularly in the early days, tended to keep the church pure. On the other hand, it was in the periods of rest, when the church was becoming popular and important, that apostasy was most rapid. For example, Eusebius, a historian who lived at the time of the Emperor Constantine, writes about the state of the church immediately preceding the Diocletian persecution, as follows:

> When by reason of excessive liberty we sunk into negligence and sloth, one envying and reviling another in different ways, and we were almost, as it were, upon the point of taking up arms against each other with words as with darts and spears; prelates inveighing against prelates, and people rising up against people, and hypocrisy and dissimulation had arisen to the greatest height of malignity; then the divine

judgment, which usually proceeds with a lenient hand, whilst the multitudes were yet crowding into the church, with gentle and mild visitation began to afflict the episcopacy, the persecution having begun with those brethren in the army. But as if destitute of all sensibility, we were not prompt in measures to appease and propitiate the Deity; some indeed like atheists, regarding our situation as unheeded and unobserved by a Providence, we added one wickedness and misery to another. But some that appeared to be our pastors, deserting the law of piety, were inflamed against each other with mutual strifes, only accumulating quarrels and threats, rivalship, hostility and hatred to each other, only anxious to assert the government as a kind of sovereignty.

The fact of the apostasy lays on the disciples of today a special obligation of vigilant faithfulness. We need to keep in mind that apostasy cannot be departmentalized. The church did not abandon her doctrines and retain her gifts; she did not lose communion with God and retain an inspired ministry; she did not lose her sense of humble service and retain her authority. The vital characteristics of the church are related to each other; and weakness in any phase of church life leads to inadequacy and loss of power in every other phase. Apostasy is a poison which, in time, reaches out to destroy the whole body.

Study Outlines

What Was Lost by the Apostasy

Lesson Purpose

To show what was lost in the apostasy, and to prepare the way for enhanced appreciation of the Restoration.

High Points of the Lesson

The apostasy resulted in the loss of genuine spiritual authority both among the ministry and in the life of the body; in the cessation of clear guidance through divine revelation; in loss of the pure doctrines and ordinances of the gospel; and in withdrawal of the gifts and blessings of the Spirit.

Loss in any one phase of church life was inevitably followed by weakening of all other aspects of church life.

Questions and Discussion Topics

(1) What is the basic cause of the doctrinal differences between Christian people?

(2) What was the first and most distinctive loss occasioned by the apostasy?

(3) In what way did the apostasy affect the authority of the ministry? What was its influence on church organization?

(4) Discuss the progress of apostasy in connection with the principle of divine guidance.

(5) What was the relation of the apostasy to the ordinances of the gospel? Name some of the specific doctrines and ordinances affected.

(6) Enumerate some of the characteristic gifts of the gospel lost through apostasy. Were these gifts needed at this period? Give reasons for your answer.

(7) During what periods was the apostasy most rapid? Why?

(8) What are our major safeguards against apostasy?

What the Lesson Means Today

It is possible to retain the form of godliness but to lose the spirit. It is also possible to emphasize spirituality to the neglect of those ordinances and sacraments on which it is nourished. These two must be balanced in effective Christian living.

No member of the church can be truly unconcerned in any phase of church life. Loss at any one point means weakness at every other.

The ultimate test of our acceptance with God is demonstrable spiritual power.

Lesson Twenty-nine

III—REFORMATION AND RESTORATION

Most Protestant authorities believe that the state of apostasy which we have discussed continued for eight hundred years or more, and was brought to a close by the Protestant Reformation under Luther and his associates. We do not believe that the Reformation corrected all the abuses of the apostasy or restored the spirit and power of the early church; nevertheless it prepared the way for the restoration of the gospel which was yet to come.

Roman Catholic authorities admit quite freely that there was a widespread corruption of morals in the sixteenth century, but they do not admit that there was any basic doctrinal inadequacy. Cardinal Gibbons states the Roman Catholic position very ably:

> The church is the work of an incarnate God. Like all God's work, it is perfect. It is, therefore, incapable of reform. Is it not the height of presumption for men to attempt to improve the work of God? Is it not ridiculous for the Luthers, the Calvins, the Knoxes, and the Henries, and the thousand lesser lights to be offering their amendments to the constitution of the church, as if it were a human institution?—*Faith of Our Fathers,* page 94.

There is something to be said for the position taken by the Roman Catholic theologians. They are entirely right in their contention that the church is a divine institution and not a human organization. Its nature and authority are derived from Divinity, and are not to be adjusted by mutual agreement among the membership. The difficulty with their position, however, lies in the fact that the most significant characteristic of the Church of Jesus Christ is her communion with her Lord and Master and her obedience to the nature and purpose of her being. So long as God is with his church, then no outside authority has the right to reform it. But when the church has departed from him, and a different organization, directed by human authority and having a form of godliness but denying the power thereof, has taken her place, then obviously neither readjustments from within nor reforms from without can refashion this organization like its earlier self. Nothing but rebirth from above will do.

We are therefore faced with a dilemma of major proportions. The church had in fact "gone into the wilderness" (Rev. 12: 6), and was no longer available among men. No purely human authority or ingenuity could restore it. It is conceivable that men might organize a body, like the body of the apostolic church, but there would still remain the much more important task of endowing this body with the life of God. God alone could do this.

We are here attempting to face facts and to note their bearing on our own spiritual destinies. There is neither desire nor intention of disparaging the great and noble work done by the men of the Reformation period, nor, for that matter, by the heroes of Roman Catholic history. Their situation was akin to that of good men who lived during previous eras of apostasy. Something of the afterglow of the ages of revelation was left to them. Certainly God had not ceased to love them, nor had he deserted them, but they were trying to work out by the process of trial and error the insight which God would have had them gain by the process of revelation and obedience. They learned by the things they suffered, and with courage, devotion, and hope they faced the facts of their time and sought to recapture something of the earlier power of the Christian evangel. They failed in the sense that it was not given to them to restore the Church of Jesus Christ and its former beauty. They succeeded in that they did much to pave the way for the Restoration which lay ahead.

The Reformation made three notable contributions to the religious growth of humanity: It broke the strangle hold of the papacy, it promoted a new freedom throughout Europe, and it restored the Bible to the homes of the masses. Of course there were changes in doctrine; but none of the vital losses of the apostasy were made up. There was no restoration of an inspired priesthood, no return to the simple but beautiful doctrines of the earlier years unimpaired by later accretions, no recapture of the unique spiritual power of apostolic Christianity.

Without the Reformation, the Restoration of the gospel would have been impossible. The Reformation prepared the way. Much can be said against the various sects which sprang up within a few years of the time of Luther. They were quarrelsome and dictatorial and did not hesitate to resort to the same persecution which they had deplored under the pope. But their errors, painful and far-reaching as they were, for the most part were the errors of men who recognized a great need and sought to supply it, but who had not yet grown to the point where they were ready to give first place to the guidance of heaven, which was vital to their success. When they would do good, evil was present with them. The body of the years of the apostasy still remained. Their thinking and planning were clouded over by the experiences of blind and dead centuries. The past lived within, and they could not forget it. They and the church needed to be reborn.

Some of the reformers recognized the limitations of their own work. Martin Luther, for instance, said: "I cannot tell what to say of myself. Perhaps I am Philipp Melanchthon's forerunner." Roger Williams, the great Baptist reformer of this country said: "I can see that the apostasy of anti-Christ has so far corrupted all that there can be no recovery out of that apostasy until Christ shall send forth new apostles to plant churches anew." John Wesley said:

> The times which we have reason to believe are at hand, if they are not already begun, are what many pious men have termed the latter-day glory . . . . and yet the wise men of the world, men of learning and renown, cannot understand what we mean by talking of an extraordinary work of God. They cannot discern the signs of these times. They can see no sign at all of God arising to maintain his own cause and set up his kingdom over all the earth.

This statement was made less than half a century before the Restoration Movement was initiated. A contemporary of Joseph

Smith's, Alexander Campbell, was in full agreement with this when he said: "The primitive gospel in its effulgence and power is yet to shine out in its original splendor and regenerate the world." These great reformers looked for the coming of a greater gospel than they themselves had yet conceived. We believe that history has vindicated their insight.

Study Outlines

Reformation and Restoration

Lesson Purpose

To note the contributions and inadequacies of the Reformation Movement and to restate the nature of the church of Jesus Christ.

High Points of the Lesson

The Reformation broke the strangle hold of the papacy; it promoted a new freedom throughout Europe; and it restored the Bible to the homes of the people. But it brought no clear recommitment of divine authority, no re-endowment of spiritual gifts, and no restoration of the purity and completeness of doctrines and ordinances.

When the way had been prepared by the various reformation movements, and a new land of opportunity had bred a race of pioneers, the lines of preparation converged and the Restoration took place.

Questions and Discussion Topics

(1) What position is taken by Roman Catholic authorities with regard to the apostasy and recovery therefrom? What is the strength or weakness of this position?

(2) Outline the characteristics of the church during the period of apostasy.

(3) What notable contributions to religious growth were made by the Reformation Movement? In what way did the Reformation fall short?

(4) How did the reformers feel about their own work? Give reasons for your answer.

(5) Refer to some of the New Testament indications of the coming Restoration.

(6) What political preparation was made for the Restoration? What social preparation? What contribution was made by science?

(7) Discuss briefly the spiritual situation in the United States and Europe immediately prior to the Restoration. How did this affect the various denominations?

(8) Name some of the leaders of the Reformation. Discuss the work of each one appreciatively.

What the Lesson Means Today

Those who promote social well-being in the right spirit are divinely blessed. But the kingdom of God is not merely an improvement on the present world order. It is a new order of social life made possible by our faithfulness, divine guidance, and blessing.

We face many inducements to abandon the work of building the kingdom. Some of these are trivial and have little attraction. Others become more attractive the more eager we are to serve men. The worst enemy of the best is the second best; for many people become so immersed in good work that they never go on to do their best work.

Lesson Thirty

IV—THE BACKGROUND OF THE RESTORATION

It is not a pleasant task to narrate the story of the apostasy, but it is better to face facts than to ignore them; the fact is that sin blinds and misleads men and groups of men. Our Heavenly Father did his utmost to persuade the people of post-apostolic times to take full advantage of the opportunities of the gospel. They refused to do so, and became the servants of the law of sin, which they chose to obey. The apostles knew that the apostasy was coming and foretold it. They knew that their world-wide mission would apparently be brought to nothing. Yet they endured, strong in the prophetic assurance which guaranteed them final triumph. Everyone of them had three facts well in mind—the present fact of the truth committed to him, the coming fact of the apostasy, and the final fact of the great victory of truth in the triumphant return of the Lord Jesus. Peter, Paul, and John each bore witness of all these facts.

As Peter and John were on their way to the temple for prayer, not long after the day of Pentecost, they came on a maimed man sitting beside the Gate Beautiful, asking for alms. The lame man had never walked, and there was no power in him by which he could learn to walk. Friends had done all they could for him; but he had lost hope. All that he asked was help in carrying on a meager existence. But the love of Jesus exceeded his expectation, and power such as the man had never known was made available to him through faith. At the command of Peter, he stood with "perfect soundness" in the presence of them all (Acts 3: 16). The people of the vicinity had known the lame man all his life, and were astonished by what had taken place. Peter took advantage of their amazement to tell them the true story of the Crucifixion. Then he made the miracle which they had witnessed a parable of what God wished to do for them. They, too, were needy and helpless. They, too, had asked only a pittance of life. They needed to repent and be converted, to expect great things from God, and to look forward to the time of refreshing which would come from the presence of the Lord. Enlarging the circle still more, he used the miracle as a parable against the background of all time. Reaching beyond the immediacy of the present, he told them of a greater restitution yet far in the future, a "restitution of all things which God hath spoken by the mouth of all his holy prophets since the world began" (Acts 3: 21). Not even the ministry of Jesus had brought such a glorious consummation, for he had been handicapped by the lack of faith of many to whom he would minister. But Peter looked to a great day when humanity should rise from the debility of sin, and should walk in newness of life, a time of restitution where the righteous would, at last, be fully responsive to the victorious leadership of Jesus.

It was a great experience for Peter to feel the Spirit of God surging through him and to be God's minister in bringing new life to a man who had lost hope. It was an even greater experience to realize that this was part and parcel of the total movement of God for men, to see that this physical healing was typical of the spiritual vigor which few have ever known but which is available to all who put their trust in Christ, to realize that such an endowment of power will come to a sustained climax when we welcome Christ as King. It was in the strength of this conviction that Peter went ahead with his work in spite of his knowledge about the coming apostasy. It is to his great glory that when the time came he played an important part in the Restoration about which he had prophesied.

The Apostle Paul had learned the riches of Christianity by the revelation of Jesus Christ (Gal. 1: 12). Although his approach was the very reverse of that made by Peter and John, he shared the convictions which Peter had expressed to the Jews gathered on Solomon's porch. Writing to the saints in Ephesus, for example, his heart overflowing with a sense of the greatness and majesty of the love of God for needy men, he told them that the faithful have been blessed with all spiritual blessings in heavenly places in Christ (Eph. 1: 3). He told them of the preparation made before the foundation of the world for winning men to the love of God (Eph. 1: 4). The vision which had taken him back into the morning of creation then reached forward and caused him to write that those who "have redemption through his blood, the forgiveness of sins according to the riches of his grace" (Eph. 1: 7), are won through Christ, "that in the dispensation of the fullness of time he might gather together in one all things in Christ, both which are in heaven, and which are on earth; even in him."—Ephesians 1: 10.

Peter and Paul both knew of the successive apostasies of the past. Both of them knew of the apostasy which was to follow their own ministry, for they could see "the mystery of iniquity" already at work. It is not surprising, therefore, that their hearts were sometimes sad, and that they asked themselves whether the gravitation of ungodliness would ever be overcome, and the fullness of the gospel of Christ ever be established among men, never again to be overcome. Nothing but the testimony of the Spirit of God could have brought them the assurance they needed and which they evidently received—the assurance which shines through these two messages and which held steady in their contribution to the great day of culmination and of triumph.

The Apostle John outlived Peter and Paul and all the other apostles. Before the end of his life, the beginnings of the apostasy were clearly apparent. He was required to write to the seven churches of Asia, chiding them for the loss of their first love, and that they were lukewarm. Yet the very revelation which required him to warn the churches of their danger also gave him a reassuring vision of the future. He was shown what was to take place "in the hour of God's judgment"; he continued:

> And I saw another angel fly in the midst of heaven having the everlasting gospel to preach unto them that dwell on the earth, and to every

nation, and kindred, and tongue, and people. Saying with a loud voice, Fear God, and give glory to him; for the hour of his judgment is come; and worship him that made heaven, and earth, and the sea, and the fountains of waters.—Rev. 14: 6, 7.

This experience lifted John far above the limited interests of the moment. He saw to the end of time, when "every nation, and kindred, and tongue, and people" would be recalled to the word of the true God. He saw their need supplied by the coming of a messenger from the courts of glory with a message worthy of his dignity and suited to their need—the everlasting gospel.

By the beginning of the nineteenth century, there was a widespread yearning for some great act of God which should set aside the blindness and spiritual inertia of the age and restore the true faith. The American people were alert with an eager expectancy which reached into every hamlet and inspired both material and spiritual endeavor. In Europe the devastating Napoleonic wars had been terminated on the field of Waterloo, and the sigh of relief which arose from that stricken continent had been echoed here. Men were setting their faces toward a new and better day and were eagerly awakening to the wonderful opportunity of the land of promise which was theirs.

In other countries, the opportunity for free expression was limited by the terrible inertia of tradition. In the new world, all the gains of the past were available; men of pioneer vision and courage were free to use or adapt or scrap these traditions as their expanding experience showed wise. It was out of this background of opportunity that the new nation fashioned its doctrine of the value of individual initiative. Such a faith called for leaders of tried power, and when these took their places, their attitude was a prophecy of what was to come.

The restless energy, the capacity for making decisions of moment and the sure belief in freedom of opportunity which characterized the times could not be limited to material things. The expectancy of big things which is the companion of achievement was felt in literature and in science and in religion. With but little patience for the niceties of ordered worship, the men of the advancing line of population were nevertheless too close to the reality of things to be irreligious. On the contrary, they were deeply concerned about the fundamental truths of life. Religion was their outstanding interest. The Bible was the most available piece of literature and was so studied that it left an indelible mark in the thought and speech of the time. It was believed simply and literally, and Bible heroes became the embodiment of frontier ideals.

This spiritual expectancy manifested itself in the rapid growth of the older denominations, their break-up into fragments, and the creation of new organizations. Religious revivals were frequent and intense, a notable one being the Kentucky revival of 1800. The Methodists and Baptists and Universalists grew rapidly stronger in numbers, the Unitarians definitely separated themselves from the Congregationalists, and the Disciples, or Christians, first came into being. Numerous humanitarian agencies also sprang up in response to the general concern about the common welfare. In every realm it was the day of great men and of great doings. Thus it was that in 1820 the stage was set, the players were awaiting their cues, and God, the great author of the drama of the Restoration, was about to order the drawing of the curtain on the opening act.

V—THE RESTORATION

Prophets, apostles, and reformers had looked forward to the time when the church should be reborn, when the angel should "fly in the midst of heaven, having the everlasting gospel to preach to them that dwell on the earth" (Rev. 14: 6). Now history had converged to the point where their expectations could be fulfilled.

In the closing decades of the eighteenth century and the early years of the nineteenth century, the deep religious concern of the frontier people resulted in great camp meetings and other gatherings where excitement and religious fervor sometimes went to extravagant lengths. Such a revival was held among the Methodists in the winter of 1819, and spread from hamlet to hamlet and from village to village so that the whole western country was soon deeply affected thereby.

At this time the family of a farmer named Joseph Smith lived at Manchester, New York. With the other members of the community, the Smiths attended the joint revival held in the vicinity of their home, and, like their neighbors, they became greatly concerned about their spiritual destinies. The rather extravagant manifestations of emotional fervor which he saw during the revival particularly impressed young Joseph, who was then about fourteen years of age. While he did not participate in these activities, he did sense a certain reality behind them, and he was eager to respond. The many differences among those who had "found religion," however, greatly perplexed him, as he sought to determine what course he should pursue, until he read and was greatly impressed by the statement of James, "If any of you lack wisdom, let him ask of God, that giveth to all men liberally; and upbraideth not; and it shall be given him" (James 1: 5). This appealed so strongly to Joseph that he read and reread it; with each reading it seemed more necessary that he should receive the divinely imparted wisdom that James promised. Accordingly, one beautiful morning in the early spring of 1820, Joseph repaired to the woods near his home, and with his heart full of concern about the great issues before him, but with the utmost faith in the promises of the Lord, he asked for the wisdom which he needed. Perhaps no other words but his own can fittingly describe what transpired. He says:

> Having looked around me and finding myself alone, I kneeled down and began to offer up the desires of my heart to God. I had scarcely done so when immediately I was seized by some power which entirely overcame me, and had such an astonishing influence over me as to bind my tongue so that I could not speak. Thick darkness gathered around me, and it seemed to me for a time as if I were

doomed to sudden destruction. But exerting all my powers to call upon God to deliver me out of the power of this enemy which had seized upon me, and at the very moment when I was ready to sink into despair and abandon myself to destruction, (not to an imaginary ruin, but to the power of some actual being from the unseen world, who had such marvelous power as I had never before felt in my being), just at this moment of great alarm, I saw a pillar of light exactly over my head, above the brightness of the sun, which descended gradually until it fell upon me.

It no sooner appeared than I found myself delivered from the enemy which held me bound. When the light rested upon me I saw two personages (whose brightness and glory defy all description) standing above me in the air. One of them spoke to me, calling me by name, and said, (pointing to the other), "This is my beloved Son, hear him."

My object in going to inquire of the Lord was to know which of all the sects was right, that I might know which to join. No sooner therefore did I get possession of myself, so as to be able to speak, than I asked the personages who stood above me in the light, which of all the sects was right . . . . and which I should join. I was answered that I must join none of them, for they were all wrong, and the personage who addressed me said that all their creeds were an abomination in his sight; that those professors were all corrupt; "they draw near me with their lips, but their hearts are far from me; they teach for doctrine the commandments of men, having a form of godliness, but they deny the power thereof." He again forbade me to join with any of them: and many other things did he say unto me, which I cannot write at this time.—*Church History,* Volume 1, pages 9, 10.

This vision of Joseph's has become one of the landmarks of our spiritual history. It was the beginning of the work of the Restoration, and was so recognized by the Prophet and his associates in the latter years of their ministry. In spite of Joseph's youth and inexperience, it committed him to certain fundamentals from which he never turned, and which will be impressed on the philosophy of the Restoration till the end of time.

Perhaps the first significance of this vision is its clear presentation of the fatherhood of God. As the initial pronouncement of a great spiritual movement, nothing could have been more fitting. In laying the foundation of the church in these last days, nothing could be more fundamental and in all the realm of spiritual values, nothing is more vital. The vision of 1820 committed Joseph and the church to deep-seated convictions regarding the fatherhood of God.

Parallel with this pronouncement, and as part of it, is the clear recognition of the mission of Jesus Christ among men. In the centuries which had passed since the close of the apostolic age, this ministry had been obscured, except in the personal devotion of a comparatively small number of saintly men and women. But in this key vision received by Joseph, the central command was, "Hear him." In the Restoration Movement the authority of the Lord Jesus Christ is central.

Then, again, the vision itself is a marvelous testimony of direct answer to the prayer of faith and an equally outstanding vindication of the principle of divine revelation. Both of these, so intimately related to each other, are also fundamental to deep, spiritual experience. Indeed, there is no spiritual life without them. If the prayer of faith does not evoke response from God, then he is not in fact our Father; if his response does not reveal his nature and purpose to us, then it is futile. It is not likely that Joseph sensed at the time how very much was involved in this simple but inspiring experience. But as the years have passed, it has become more and more clear that from the very beginning, by reason of this vision, the church has been committed to the practice of fervent prayer and to the expectancy of divine guidance.

Finally, this experience of Joseph's indicated clearly the attitude which he should take toward the denominations of his time. The Lord proposed to build his church. As in other ages, he did not intend to do this by reforming existing organizations but by the demonstration of his own power. Since Joseph was to be one of the chief instruments of Divinity in bringing forth the Restoration, it was not fitting that he should become affiliated with the divided and uninspiring religious societies of the neighborhood. The expectancy of the times was being justified in the response of Divinity. The American people were moving out into a new country, and the people of God were moving out into new realms of spiritual experience and power.

THE VISION OF EIGHTEEN HUNDRED TWENTY-THREE

The three and a half years which passed between the vision of 1820 and the next outstanding revelation which Joseph Smith received were years of preparation and testing. The immediate effect of his remarkable experience in the woods at Manchester was to deter him from joining any of the denominations which had participated in the revival, and whose claims had previously attracted him. His quiet but steadfast assertion that he had received the ministry of both the Father and the Son brought persecution and ridicule, but apart from these things the years were apparently uneventful.

These three years were not without their mistakes. It is difficult for the most mature of us to maintain any marked spiritual tension over an extended period. This becomes many times more difficult when the exalted level of a great experience is to be maintained without some corresponding activity. To wait in quiet contemplation of the instruction he had received and to recenter his every thought and deed in the revelation which had been embodied in this instruction was too much for Joseph. He tells us that at times he became involved in the follies of the world. There is no reason to believe that this means that he became vicious or degenerate, but only that he became tired of the constant endeavor to discipline himself in the great school of God. The adolescent wanted action; missing it, he became lethargic; then, realizing his mistake, he repented.

All men of spiritual genius have had a horror of sin. This horror Joseph shared. Accordingly, when he sensed the fact that he had not been true to his knowledge of God, this fact burned into his inner consciousness and made him yearn for a gesture of divine forgiveness. In this mood Joseph retired to his room on the evening of September twenty-third, 1823. Here he prayed for forgiveness of his sins and for knowledge of his standing before God. How long he thus prayed we do not know, but Joseph has himself preserved for us a picture of what transpired as a result of his prayers. He says:

While I was thus in the act of calling upon God I discovered a light appearing in the room, which continued to increase until the room was lighter than at noonday, when immediately a personage appeared at my bedside standing in the air, for his feet did not touch the floor. He had on a loose robe of most exquisite whiteness. It was a whiteness beyond anything earthly I had ever seen; nor do I believe that any earthly thing could be made to appear so exceedingly white and brilliant; his hands were naked, and his arms also a little above the wrist. So also were his feet naked, as were his legs a little above the ankles. His head and neck were also bare. I could discover that he had no other clothing on but this robe, as it was open so that I could see into his bosom. Not only was his robe exceedingly white, but his whole person was glorious beyond description, and his countenance truly like lightning. The room was exceedingly light, but not very bright as immediately around his person.

When I first looked upon him, I was afraid, but the fear soon left me. He called me by name, and said unto me that he was a messenger sent from the presence of God to me, and that his name was Nephi (Moroni). That God had a work for me to do, and that my name should be had for good and evil, among all nations, kindreds, and tongues; or that it should be both good and evil spoken of among all people. He said there was a book deposited written upon gold plates, giving an account of the former inhabitants of this continent, and the source from whence they sprang. He also said that the fullness of the everlasting gospel was contained in it, as delivered by the Savior to the ancient inhabitants. Also that there were two stones in silver bows, and these stones fastened to a breastplate constituted what is called the Urim and Thummim, deposited with the plates, and the possession and use of these stones were what constituted seers in ancient or former times, and that God had prepared them for the purpose of translating the book.—*Church History,* Volume 1, pages 12, 13.

After telling of the coming forth of the Book of Mormon, the heavenly messenger proceeded to quote numerous Biblical prophecies and to explain their significance and imminent fulfillment. Then the vision closed, and the room was left in total darkness, while Joseph meditated on that which he had heard. Suddenly, the messenger again appeared, and the vision was repeated and embellished. Again Joseph was left to meditate, and again the vision was opened to him, the messenger repeating all that he had said before.

The day after this remarkable experience, Joseph went to a hill of considerable size, convenient to Manchester, Ontario County, New York, as directed by his heavenly guide. Here he saw the plates and other articles. At first he sought to take them, but he was not permitted to do so. Instead he was instructed to return to this place every year.

In accordance with the command of the messenger Joseph returned to the hill again each year and was met by Moroni who gave him instructions regarding both the Book of Mormon and the great work which the Lord was to do in the coming days. It seems that each year Joseph expected to have the plates committed to his care; but each time he was told that he must wait a little longer.

On the twenty-second of September, 1827, Joseph went to the hill for the fifth time. He was now in his twenty-second year, and responsibility and preparation had left their marks on him. On this occasion Moroni met him as before. Moroni took the sacred plates and the other things which had been deposited with them, including the Urim and Thummim, and presented them to the young man, with the charge that he was now responsible for them, to guard them with the utmost care.

Study Outlines

The Background of the Restoration

Lesson Purpose

To recount the earlier events of the Restoration and to emphasize their spiritual significance.

High Points of the Lesson

The vision of 1820 created in Joseph a spiritual appetite which could not be satisfied among people who denied the reality of present revelation.

The three years following 1820 are remarkable for two things: the absence of spiritual extravagance, and the growth of steadfast spiritual purpose.

The coming forth of the Book of Mormon fits in to the pattern of the Restoration Movement. The dispensation of the fullness of times was ushered in by the enrichment of the Scriptures.

QUESTIONS AND DISCUSSION TOPICS

(1) Tell the story of Joseph's first vision. What spiritual truths become apparent because of this vision?

(2) Give reasons why Joseph could not reassociate himself with any of the various denominations after this experience.

(3) Describe the period between 1820 and 1823 in the life of Joseph Smith. What were the major characteristics of this period?

(4) Describe the vision of 1823. What led up to it? What remarkable promise was made to Joseph at this time? Has this been fulfilled?

(5) Recall the events immediately following the vision of 1823.

(6) What were the major happenings of the period between 1823 and 1827? In what way was Joseph prepared for his further work during this period?

(7) What is the relation of the Book of Mormon to the Restoration Movement?

(8) Discuss briefly the place of the Book of Mormon in the life of the church.

WHAT THE LESSON MEANS TODAY

Latter Day Saintism began as a religion of experience. It will be strong only as it continues to be a religion of experience.

The Book of Mormon has been made available to us at such tremendous cost that it has obvious claims on our consideration and study.

The early years of the Restoration Movement were years of power because the Saints were gripped by great convictions. We need to seek convictions which are adequate to our day and time, because they are rooted in eternity.

Lesson Thirty-one

RESTORATION OF THE AARONIC PRIESTHOOD

After the plates were delivered into the keeping of Joseph Smith in September, 1827, he translated them by the inspiration of God through the Urim and Thummim as fast as his circumstances permitted. For a time it seemed that the cares of life—the necessity for providing for his own needs and those of his wife, and particularly the difficulty of securing a scribe would make it impossible to push the work as he desired. Yet somehow each need was supplied as it arose, and the work went forward. The actual translation was quite an education for Joseph and those who wrote for him, particularly Oliver Cowdery. This was because they did not merely render word for word, but in the process of rendering the record into the English language they sought to understand what they wrote. (Consider Doctrine and Covenants 9: 3, in this connection.)

As Joseph and Oliver were engaged in this work of translation and of understanding, they came to an exposition of the doctrine of baptism. The force of the Book of Mormon statement was such that both Joseph and his scribe became greatly concerned. Following the course which had previously brought them light, they went into the woods, knelt down, and asked God that he would give them instruction regarding this great principle. As they knelt before the Father, their experience of the past was repeated. God revealed himself to them in a way and in terms that were beyond denial or misunderstanding. Joseph has recounted the experience as follows:

We still continued the work of translation, when in the ensuing month (May, eighteen hundred and twenty-nine) we on a certain day went into the woods to pray and inquire of the Lord respecting baptism for the remission of sins, as we found mentioned in the translation of the plates. While we were thus employed, praying, and calling upon the Lord, a messenger from heaven descended in a cloud of light, and having laid his hands upon us, he ordained us, saying unto us, "Upon you, my fellow servants, in the name of Messiah, I confer the priesthood of Aaron, which holds the keys of the ministering of angels, and of the gospel of repentance, and of baptism by immersion, for the remission of sins; and this shall never be taken again from the earth, until the sons of Levi do offer again an offering unto the Lord in righteousness." He said this Aaronic priesthood had not the power of laying on of hands, for the gift of the Holy Ghost, but that this should be conferred on us hereafter; and he commanded us to go and be baptized, and gave us directions that I should baptize Oliver Cowdery, and afterwards that he should baptize me.—*Church History,* Volume I, pages 34-36.

The messenger said, further, that he was John the Baptist mentioned in the Scriptures, the forerunner of Jesus Christ, that he was then ministering in accordance with the authority of God vested in him under the direction of Peter, James, and John. He promised the two young men that this greater priesthood which Peter, James, and John held should yet be conferred on them, but for the time assured them that they were to function in accordance with this Aaronic priesthood mentioned in the narrative of Joseph.

Until this time Joseph had been the sole recipient of these manifestations of the power and revealing love of God, but from then on Joseph was associated with other men, sometimes one, sometimes more—and thus his testimony was now reinforced by their testimony. In this experience Joseph was accompanied by Oliver Cowdery, and Oliver has borne testimony to this same experience in words of equal soberness, though perhaps somewhat more fluently than Joseph.

In accordance with the instruction of this messenger, Joseph proceeded to baptize Oliver, and Oliver in turn baptized Joseph. Then, still following the instruction which had been received, Joseph ordained Oliver to the Aaronic priesthood. Immediately Oliver stood up and spoke in prophecy, foretelling many wonderful things that were yet to happen. He then ordained Joseph, and this divine unction descended on Joseph. He, too, foretold many things connected with the rise and coming glory of the church.

Because there had been so much persecution of their previous testimony, these two young men (Joseph at this time was not yet twenty-four; Oliver Cowdery two or three months younger) tried to keep the fact of their baptism and ordination secret for a short time. But the power of their new experience outdid all their attempts at secrecy. As they broke the news to their neighbors and relatives, they found that the Spirit of God had been working before them. For example, they talked with Samuel, the younger brother of Joseph, and there came to him such conviction of the truth that he demanded baptism.

Joseph and Oliver were now members of the Aaronic priesthood. They were called to hold the keys of the ministering of angels, because they knew with assurance that God had ministered to them by angelic power. They were called to preach the good news of repentance because the good news of repentance had found fruitage in their lives. They were called to preach the principles of baptism, because they had been reborn themselves and their lives recentered in the things of God. And they were called to bring men to a new knowledge that temporal things can become means of spiritual blessing in the hands of men of God, because all their temporal interests had thus been dedicated to the achievement of spiritual ends.

RESTORATION OF THE MELCHISEDEC PRIESTHOOD

Joseph tells of the next outstanding event of this period in the following words:

Meantime we continued to translate, at intervals, when not necessitated to attend to the numerous inquirers, that now began to visit us; some for the sake of finding the truth, others for the purpose of putting hard questions, and trying to confound us. Among the latter class were several learned priests who generally came for the purpose of disputation: however the Lord continued to pour out upon us his Holy Spirit, and as often as we had need, he gave us in that moment what to say; so that although unlearned, and inexperienced in religious controversies, yet were we able to confound those learned rabbis of the day, whilst at the same time, we were enabled to convince the honest in heart, that we had obtained (through the mercy of God) to the true and everlasting gospel of Jesus Christ, so that almost daily we administered the ordinance of baptism for the remission of sins, to such as believed.

We now became anxious to have that promise realized to us, which the angel that conferred upon us the Aaronic priesthood had given us: viz., that provided we continued faithful we should also have the Melchisedec priesthood, which holds the authority of the laying on of hands for the gift of the Holy Ghost. We had for some time made this matter a subject of humble prayer, and at length we got together in the chamber of Mr. Whitmer's house in order more particularly to seek of the Lord what we now so earnestly desired: and here to our unspeakable satisfaction did we realize the truth of the Savior's promise, "Ask, and you shall receive, seek, and you shall find, knock and it shall be opened unto you;" for we had not long been engaged in solemn and fervent prayer when the word of the Lord came unto us in the chamber, commanding us that I should ordain Oliver Cowdery to be an elder in the Church of Jesus Christ, and that he also should ordain me to the same office, and then to ordain others as it should be made known unto us, from time to time: we were, however, commanded to defer this our ordination until such times as it should be practicable to have our brethren, who had been and who should be baptized, assembled together, when we must have their sanction to our thus proceeding to ordain each other, and have them decide by vote whether they were willing to accept us as spiritual teachers, or not, when also we were commanded to bless bread and break it with them, and to take wine, bless it, and drink it with them, afterward proceed to ordain each other according to commandment, then call out such men as the Spirit should dictate, and ordain them, and then attend to the laying on of hands for the gift of the Holy Ghost upon all those whom we had previously baptized; doing all things in the name of the Lord.—*Church History,* Volume 1, pages 60, 61.

It is probable that the spiritual instruction here referred to was received in the house of Father Whitmer some time during June, 1829, or about a month after the bestowal of the Aaronic priesthood. It is probable, too, that the revelation regarding the call of the twelve apostles was given at this time. As you will have noticed, however, Joseph and Oliver were commanded to defer their ordination until the time should arrive for the organization of the church, and they therefore continued under the authority of the Aaronic priesthood until the next April. During these months, however, they continued to bear testimony until the whole neighborhood became aware of their calling.

On April 6, 1830, the church was organized. At least six men were present, and possibly two or three others. The laws of the state of New York required that number for an organization of this nature.

At this initial meeting, one of the fundamental doctrines of the church was emphasized. This is the "doctrine of common consent," by which we mean that the administration of the church is conducted with the expressed consent of the people concerned. In accordance with this principle, Joseph and Oliver had been instructed not to proceed with their ordination until the other members of the infant church should express their willingness to accept them as leaders in spiritual things. After this expression of approval was received, each of them then ordained the other to the Melchisedec priesthood. Following this ordination they confirmed those who had previously been baptized, this rite of confirmation being performed by the laying on of hands.

The church was then ready to commence its work in the world. Prior to this time, we believe, no one had the authority necessary to reorganize the church. At first this may seem extremely narrow; but when we consider that the right to act for God depends primarily upon humility, love, and recognition of the divine nature and purpose, we shall see that other good men were barred from service as pioneers of the Restoration, because their traditions prevented them from realizing that God still desires to manifest himself to the world. No man can act for God acceptably who does not recognize that God still lives and loves and reveals himself to his people. Unless a man recognizes this, he will not see the necessity for being definitely called of God to the work which the Father wants him to do. Joseph and Oliver had authority to minister in the lesser ordinances of the gospel, but the right of presidency or of direction in the affairs of the church belongs to the Melchisedec priesthood. This has been true in every dispensation of the gospel, and God recognized it in the organization of his church in this age by commanding Joseph and Oliver to wait until this priesthood had been bestowed upon them before they should proceed to bring his church into being.

During the one hundred years of our church experience, the rights which these young men claimed had been bestowed on them have repeatedly been vindicated. In the course of time they ordained other men, who in turn ordained others, so that a great chain of authority was created, reaching out through them from God. Those holding this authority have acted in line with their priesthood, and all of us can bear testimony to the fact that through the ministry of these elders of the church, the Spirit of God has come into our lives by way of confirmation or of blessing or of healing or of ordination or of any several of these. It was comparatively easy for that small group to make such claims as they did; but nothing short of the power of God could bring the validation of their claims which have come to us during the past century and a quarter.

Study Outlines

Restoration of the Priesthood

Lesson Purpose

To tell the story of the restoration of the priesthood, to show its necessity, and to emphasize its importance.

High Points of the Lesson

The restoration of the Aaronic priesthood followed careful study of the Book of Mormon.

The procedure in the restoration of the priesthood ties the new dispensation to the old and indicates the continuity of the work of God from age to age. It also emphasizes the importance of authority in spiritual things.

The procedure followed in the organization of the church included the work of preparation by the Aaronic priesthood, the presidency of the Melchisedec priesthood, the free consent of the membership, the declaration of fundamental principles, and the endowment of spiritual power. This procedure has been vindicated in our subsequent experience.

Questions and Discussion Topics

(1) Tell the story of the restoration of the Aaronic priesthood. When did it occur? Who were involved?

(2) What is the work of the Aaronic priesthood?

(3) What church ordinance was now administered for the first time in this dispensation? What was its purpose?

(4) What further promise was made to Oliver and Joseph at this time? When was this promise fulfilled?

(5) Tell the story of the restoration of the Melchisedec priesthood. When and under whose authority did this take place?

(6) Why was the ordination to the Melchisedec priesthood deferred?

(7) In what way is the priesthood of today related to that of Joseph and Oliver? In what way is it related to that of Jesus and the apostles?

(8) What does priesthood mean in your life? Is it possible to have a branch of the church without priesthood? Do the members of the church have the right to appoint the ministry?

What the Lesson Means Today

Evidently the translation of the Book of Mormon was not an automatic procedure, but Joseph and Oliver gave careful attention to every principle involved. Similarly careful study of the Scriptures is the best kind of preparation for ministry today.

The importance of priesthood is indicated in the fact that the ministry of an earlier day returned to earth to recommit it to men.

Every time a minister functions in the ordinances of the gospel, those participating are joined together by a chain of priesthood authority which reaches back through Joseph and Oliver to Peter, James, and John and to the Master himself.

Chapter XIV

THE GIFTS OF THE SPIRIT

The spiritual gifts—The primary gifts—Divine healing—Miracles—Prophecy—The discernment of spirits—Tongues and interpretation.

Lesson Thirty-two

I—SPIRITUAL GIFTS

WHEN A MAN CHANGES HIS ATTITUDE toward God, he changes the direction of his life and opens many doors which have hitherto been bolted and barred against the coming of the Holy Spirit. In a sense he is the same man, for he has the same name, the same heritage, the same native endowment, and the same possessions. But in another sense, he is entirely different, for he has different purposes, different objectives, and a different point of view, and he is motivated by a different power. The Spirit of God can now search out in his life those abilities and powers which can be developed for his own good and for the good of the kingdom. Such a man is now eager for his best abilities to be discovered and enriched and used, and therefore yields himself willingly, with intelligence and with deep concern regarding what is happening, and opens the gates of his soul so that no impediment shall prevent the full and free influx of the Spirit of God. It is perfectly natural that under these circumstances the Spirit of God shall quicken his normal abilities and shall at times give him insight and understanding which he could not win for himself.

There is abundant evidence in the New Testament that this indwelling of the Spirit was widely experienced among the early disciples, and that as a result they were greatly blessed. The natural powers of many of the saints were augmented by an additional spiritual endowment which was given them for their own good and also for the good of the church. Paul explained this to the saints in Corinth as follows:

> But the manifestation of the Spirit is given to every man to profit withal. For to one is given by the Spirit the word of wisdom; to another the word of knowledge by the same Spirit; to another faith by the same Spirit; to another the gifts of healing by the same Spirit; to another the working of miracles; to another prophecy; to another discerning of spirits; to another divers kinds of tongues; to another the interpretation of tongues. But all these worketh that one and the self-same Spirit, dividing to every man severally as he will.—I Corinthians 12: 7-11.

These gifts are signs of the presence and direction of the Spirit of God. As James wrote, "the body without the spirit is dead."—James 2: 26.

But he who is enlightened by the Spirit of God has the abundant life which Jesus came to bring (John 10: 10). He "walks in newness of life" (Rom. 6: 4) and by manifesting the powers of goodness and of insight shows that he really is alive and is no longer "dead in trespasses and sins."—Eph. 2: 1.

The gifts of God are shared among the disciples through the ministry of the Holy Spirit, and are divided to every man severally as the Spirit wills (I Cor. 12: 11). Several of these gifts are mentioned in the Scriptures; but it is not inconceivable or in any sense unscriptural that in addition to those mentioned, special gifts of poetry, music, paintings, sculpture, or of any other helpful nature shall be bestowed on the children of God in harmony with their natural callings and the endowment of the Spirit. How greatly we should be enriched if we could but realize how generously the love of God flows toward us. How much closer we should come to the great destiny prophesied in our finely-wrought bodies and minds if we would but show ourselves worthy of the special gifts of divine love by our consecrated use of the gifts already submitted to our care.

The function of the Spirit in the life of man is to continue the work of creation and redemption. We are not yet completely fashioned in the image of God, but need to become more like him in spirit and in truth. The work of God in us is therefore designed both to eradicate evil and to bring good to flower. The divine intention is not to produce uniformity in us by pressing all men into the same mold, but to lift us to new levels of life by setting us on fire with love for God and our fellows. Out of this love for God will come the possibility of rich endowment. And out of our love for our fellows will come the inspiration to use our several endowments for the common welfare.

While the Holy Spirit works with us individually, it works with us, also, as members of the church. Much of the vigor and strength of the body of Christ is ministered to us through our connection with this body. We live in the body and for the body, and are blessed in order that we may bless the members of the body and, of society as a whole and may "grow together in love" (Eph. 4: 15, 16). The church as a whole as well as every member of the church is called to be "the habitation of God through the Spirit" (Eph. 2: 22). We may therefore rightfully expect that many of the gifts of the Spirit will be exercised in association with the Saints, and that not infrequently the gifts which are given to us as individuals await completion in gifts which are given to others. Our Heavenly Father is seeking to unite us in a creative spiritual fraternity; it is like him to bless us in such ways as will require us to serve him together.

Study Outlines

The Spiritual Gifts

Lesson Purpose

To show the nature of the spiritual gifts and to indicate that these are inseparably connected with the gospel of Christ.

High Points of the Lesson

While a member of the church may not enjoy any of the specific gifts listed by Paul, every true disciple will find himself quickened in some way for the general good.

Many of the gifts which we exercise individually are made possible through the church, and belong to us as members of the body. A fundamental test of the value of the gifts is in their contribution to the good of the body.

Questions and Discussion Topics

(1) Do we learn best when we are entirely free, or when we are under the direction of a recognized authority? Under what direction do the members of the church learn about God and his kingdom?

(2) For what purposes are the gifts of the gospel given to the Saints? What is the relation between these gifts and our natural gifts?

(3) How does the agency of the individual operate in relation to spiritual gifts? Can a church member choose which gifts he will exercise?

(4) Enumerate the gifts mentioned in Paul's letter to the Corinthians. Name some other spiritual gifts which well might be enjoyed in the church.

(5) The work of the Spirit is not to promote uniformity by pressing men into the same mold, but to transmit life by setting men on fire with love for God and their fellows. Discuss this briefly.

(6) How are the spiritual gifts of individuals augmented by the spiritual activity of the group?

(7) What is the relation between the spiritual gifts and charity?

(8) In what way may we rightly promote the exercise of the spiritual gifts? What gifts are most needed in your branch?

What the Lesson Means Today

We have each been endowed with many gifts. Some of these have been matured and used. Others have been completely hidden. Every gift should be fully developed and fully used. This can best be done in such an enterprise as the building of the kingdom.

No man's life is really profitable to God until the Spirit can bless him with gifts over and above those which he normally uses. The best preparation we can make for such gifts is to use what we have in the service of the Master.

The gifts of the gospel are given to enrich the life of the church. They are lost when they are sought for personal aggrandizement or are pursued as ends in themselves.

Lesson Thirty-three

II—THE PRIMARY GIFTS

It is interesting to note that when Paul listed the gifts of the Spirit for the benefit of the saints in Corinth, he thought of wisdom and knowledge and faith before he thought of healing or miracles or tongues. I do not think this means that Paul was seeking to list these gifts in the exact order of their importance; but it means at least that he held these all in sufficiently high regard to include them early in his catalogue.

Paul had been a devout Jew and knew the sacred literature of his people. It is not unlikely, therefore, that consciously or otherwise, he was influenced by Isaiah's prophecy of Jesus when he gave first place among the spiritual gifts to wisdom and knowledge. Of the coming of Jesus, Isaiah had said:

> The Spirit of the Lord shall rest upon him, the spirit of wisdom and understanding, the spirit of counsel and might, the spirit of knowledge and of the fear of the Lord; and shall make him of quick understanding in the fear of the Lord; and he shall not judge after the sight of his eyes, neither reprove after the hearing of his ears; but with righteousness shall he judge the poor, and reprove with equity the meek of the earth.—Isaiah 11: 2-4.

The first of the gifts enumerated by Paul is the gift of wisdom. If we have studied the other writings of Paul, it is immediately apparent that by wisdom the apostle does not mean mere shrewdness. Men may be very able in a limited field, but very foolish with regard to the total purpose of life. Many a business man who is feared by his competitors is not wise enough to order his home life so that he can enjoy in peace the fruits of his business successes. Nor does the apostle mean cleverness when he discusses wisdom, for a rogue is likely to be as clever as a saint. Such a man spends his thought and his skill on himself and becomes ruthlessly expert in the narrow circle of his selfish interests, while he remains blind to the larger issues of life. Nor, again, did Paul refer to carefully amassed information, when he wrote of wisdom. Information does not necessarily make a man wise, although it may easily make him conceited. What the apostle had in mind was something over and above mere information, something which uses information and avoids the pitfalls of conceit.

If we are to understand what Paul meant, we must go back of Paul to Jesus. To the Master, wisdom is the attitude of heart and mind which seeks to know the will of God, and to bring every act into relation to his total purpose. In the eyes of Jesus, the man who built bigger barns but failed to cultivate his soul was a fool. So is every other man who permits the immediacy of the present to cloud the long vision, and becomes so wrapped up in the things that lie at hand that he has no time to live in the light of eternity. Paul learned this from Jesus, not because of anything the Master said as much as because of everything the Master was. The gift of wisdom to which Paul refers is therefore the inspired good sense to follow the example of Jesus in the affairs of daily life. Such wisdom is not an abstract quality. Though it may be won in the secret places where men walk with God, it is confirmed in the experiences of daily life. It is the wisdom of experience shared with Divinity.

Paul calls this gift "the word of wisdom," which seems to indicate that the wisdom of which he is speaking is born in communion, confirmed in experience and shared with the saints for the edification of the body of Christ. It is not a cloistered insight reserved for the elect among the wise, but is nevertheless far above the understanding of ungodly men. In the last analysis it is the gift of God, shared with good men, that they in turn may share it with their fellows.

James confirmed the conviction of Paul as to the importance of wisdom. In a passage which has become famous in Latter Day Saint history and theology, he advises the man who lacks wisdom to "ask of God, that giveth to all men liberally, and upbraideth not; and it shall be given him" (James 1: 5). Then, lest any should mistake the type of wisdom of which he is writing he says:

> Who is a wise man and endued with knowledge among you! let him show out of a good conversation his works with meekness of wisdom . . . . the wisdom that is from above is first pure, then peaceable, gentle, and easy to be entreated, full of mercy and good fruits, without partiality and without hypocrisy.—James 3: 13, 17.

The second gift mentioned by Paul is the gift of knowledge. If we are to enter truly into the thought of the apostle, we must again consider what he means in the light of all that we know about Paul. For example, we must take into account what Paul wrote in a later letter to the Corinthians:

> God, who commanded the light to shine out of darkness, hath shined in our hearts, to give the light of the knowledge of the glory of God in the face of Jesus Christ.—II Corinthians 4: 6.

There is nothing small or narrow about knowledge such as this. It is knowledge quickened in the soul by the indwelling of the Spirit of God, but dependent on all that we believe and are. It is the kind of knowledge which makes wise the simple, and gives assurance which makes for steadfastness. It is knowledge which leads unto eternal life (John 17: 3).

The seers among the poets have always been aware of our deep need for this knowledge, which comes to us in the presence of God, and which mellows and informs all our lesser understanding. This is what Tennyson had in mind when he wrote:

> Let knowledge grow from more to more,
>   But more of reverence in us dwell;
>   That mind and soul, according well,
> May make one music as before
> But vaster.

It may appear at first that we are not justified in applying the term "knowledge" to this larger understanding born of the Spirit. Knowledge, we are told, has to do with that irrefutable assurance which comes from adding fact to fact, and observing their joint significance. But the difference between these two points of view is far more apparent than real. Actually, the acquisition of knowledge in any field is a miraculous affair. No one can explain why and how it happens. It is a gift of insight granted when we, who were previously in the dark, are blessed because God again says, "Let there be light."

As might be expected, the knowledge with which the Apostle Paul is concerned warms the heart and makes resolute the will, as well as enlightening the mind. It enriches the whole man. It avoids the pitfalls which constantly beset all lesser understanding. It is knowledge that "vaunteth not itself, is not puffed up, doth not behave itself unseemly, seeketh not her own, is not easily provoked, thinketh no evil, rejoiceth not in iniquity, but rejoiceth in the truth."—I Corinthians 13: 4-6.

This priceless gift of knowledge does not become complete and all-inclusive in a moment; it is granted us, rather, as we grow in capacity to receive and use it. Moreover, it is not given to any of us in isolation, but is given to us individually and is also extended within us as members of the body of Christ. No man can come to know the riches of the grace of God as a result of his solitary explorations. He must do his part; there are times when he must go bravely forward by himself; but, in the long run, here, as elsewhere, great achievement is a social affair.

Faith is the third gift in the initial group mentioned by the Apostle Paul. The principle of faith is one of the basic principles of the gospel, but here we are not discussing the principle but the gift.

To all of us is given some wisdom and some knowledge, but to certain chosen ones these gifts are given in greater abundance than to others. So it is with the gift of faith. Faith in God is one of the basic qualifications for discipleship, but the gift of faith to some seems to be greater than ordinary people possess and is an outstanding endowment of confidence in God. This keener insight, this finer understanding, this surer confidence is given because the recipient has opened the windows of his soul to the light of God. It is not blindness to disturbing facts, or unusual credulity, for these are negative things. The faith which we are discussing is the positive work of the Spirit of God in the soul of man. It is the power to endure, as seeing him who is invisible (Hebrews 11: 27).

The gift of faith may come to an earnest disciple in a brief period of superlative insight and confident trust for which he may have prepared by fasting and prayer, or which may result from the spiritual uplift of a good prayer meeting. Such brief gifts are not to be despised, even though their intensity is not maintained. They cast a glow of understanding and power over the months and years which lie ahead. But while it is less spectacular, the gift of faith which is matured steadily in a good man's life and nourished by his unfailing devotion is likely to be of more permanent value than its briefer counterpart. It is unfortunate that many of us tend to think of the gift of faith as being necessarily brief, flashing into consciousness and then being lost except to memory. This does not seem to have been within the thought of the Apostle Paul. His concern was with a faith which gives poise and power when those who lack such faith are vacillating and feeble.

Our Heavenly Father has blessed us with many gifts which he did not entrust to men of earlier generations. Tools which he has placed in our hands have annihilated the older concepts of time, space, and might. Such gifts can obviously be great means of blessing; but we all know from experience how easily they might be turned to our destruction. The gift of faith in God, the quiet and confident assurance that he will bring to pass his eternal purpose, is especially important in such a day as this. By the light of such a gift, we know that we do not struggle alone amid the titanic forces of darkness. We work with a keen sense of responsibility, but we work also with a knowledge that the light and power and truth of God shall never be snuffed out.

The most valuable gifts must be earned. I cannot give my boy an education; all I can do is to make an education available for him. He gains the education as he shows that he merits it. So the gifts of wisdom and knowledge are only added to persons of such quality that these gifts will round out the gifts which they have already demonstrated. Similarly, faith is not handed out like a parcel; it is added, step by step, as the way of insight is prepared in the process of living.

Here, then, are some of the primary gifts of the Spirit: the word of wisdom, the word of knowledge, the gift of faith. Looking backward into the world which Paul knew, we can see how imperative these gifts were in the life of the early church. Are they not equally necessary today? Looking back, we know that the wisdom, knowledge, and faith which characterized the outstanding saints of that age were not the products of their times, but came down from above. The wisdom and the knowledge and the faith which we need must also come from above. Our Heavenly Father, who loves us even as he loved his older children, will bless us with all necessary gifts as we humbly seek his guidance to walk in the ways of righteousness.

Study Outlines

The Primary Gifts

Lesson Purpose

To discuss the gifts of wisdom, knowledge, and faith so as to show their place in the life of the believer and of the church and to lay the foundation for their greater expression.

High Points of the Lesson

Wisdom, knowledge, and faith are essentially spiritual achievements. They are vital to effective Christianity in any age. These primary gifts imply a natural endowment which is augmented by the Spirit of God. They are given for the blessing of the body. Their very presence is indicated by the wisdom and understanding and confidence in which they are shared.

Questions and Discussion Topics

(1) What do you mean by the gift of wisdom? Analyze the meaning of the statement: "It is not wisdom to be only wise, and on the inward vision close the eyes."

(2) Indicate the distinction between wisdom and shrewdness. Between wisdom and cleverness. Between wisdom and knowledge.

(3) What did Paul mean by the gift of knowledge? Discuss, briefly, the meaning of Tennyson's statement that "knowledge comes but wisdom lingers."

(4) How is the gift of knowledge related to the intellect? How is it related to the heart?

(5) What is the relation of the gift of knowledge to spiritual certitude? Discuss this in relation to the necessity for living one's religion.

(6) What did Paul mean by the gift of faith? What is the relation of this gift to the principle of faith?

(7) "The most valuable gifts must be earned." Is this true? Discuss it briefly.

(8) In what sense are wisdom, knowledge, and faith the primary gifts? In what way are they related to the daily activities of the Saints?

What the Lesson Means Today

These less spectacular gifts are greatly needed in the church today. They promote the best use of the other gifts and should be sought after by all.

The atmosphere most congenial to these gifts is one of eager devotion to the tasks of the kingdom. They will be best enjoyed as the kingdom is earnestly advanced.

These gifts are essential if we are to see things in their proper proportion, putting first things first and not being influenced unduly by superficial appearances.

Lesson Thirty-four

III—DIVINE HEALING

The organization of the social structure in Palestine at the time of Jesus was extremely crude and rudimentary. Perhaps we could get the best picture of those far-off days by traveling inland in Africa, India, or China; since so few of us can do this, a good book or missionary magazine discussing conditions in those lands would be quite helpful. Modern civilization, with all its faults, has brought us many physical blessings. It is when we get away from this civilization that we realize the awful squalor in which our remote ancestors lived. In Paul's day there were only the most primitive and fragmentary hygienic arrangements, medicine was just at its beginning, and a dark cloud of ignorance and fear made mutual helpfulness almost impossible. In such a world the gospel of health was inseparably connected with the gospel of the kingdom.

Today we are proud of the advances of modern medicine, take for granted miracles of healing which doctors and nurses have died to make possible. Yet in spite of the great work of healing associated with such names as Pasteur, Jenner, Lord Lister, Sir Robert Jones, and others, everyone knows that disease still ravages the earth and that cancer, tuberculosis, circulatory diseases, and a thousand other ills still bring pain and futility, and cut people off before their time. The ministry of healing is still important; religion has a significant part to play in the field of preventive medicine which is now opening up.

Good men have long realized the close connection between religion and healing. Many years ago David sang of the Lord "who forgiveth all thine iniquities; who healeth all thy diseases; who redeemeth thy life from destruction; and crowneth thee with loving-kindness and tender mercies" (Ps. 103: 3, 4). Against the background of the great need of the people of his time, we can see Jesus moving constantly among them as a minister of life and health. He "went about in all Galilee, teaching in their synagogues, and preaching the gospel of the kingdom, and healing all manner of diseases and all manner of sickness among the people" (Matt. 4: 23). As Jesus shared his mission with his apostles they, too, preached "that men should repent. And they cast out many devils and anointed with oil many that were sick, and healed them" (Mark 6:12, 13). It was in this spirit and with this understanding of the close relation between the gospel of the kingdom and the gospel of good health that James wrote:

> Is any sick among you? let him call for the elders of the church; and let them pray over him, anointing him with oil in the name of the Lord; and the prayer of faith shall save the sick, and the Lord shall raise him up; and if he have committed sins, they shall be forgiven him. Confess your faults one to another, and pray one for another, that ye may be healed. The effectual fervent prayer of a righteous man availeth much.—James 5: 14, 16.

Jesus and his chosen disciples exercised a threefold ministry: the ministry of preaching, the ministry of teaching, and the ministry of healing. These three ministries have been carried forward into the church of Jesus Christ at this age. They are not separate ministries but are related to each other. Thus in inspired instruction received soon after the organization of the church, the Saints were told:

> Mine arm is not shortened, and I will show miracles, signs and wonders, unto all those who believe on my name. And whoso shall ask it in my name, in faith, they shall cast out devils; they shall heal the sick; they shall cause the blind to receive their sight, and the deaf to hear, and the dumb to speak, and the lame to walk; and the time speedily cometh that great things are to be shown forth unto the children of men; but without faith shall not anything be shown forth except desolations upon Babylon.—Doctrine and Covenants 34: 3.

The effectiveness of the church in the field of health is not fully revealed by enumerating the known cases of miraculous healing. The influence of the church is much wider than this. The Christian life is in itself a major factor in promoting good health. Temperance in eating and drinking and freedom from the excesses of lust and of personal strife do much to prolong life. The Christian attitude of mind makes for strength and vigor. Faith, love, and peace are healing agents. Like sunshine, they do away with disease; like food, they build strength. These spiritual forces are just as effective because they operate as part of a program of righteousness as they would be if they were pursued as part of a program of health.

The remarkable revelation known as the "Word of Wisdom" (Doctrine and Covenants 86), contains valuable instruction looking toward the conservation of the health of the people of God. This revelation warns the Saints to beware of the dangers to health which arise out of "evils and designs which do and will exist in the hearts of conspiring men in the last days." That this warning is necessary has been attested by the fact that practically all civilized nations have been forced to protect their citizens by pure food acts.

Another important prohibition of the Word of Wisdom is directed against the use of strong drinks and hot drinks, and it should be noted that in the revelation these are treated separately. Members of the medical profession are united in affirming that hot drinks are injurious. It is not likely that the early Saints interpreted "hot drinks" as meaning only tea and coffee, but it is practically certain that tea and coffee were included in this category.

The revelation says that strong drinks and tobacco are to be used for their medicinal value, "with judgment and skill." The drinking of alcohol and the use of tobacco tend strongly toward habit formation, and the more alcohol and tobacco are abused in these ways, the less becomes the likelihood that they will be used "with judgment and skill."

The growth of the modern emphasis on dietetics has done much to increase our respect for the instruction contained in this revelation. It is not likely that "all wholesome herbs God hath ordained for the constitution, nature and use of man, every herb in the season thereof, and every fruit in the season thereof" means that vegetables and fruits should not be used out of season. It is a wise provision of nature, however, that fruit and herbs are particularly beneficial when they are in season in the various localities. Not only this instruction, but the instruction regarding grain foods and the sparing use of meat have been amply vindicated. The study of vitamins and calories in a well-balanced diet is of major concern to those interested in maintaining health and vigor.

In view of the foregoing, it is clear that the church has an affirmative and constructive approach to the matter of health. It is nevertheless all too apparent that many are sick and incapacitated by reason of disease or accident. This is not a natural situation, for the natural way to live is the healthy way to live. The gospel, nevertheless, has a message of hope for us when we are suffering. In harmony with the pattern set forth in the New Testament church and confirmed to us in modern revelation and in the experience of many of the elders, we practice the rite of administration to the sick by laying on of hands, anointing with oil accompanied by the prayer of faith. Without question, many sick people are greatly blessed through this ministry. There are very few elders of mature experience who cannot relate incidents of the blessing of God received through them in this way. Nor are these blessings confined to stories of the past. There are current evidences of the blessings of healing among people of faith and devotion.

There is a close correlation between the healing of the body and the forgiveness of sin. This is illustrated in the healing of the man sick with palsy. When this man was first brought to Jesus, the Master greeted him: "Son, be of good cheer; thy sins are forgiven" (Matt. 9: 2). Then, seeing that the scribes thought he was blaspheming, he continued, "but that ye may know that the Son of man hath power on earth to forgive sins . . . . arise and take up thy bed, and go unto thy house" (Matt. 9: 6). The same thought was evidently in the mind and heart of James when he so closely connected healing by administration of the elders with the forgiveness of sin.

Before medicine reached its present high state of development, people frequently sought relief from pain but neglected their more fundamental needs. Nowadays doctors recognize pain as a danger signal which calls attention to a deeper need demanding attention. In the same way sickness itself may be a danger signal which points to a moral lack. The healing of the sick is designed to remove any such underlying moral maladjustment. It is at this point, therefore, that the problem of sin and the problem of physical healing are merged. It is not the function of the elders of the church to distract attention from our basic needs. It is their responsibility to act as the ministers of God in calling attention to these basic needs. They seek to dispel disease and stay the hand of death in order to set our feet firmly in the way of righteousness and truth, which is the way of life.

In separating healing from redemption, many of the groups which make a point of faith healing do a great disservice. Redemption means not only that men "do not perish" but also that they "have everlasting life." It means that people are not only saved from being sinners but that they are also saved to be saints; it means that they are both rescued and strengthened. Suppose the faith healer does heal men and women of ills which result from sin. His work is good as far as it goes, but has he the power to complete his work? Does he lift life to a higher level? Physical or mental healing which has no connection with the forgiveness of sins may be a dangerous thing, rather than a hopeful thing, when looked at from the point of view of an immortal soul. It may mean that the danger signal has been removed but that the danger remains.

Not all who are administered to are healed. This has always been true. Jesus was prevented from doing many mighty works because of the lack of faith of people who needed him. Lack of faith however is not the only factor operating against the effective functioning of the power to heal. Apparently Paul had every confidence in his "son in the gospel," but he nevertheless advised Timothy to watch his diet (I Timothy 5: 23).

Modern revelation which covers this point is as follows:

.... And whosoever among you are sick, and have not faith to be healed, but believe, shall be nourished with all tenderness with herbs and mild food. .... And the elders of the church, two or more, shall be called, and shall pray for, and lay their hands upon them in my name; and if they die, they shall die unto me, and if they live, they shall live unto me.—Doctrine and Covenants 42: 12.

At the conference of 1906 President Joseph Smith made the following statement:

We appear before the world as advocates for what are called signs of the gospel, the accompaniments of the gospel economy as instituted by the Christ. A great deal of comment has passed among our elders, and among our membership, very largely, in our large branches, as to why it is that there are not more persons healed by the administration of the oil and the laying on of hands than there are. My observation leads me to the conclusion that there are a great many more healings occur than are taken notice of, or than we are given credit for, while there are a great many that are lost as a matter of course.

The thought which was presented to me was this: that we ought as a people to .... establish a sanitarium or a hospital .... that shall be under the supervision of some earnest, upright, and spiritual-minded officer of the church; and that this sanitarium shall be a place where our sick who may not be properly treated at their homes may be treated by the laying on of hands, by the nursing as provided for under the law, and by such careful treatment as medical knowledge within the province of our own membership may give, and thus see whether or not we may try the spiritual forces for which we have been so long contending, and at last put our hands and our sacred honors in juxtaposition and say to the world, We are willing that it shall be given a trial, an open trial.—General Conference Minutes, 1906, p. 882.

In harmony with the counsel of the president of the church, the Conference entered upon a season of fasting and prayer, and before the Conference adjourned, inspired instruction was given regarding the building of the Independence Sanitarium.

In this revelation there is provision that in the Sanitarium the Saints shall receive careful nursing which is not always possible in their homes, and all possible benefit from medical knowledge and skill. In addition to this, the institution is intended as a place where healing by the laying on of hands may be most effectively practiced. The Sanitarium is therefore designed to be a center of spiritual ministry, supplemented by intelligent and faithful medical practice. It is intended as a place where we can try the spiritual forces for which we have so long contended; and can say to the world, "We are willing that it shall be given a trial."

The health program of the church is intimately related to the other phases of our kingdom-building work. The Lord desires his people to be well and strong. The greatest factors making for this mental and bodily vigor are the forces which make for righteousness. When the work of these forces has been disrupted, or where ill-health has occurred from other causes, the Lord works for the benefit of his people in ways that seem good to him. Without doubt a larger devotion and a more valiant faith would bring many more marvelous illustrations of the healing power which is committed to his ministry; it is in full harmony with the nature and will of God, and with his way of working among men that he should also use as his ministers doctors who have spent years of study learning how to assist him in the care and nurture of the body. The doctor who brings his skill and the elder who brings his faith may both rightfully expect the blessing of God to follow their ministries.

Study Outlines

Divine Healing

Lesson Purpose

To show the importance of health and its relation to the forgiveness of sin; to indicate the general field of the health program of the church.

High Points of the Lesson

The effectiveness of the church in the field of health lies not only in miraculous healings, but also in the physical values of righteousness.

Physical healing which is not related to spiritual renewal may easily be vicious.

The health program of the church is best illustrated in the basic purpose of the Sanitarium. Here it is designed that the best knowledge and skill shall be made available to invite and support the ministry of the Spirit.

Questions and Discussion Topics

(1) Is sickness ever the will of God? Discuss this briefly.

(2) What are the teachings of the Scriptures concerning the connection between religion and health?

(3) Discuss, briefly, the physical significance of such spiritual qualities as love, joy, peace, and their opposites, hatred, despair, and strife.

(4) Discuss the bearing of the Word of Wisdom on the adulteration of foods and on the use of judgment and skill in diet.

(5) Why do the Scriptures associate the gift of healing with forgiveness of sins? Is it desirable that we shall receive physical healing without regard for the state of our souls?

(6) Why is it that some who receive administration are not healed? What scriptural evidences are there that this was true in early Christian times?

(7) What are the major purposes of the Sanitarium?

(8) What is the major purpose of divine healing?

What the Lesson Means Today

The gift of healing is most likely to be exercised in the church when we give heed to the constructive aspects of the church program of health.

Our Heavenly Father prefers us to carry as much of the cost of life as possible in order that we might grow thereby. There is therefore no conflict between the reverent practice of the healing arts and divine healing.

Lesson Thirty-five

IV—MIRACLES

Fourth in his list of the gifts of the Spirit, the Apostle Paul puts "the working of miracles." The saints of that day had experiential knowledge of this gift. But in our day there is a feeling abroad among some shallow-thinking persons that the day of miracles has passed. It is amazing that this should be so in an age when we take for granted things which would have seemed positively miraculous a generation ago. It should not be too much to assume that our Heavenly Father has power beyond our present understanding, and that his use of such power would still produce miraclous results.

Difficulties concerning belief in miracles have apparently centered in two questions: Can God break into our orderly universe to perform miracles, and, even if he can do so, will he break into an orderly system which he himself has set up?

Let us look at the first of these difficulties. The people of the twentieth century have almost childlike faith in science, and science is grounded in belief in the universal operation of law. Unless the scientist took it for granted that the world would function tomorrow according to the same laws that it does today, he could not even begin his work. He has observed that under a variety of conditions, and without exception, when sulphuric acid is poured on salt it always bubbles and gives out fumes of hydrochloric acid gas. He knows, moreover, that the sequence of cause and effect illustrated here can be relied on in millions of like situations. So the scientist builds his life and his life's work on this constancy, and it is this very constancy that makes possible the modern "miracles of science."

There is nothing about the nature of the laws of the universe that excludes the possibility of miracles. Miracles do not break laws, they merely involve the use of laws by someone whose understanding goes beyond that of any given generation. This implies that many things which appear miraculous to the persons of one generation would not appear to be miraculous to persons of a more enlightened generation. But it also implies that since the thoughts of God are so far above our thoughts, some of his doings will be miraculous even in the eyes of our generation.

It is because our Heavenly Father works in an orderly fashion that the universe is stable and predictable. In such an orderly universe, an intelligent person can utilize the laws of nature so as to achieve his ends, and it is the reign of law which makes this possible. By our faith, our ingenuity, and our labor, we remove mountains and cast them into the sea; we join oceans to each other and bring continents closer together, so that the fellowship of nations is brought from the realm of dreams into the realm of possibilities. These things are not possible because law is denied but because personality is introduced.

It is not because man is kin to the animal that he shares this creative power with God. Discovery and invention call on the finest and most qualitative characteristics of human nature. We are building a new and better world by use of powers which link us most closely to God. In the light of our experience, it is not too much to say that in both Divinity and in humanity personality plus advanced knowledge equals miraculous performance. Certainly, the fact that we live in an orderly universe is no reason to deny the possibility of miracles unless we are also ready to deny the personality of God.

The foregoing is well illustrated by a story which Dr. Emerson Fosdick tells concerning a man whose house was near a railway. This man noted carefully the time when the various trains passed his house and in a few weeks constructed an accurate timetable. It appeared that he had everything carefully noted so that he could prophesy just what train would pass during any given period. But, one day a train flashed passed the house at a time not called for on the schedule. Then everything returned to normal for a few days. After a week or so, another train which was not called for on his schedule thundered down the tracks. A few weeks later this happened a third time. It seemed to the bewildered amateur that the railroad officials had become completely irresponsible and that they knew nothing whatever about the orderly operation of a railroad. Then one of the engineers told him that the regular system was being followed all the time, but that special trains were put on when occasion demanded to accommodate key railroad officials who had special business for the company. In like manner the scientists have assured us that the universe is run according to schedule. We do not need to abandon this belief because we find that God sometimes chooses to run special trains when his people are in special need of help.

Belief in miracles is not one of those matters on which we can afford to take up a position of mild scepticism. To deny the possibility of miracles is to deny to God freedom of personal action. This, in turn, is to deny that God is truly a person and to regard him as a machine. This flouts all our observation of the order and rationality of the universe. If there are no miracles, then it would seem that this world is governed by a mechanical sequence of cause and effect into which no one can obtrude; if this were true, it would be tragic indeed.

The universe is not a closed system. It is an expression of the love of our Heavenly Father, and he did not set things in motion many generations ago and then leave them to run themselves. God is behind the scheme of things, shaping the destinies of men and of nations. He leaves us free to choose so far as we can be left free; but he, too, has his agency and can exercise his will in the world just as we exercise our wills. He will not coerce us, but he can and will surround us with inducements to righteousness. If this sometimes requires that he shall intervene in the order of things as we have observed them, then who are we to say that he shall not do so.

But God is not an irresponsible miracle worker. He does not work beyond the realm of our understanding just to mystify us. Nor does he ever ignore his own fundamental provision that a man is truly blessed by what is accomplished within him rather than by what is done for him. This is illustrated in the fact that the miracles of Jesus were always directed toward the accomplishment of some Godlike purpose. With a little stretch of the imagination, it is possible to concede that the Devil might have raised the widow's son from the dead. What is not possible to imagine is that the Devil might raise the dead to heal a mother's broken heart. It is the divine motivation of miracles that we need to keep well in mind. The truly marvelous aspect of the wonders done by Jesus is not in the power and knowledge displayed, but in the unfailing love disclosed in his every act.

On those occasions when we become discouraged because God does not appear to come to our rescue as quickly as we think he should, it is well for us to remember that it may not be the times when he intervenes, but the times when he refrains from performing miracles that reveal his divinity. If we had his power, but lacked his love and his wisdom, we would tend to use that power indiscriminately. We would heal our loved ones, or would extend their lives for a few years, without regard to any deeper issues which might be involved. But one of the reasons why our Heavenly Father rightfully commands our adoration is that while he loves us to the uttermost, yet he sometimes withholds his help for our sakes. The greatness of God is revealed both in the wonders wrought by his power and in the restraint with which that power is used.

As we might well expect, some of the most significant miracles of all time are connected with the life and ministry of the Lord Jesus. There is a theory which has found lodgment in a few places that belief in miracles is a superstition which grew up after the death of Jesus and fastened itself on the gospel, because of the credulity of the early disciples. Nothing could be further from the truth. The most authentic record that we have regarding the character of Christianity at the beginning of the Christian era is contained in the Gospel of

Mark, and this book records more miracles than any other. As Professor Cairns has pointed out, the miracles are not additions to the gospel story, but form an inseparable part of what God revealed to the world in his Son, Jesus Christ. When properly understood, they help us to see the heart of that revelation. They show us God at work in the world today, and convince us that under proper circumstances he is willing to use for our good laws which we do not as yet understand. *(The Faith That Rebels* and *The Reasonableness of the Christian Faith.)*

The life of Jesus was in itself a miracle of purity, love, and holiness. Jesus is quite unexplained by the Jewish race from which he sprang. Nor is he explained by the times in which he appeared. He is indeed "a new creation" different from and greater than anyone who preceded or came after him.

The death of Jesus, moreover, was a miracle of sacrifice and of devotion. The Master truly laid hold of powers which we have never fathomed, when he who felt the stark depravity of his murderers so keenly, still retained the spirit of understanding and forgiveness to such a degree that he prayed for the very ones who crucified him. To anyone else, those last moments on the cross would have seemed utterly devoid of opportunity and could only be endured. Yet Jesus used them to give us a final picture of love stronger than evil; a love which could triumph over pain.

It is true, furthermore, that Christianity took its rise in the miracle of the Resurrection. What does the Resurrection say to us? It says that no weapon that is formed against God shall prosper. It says that the ultimate destinies of humanity are in the hands of God, and not in the hands of wicked men. It says that God will leave sinners free to follow their own course; but that he is still free to use even their wrath to minister to the needs of those who can be persuaded to love him.

The Latter Day Saint view of the universe, then, is that there is a "natural world" in which law and order rule; but above, beneath, beyond, and around is a "spiritual world" of which God is the center. These two worlds are not shut off from one another, but the spiritual world constantly penetrates into and influences the natural world. Creation is pushing forward into a more richly spiritual phase in which the laws of life will more and more steadfastly minister to the purposes of men of good will.

In a mechanical world, everything encourages men to believe that they are governed by a fate which leaves no room for freedom, either to men or to God. But the miraculous events of the gospel are a declaration of the poverty of this point of view. Far from being a slave, the Creator of the universe is its undisputable Master. He moves therein with wisdom and restraint, but he always acts freely and for the best good of his children.

Study Outlines

Miracles

Lesson Purpose

To show that the working of miracles is to be expected in the church of Jesus Christ.

High Points of the Lesson

Intelligent persons constantly bring some laws into play so as to offset others. The universe is not therefore governed by law alone, but by personality and law.

God is a person. He loves us. He knows and can use many laws which we do not yet understand. Under proper conditions we shall therefore expect him to do things which cannot be explained by what we already know.

God does not work miracles just because he knows how to do so. He does so when this is necessary to further his purpose.

Questions and Discussion Topics

(1) Is the reign of law a help or a hindrance to free men? Discuss this briefly.

(2) Name some of the accomplishments of modern men which would have seemed miraculous fifty years ago.

(3) What is a miracle? Does it involve the breaking of natural laws?

(4) "Denial of our Father's freedom to use his great knowledge for our good is a denial of his existence." Discuss this briefly. Is it true?

(5) What scriptural basis is there for our belief that the working of miracles forms an essential part of the gospel of Christ?

(6) Under what circumstances may we expect the miraculous powers of the gospel to be most fully in evidence?

(7) To what extent does effective Christianity involve the constant touch of Divinity? In what way may we say that the Christian life is essentially miraculous?

(8) What part should miracles play in the life of the church today?

What the Lesson Means Today

There is no reason why what now seems miraculous should not become commonplace, especially in the field of personality. The "greater works" which we may do will not all be merely corrective, such as the healing of the sick. Many will be creative, such as opening the eyes of the spiritually blind.

The bestowal of miraculous power may well do three things: Assure us of our Father's concern, solve the specific problem, and show us what great things are possible with God. God is not jealous of his power. He wants to share it as soon as we can be trusted to use it well.

Lesson Thirty-six

V—PROPHECY

When the saints of Corinth read in Paul's letter "to one is given by the Spirit . . . . prophecy" this again, was no new idea but a reminder of what they already knew. The New Testament makes it quite clear that the gift of inspired insight and foresight was widely enjoyed in the early church. Thus Barnabas and Saul were indicated for the work to which God had called them (Acts 13: 1). The four daughters of Philip also exercised the gift of prophecy (Acts 21: 8, 9). So did Agabus, who foretold the imprisonment of the Apostle Paul when he should return to Jerusalem (Acts 21: 10, 11). Moreover, it was clearly expected that this gift of the Spirit would continue in the church. Paul expressed the common conviction of the disciples when he said, "God hath set . . . . in the church . . . . prophets."—I Corinthians 12: 28.

It is evident from the references given above that the gift of prophecy was widely shared among both ministers and members. Through those thus blessed the spiritual life of the body was quickened and deepened. On occasion, events yet in the future were forecast; but a much more important function of those exercising this gift was to keep the saints alive to the significance of their faith. What they had to say was not fundamentally new so much as it was an extension and application of what was implied in that which they had already received.

The agency of those exercising the gift of prophecy was carefully protected in the operation of the Spirit. The spirit of the prophet was subject to the prophet (I Cor. 14: 32). Those who prophesied were not required to yield themselves without question to the dictation of external forces, but were advised to "try the spirits" to see whether they were of God (I John 4: 1). In particular, the saints were to beware of false prophets, and consequently were to be especially vigilant lest they become false prophets themselves. The gift of prophecy was therefore an illumination of heart and mind granted to certain men and women according to the will of the Spirit. Those who enjoyed this illumination came to share something of the vantage point of Divinity, standing a little nearer the highlands of God than do ordinary mortals, and speaking with the authority of the clear and far-reaching vision thus given them for the good of all.

Prophecy is closely akin to the outreach of genius. Many have seen in it only an unusually rich endowment of the spiritual vision by which good men discern the sure issues of good or evil. While we may well suppose that those who are blessed with the gift of prophecy have a natural endowment which fits them for this experience, the clearness and certainty and spiritual quality of veritable prophecy shows that here is the manifestation of a truly divine indwelling. The Spirit does not only supplement human insight and understanding, it adds to these something which the prophets do not possess by themselves. While the message which is given them for the people may be in harmony with their own best thought, when they are uplifted by the spirit of inspiration, it has its source in the illumination of the Spirit of God.

The gift of prophecy was not exercised by all the Saints in the New Testament church; but the spirit of prophecy was shed abroad among them so generously that the church was truly the church of an inspired people. Although much of the future was hidden from them, as it is hidden from us, the veil was lifted frequently enough to give them assurance that God is indeed the Lord of the Tomorrows. Furthermore, as they became more and more devoutly aware of the nature of God, they became more and more sure of the truly significant events which lay ahead. They lived by the exceeding great and precious promises of the gospel (II Peter 1: 4). They knew that Jesus had defeated evil at Calvary, where it did its worst, and that the final triumph of good over evil was guaranteed (Rev. 20: 10). They knew that "God has chosen . . . . the things which are not, to bring to nought things that are" (I Cor. 1:

28). They were therefore confident that the hopes and dreams which as yet had no tangible reality among them would be strong enough to bear down the wickedness which seemed to be enthroned in high places. They saw the kingdom beset on every side; yet they had the sure conviction in their hearts that they were not following cunningly devised fables. They looked with confidence for the final triumph of the work of God. Death had lost its terror, for Jesus had passed through the valley of the shadow, and their hearts were uplifted with the assurance that he had prepared for them an eternal habitation.

Because of the position of the church which I have here expressed, I noticed with a great deal of interest the comment of Bishop Charles Gore on the importance of prophecy in the early church. Dr. Gore said:

We should indeed readily admit that there was in the earlier churches, especially at Corinth, a rich profusion of spiritual gifts, such as are self-evidencing, and such as the church can do no more than recognize when they occur; such as the gift of inspired utterance, or "prophecy," the gift of ecstatic praise or "tongues," the gift of interpreting tongues, the gift of miracles. One who possessed these gifts showed them by his words and deeds, and the church could only adore the divine giver and use the wonderful gifts. . . . . It has been, I think, a serious weakness in the later church that it has ceased to expect, or welcome, or use such gifts as "prophecy," or, "hearing," or "miracles," which inspired the courage and confirmed the faith of the earlier church.—*Order and Unity,* pages 108, 109.

Later in the same book, Bishop Gore says:

The inspired prophet appears, as in the Old Testament over against the priest, so in the New, side by side with apostles and evangelists, and teachers and pastors. I think the church ought to have given a great deal more attention to this fact than till quite recently it has done. Its tendency has been to relegate the prophets to the Old Testament. But they are undoubtedly prominent figures in the New.

It may be said that they were only given to the first age of the church; and that the gift of prophecy was speedily withdrawn, like the gift of healing and other miracles.

But I cannot help thinking that the church ought to have lived in more eager expectation of exceptional gifts, such as cannot be provided at demand, but can be reverently welcomed and used when they are given.—*Ibid*, pages 156, 157.

Paul says that prophecy will pass away "when that which is perfect is come" (I Cor. 12: 28). But until our partial vision is swallowed up in complete understanding and insight, prophecy remains as one of the great ministries of the Spirit and one of the great needs of individual Saints and of the church. Indeed, Paul seems to prefer prophecy to speaking in tongues, unless the gift of tongues is also prophetic. He admonishes the Corinthian saints to "covet to prophesy, and forbid not to speak with tongues."—I Corinthians 14: 39.

The Spirit chooses whomsoever he will in bestowing the gift of prophecy. No amount of preparation can guarantee that he will choose any one rather than another. But while we cannot choose ourselves or our friends as the recipients of this divinely imparted blessing, we can prepare in our own lives the background of sympathetic understanding for the receipt of such prophetic guidance. By devoted study of the Word, constant cultivation of his Spirit, and unfailing practice of self-discipline and judgment, we may prepare ourselves for such enlightenment and guidance as we need. From among such as prepare themselves God will choose those who, by his grace, can wing words of truth deep into the hearts of men.

VI—THE DISCERNMENT OF SPIRITS

The early church was beset on every side, yet the gravest dangers came from within. The sub-Christianity of some who had not caught the spirit of the gospel or who were only nominal members of the church was much more dangerous to the spiritual life of the body than all the opposition from without. The seeds of apostasy grew as a cancer grows, feeding on life and turning it to putrefaction. Those who would be faithful were in special need of an endowment of the spirit of discernment if they were to see their way aright.

This is illustrated in the struggle with the Judaizers. From almost the very beginning, the church was disturbed by those who believed that no one could be a Christian who had not first become a Jew. If these had prevailed, Christianity would have become a Jewish sect. Very few of the early Christians saw the true significance of the conflict which Paul waged against representatives of this group; yet it was a conflict vital to the life of the Christian movement. Paul, however, saw things clearly. The saints of Galatia had been particularly troubled by these Judaizers, and Paul's letter to them has been called the Declaration of Independence of the early Christian church. Against this background, note the keen discernment and the fine courage which underlies his reassuring words:

> For ye are all the children of God by faith in Jesus Christ. For as many of you as have been baptized into Christ have put on Christ. There is neither Jew nor Greek, there is neither bond nor free, there is neither male nor female; for ye are all one in Christ Jesus. And if ye are Christ's then are ye Abraham's seed, and heirs according to the promise.—Galatians 3: 26-29.

In addition to these Jews, the church was also beset by certain philosophers who spent their time in all sorts of disputation. The Apostle Paul knew a great deal about the appeal of philosophy. Indeed, he used this appeal himself when presenting Christ to the philosophers on Mars' Hill (Acts 17: 28). Yet he knew, also, and that from experience, that reason may easily mislead when it is not linked to growing spiritual experience. In emphasis on the importance of fact as the touchstone of theory, Paul is in harmony with our best modern thought. Repeatedly he admonished the followers to live rightly, and to balance their thinking with their experience. Thus he wrote the saints in Corinth:

> The weapons of our warfare are not carnal, but mighty through God to the pulling down of strongholds; casting down imagination, and every high thing that exalteth itself against the knowledge of God, and

bringing into captivity every thought to the obedience of Christ.—II Corinthians 10: 4, 5.

"We do not depend on eloquence, talent, learning, wealth, beauty, or any of the external aids on which the men of this world rely," said Paul. All these may help, but "your faith should not stand in the wisdom of man but in the power of God" (I Cor. 2: 5). The gift of discernment enabled the saints to attack "imaginations" and "every high thing against the knowledge of God" and made them meet the test of the knowledge of God possessed by those who do the will of God. The safety of the early Christians depended on the discernment born of spiritual life.

In the meetings of the saints it was particularly important that those who were spiritually immature should be protected against those who would bring in pagan philosophies, against those who would turn back to Judaism, against presumptuous men who attached the name of Divinity to their own words, and against various others whose influence tended to misdirect the life of the body. It was apparently out of such a need that John wrote, "Beloved, believe not every spirit, but try the spirits whether they are of God."—I John 4: 1.

The spirit of discernment was also needed in the life of the infant church outside of the services. Many, like Ananias and Sapphira (Acts 5: 1-10), sought to gain the benefits of Christianity without accepting its risks. Their pernicious influence was a constant threat to the spiritual standards of the church; and it was important that they should be recognized for what they were. Exercise of the gift of discernment, therefore, was one of the major qualifications of those in official responsibility, and the gift was also shared by many others for the protection of the body.

The gift of discernment is as vital to our spiritual welfare today as at any time in the history of the church. Truly the encroachments of evil are not so apparent to us as are those of the early centuries of Christianity. Yet each one of the typically sub-Christian influences listed in this chapter has its counterpart in the world and in the church today. The gift of discernment therefore needs to be exercised among us for the salvation of those who are deceived and for the protection of the body. Persons who are seeking to retain a hold on the things of this world at the expense of the kingdom, who seek to advance the kingdom without awaiting the guidance of Divinity, the Pharisees who emphasize the letter of the law and forget the spirit, or the philosophers who are so eager for spiritual blessings that they neglect the spiritual disciplines which belong with them—these, and all others who act as though the kingdom can be built in any way but God's way need the spirit of discernment as much as the wandering disciples of any other age. As the gifts of the gospel are multiplied among the Saints, so must the gift of discernment find its place in order to protect the body from imposture.

Today, as never before, we need to have it impressed upon our hearts and minds that "Zion cannot be built unless it is by the principles of the law of the celestial kingdom."—Doctrine and Covenants 102: 2.

Study Outlines

Prophecy and Discernment

Lesson Purpose

To indicate the nature and purpose of prophecy and discernment and to indicate something of the conditions under which these gifts are most likely to be enjoyed.

High Points of the Lesson

The gift of prophecy did much to bring vitality and power to the Christian movement.

As good men drew near to God and were enlightened by his Spirit, it was inevitable that they should share both his vision of the future and his insight into the true nature of their own times. Both of these were rightly called prophecy.

The early saints needed guidance at every step. They were not of themselves wise enough to distinguish between true Christianity and paganism. The gift of discernment was therefore of major importance in the early church.

Questions and Discussion Topics

(1) Refer to some of the Scriptures which tell of prophets in the New Testament church.

(2) What are the outstanding aspects of the gift of prophecy?

(3) What is the meaning of the statement, "the spirit of the prophets is subject to the prophets"?

(4) What is the meaning of the statement, "The testimony of Jesus is the spirit of prophecy"? What events yet future should be confidently expected by the disciples of Jesus?

(5) What reasons do you have for believing that the gift of prophecy should be continued whenever the church is in touch with God?

(6) Enumerate some of the conditions which indicate our deep need for prophetic guidance.

(7) Why was the gift of discernment of such importance in the early church? By whom was it important that this gift should be exercised?

(8) For what purpose is the gift of discernment exercised in the meetings of the Saints? In what larger field is this gift important today?

What the Lesson Means Today

Prophecy is not necessarily new, in the sense that it has not been uttered before. But it is new in the sense that it comes with new authority, new conviction, and new power.

The gift of prophecy, in the narrower sense, is likely to be exercised only by a few. The whole body of the Saints should, nevertheless, feel sure of such future events as the building of the kingdom, the Resurrection, and the great day of judgment.

One of our urgent present needs is the ability to distinguish between the best and the second best, between enlightened citizenship of this world and citizenship in the kingdom.

Lesson Thirty-seven

VII—TONGUES AND THEIR INTERPRETATION

The last of the gifts enumerated by the Apostle Paul are "divers kinds of tongues" and "the interpretation of tongues."

The best example of the gift of tongues is in the story of Pentecost. Luke tells us in the Acts of the Apostles that on the day of Pentecost, following the Crucifixion and Resurrection of Jesus, there were Jews in Jerusalem from Parthia, Media, Elam, Mesopotamia, Judea, Cappadocia, Pontus, Asia, Phrygia, Pamphylia in Egypt, Libya about Cyrene, Rome, Crete and Arabia (Acts 2:5).

While Jews were gathering for their ceremonial feast, the disciples of Jesus, who numbered about one hundred and twenty, spent their time in an upper room, praying for the endowment of the Spirit of God which had been promised them and under which they expected to become his witnesses in all the world (Acts 1:8). While they were thus engaged the "power from on high" rested on each of them like cloven tongues of flame, accompanied by noise as of a mighty wind. Under the influence of this Spirit they were all filled with the Holy Ghost, and spake with other tongues, as the Spirit gave them utterance (Acts 2:4), so that "every man heard them speak in his own language" (Acts 2:6). Not only did the power from on high enable them to talk the language of the visiting Jews, but it sent their message home with such convincing appeal that it burned in the hearts of all who heard it.

Some of those who looked on at Pentecost sought to explain what was happening by charging the disciples with drunkenness (Acts 2:13). "To escape the necessity of acknowledging their own ignorance, they adopted the theory that some drinks can teach languages." But Peter refuted this charge and then went on to explain that the gift of tongues might be expected under the operation of the Spirit of God. Quoting a prophecy from Joel (Joel 2:28-32), he showed that what had happened was an evidence of the outpouring of the Spirit. He then bore his own testimony so powerfully as to convince three thousand of his hearers that Jesus is the Christ.

Dr. Albert Barnes says:

Various attempts have been made to account for this remarkable phenomenon, without supposing it to be a miracle. But the natural and obvious meaning of the passage is that they were endowed by the miraculous power of the Holy Ghost with ability to speak foreign languages, and languages to them before unknown. It does not appear that each one had the power of speaking all the languages which were specified, but that this ability was among them, and that together they could speak these languages; possibly some one and some another.

Doctor Barnes then lists the following evidences leading him to accept Luke's account of Pentecost just as it stands:

This ability was predicted in the Old Testament.—Isaiah 28: 11.
It was also predicted by Jesus.—Mark 16: 17.
The gift was renewed in the church over a wide area and for a long time.—I Corinthians 12: 10, 11, 28.
It was admirably suited to their missionary task.
One result of sin had been the confusion of tongues; what better prophecy of the reign of righteousness than this triumph over many tongues?

As we have already noted from Paul, the gift of tongues was widely experienced in the early church. This gift was shared by others than the apostles. When Peter first took the gospel to the Gentile Cornelius, for example:

The Holy Ghost fell on all them which heard the word . . . . on the Gentiles also was poured out the gift of the Holy Ghost. For they heard them speak with tongues and magnify God.—Acts 10: 44-46.

On another occasion, while Apollos was at Corinth:

Paul having passed through the upper coasts came to Ephesus: and finding certain disciples, he said unto them, Have ye received the Holy Ghost since ye believed? And they said unto him, We have not so much as heard whether there be any Holy Ghost. And he said unto them, Unto what then were ye baptized? And they said, Unto John's baptism. Then said Paul, John verily baptized with the baptism of repentance, saying unto the people, that they should believe on him which should come after him, that is, on Christ Jesus. And when they heard this, they were baptized in the name of the Lord Jesus. And when Paul had laid his hands upon them, the Holy Ghost came on them; and they spake with tongues, and prophesied.—Acts 19: 1-6.

Not every baptized believer exercised the gift of tongues (I Cor. 12: 30). Nor is it necessary for the gift to be frequently exercised among members of the church who speak the same language, except as its exercise is a guarantee that the gift is available when it is needed for preaching the gospel. The first president of the church explained long ago that the gift of tongues was particularly instituted for preaching the gospel to people of other nations, and is not given for the government of the church (*Millennial Star,* Vol. 15, page 182). This seems to be in harmony with the record in Acts and with the essential philosophy of the situation.

On the day of Pentecost, the endowment of the Holy Spirit came in the form of the gift of tongues because this was the best vehicle through which the message of the gospel could reach the men of diverse nationalities. When, later, the Corinthians seemed to be overzealous regarding the possession of this and other gifts, Paul told them that they must seek to excel to the edifying of the church (I Cor. 14: 12). He reminded them that he would prefer to speak five words with his understanding, that he might teach men, than ten thousand words in an unknown tongue (I Cor. 14: 19). The emphasis, then, should be on the importance of the message, on the power which, when the people are devoted, breaks down every barrier that impedes the work of God, and on the love of God which reaches out that "every man might hear in his own tongue."

Closely related to the gift of tongues is the gift of interpretation of tongues. About this we have but little information in the Scriptures, although it would seem to be implied in the very fact that tongues appear to have been intelligently exercised. Obviously, on such an occasion as Pentecost, those hearing the gospel in their own language would not need an interpreter.

When the gift of tongues is given in a meeting of the Saints, it is of value only as an indication of the power of God to enable his witnesses to meet extraordinary demands. But when the tongue is interpreted, the message becomes available to those who hear, and confirms the wisdom and importance of the earlier gift. Not infrequently the gift of tongues is therefore prophetic as well as an evidence of power because of being expressed in an unknown language. In this way the interpretation carries with it a demonstration of the power of God in breaking down the barriers in missionary work; it has intrinsic value by reason of its own prophetic quality. It was evidently something of this which Paul had in mind when, in writing to the Saints in Corinth, he stressed the importance of edifying the church:

> Greater is he that prophesieth than he that speaketh with tongues, except he interpret, that the church may receive edifying.—I Corinthians 14: 5.
>
> But if there be no interpreter, let him keep silence in the church; and let him speak to himself, and to God.—I Corinthians 14: 28.

In view of the foregoing, the question naturally arises, "Shall we give our time to the study of other things when preparing for missionary work, since God can enable us to speak in the language of any people?" The student of modern revelation will immediately answer: "No, we are specifically commanded to study languages" (Doctrine and Covenants 87: 5), "and to seek learning by study and also by faith" (Doctrine and Covenants 85: 36). The gift of tongues and the interpretation of tongues are specific gifts made to meet emergencies, and to demonstrate the power of God. When the emergency passes, the gift is withdrawn. Our Heavenly Father greatly prefers us to grow in his likeness, and to have strength in ourselves, rather than to have us depend on him for sustenance in every emergency. He can help us to acquire languages rapidly, as part of our permanent equipment. Without doubt, he will do this where circumstances require, and our urgent devotion will be a major factor in making possible this fundamental but less spectacular blessing.

Study Outlines

Tongues and Their Interpretation

Lesson Purpose

To indicate the part which tongues and their interpretation should play in the life of the church and the conditions under which these gifts are most likely to be exercised.

High Points of the Lesson

The gift of tongues at Pentecost cannot be explained away without doing violence to both the spirit and the letter of the narrative. The gifts of tongues and interpretation continued for a long time in the early church.

The gift of tongues is primarily related to missionary work among foreign language groups. It is enjoyed in the assemblies of the Saints, but this is only a promise that it is available for missionary purposes.

The gift of interpretation belongs with the gift of tongues. The two are frequently exercised simultaneously, especially in practical missionary situations.

Questions and Discussion Topics

(1) Describe the experience of the apostles on the day of Pentecost.

(2) Why was it peculiarly fitting that the gift of tongues should be given at Pentecost?

(3) What other examples of the use of the gift of tongues are to be found in the Scriptures?

(4) What is the major purpose of the gift of tongues? Give illustrations of its use for this purpose.

(5) Under what conditions is the gift of tongues most likely to be used? Under what conditions is it most likely to be lost?

(6) Should the promise of the gift of tongues cause us to neglect the study of foreign languages? Why?

(7) What is the relation between the gift of tongues and the gift of prophecy? Which is the greater? Why?

(8) What part should the gifts of tongues and interpretation play in the life of the church today? Which members of the priesthood would you expect to be especially blessed with these gifts? Why?

What the Lesson Means Today

The fact that tongues and interpretation are gifts "set" in the church should remind us of the unfailing power of God to break down the barriers impeding our missionary testimony, and should remind us also of our continuing missionary task.

He who is glad to bestow these gifts on us in times of need will be glad to aid us in making foreign tongues part of our permanent equipment. A foreign language is of great value in such a country as the United States. It opens a new and available field of missionary effort where we can readily create a base for work in missions abroad.

Study Outlines

Lesson Thirty-eight

The Use and Abuse of the Spiritual Gifts

(Review)

Lesson Purpose

To point out some of the major values and dangers attending the exercise of the spiritual gifts as a foundation for their wider and more effective use.

High Points of the Lesson

A first test of the validity of a spiritual gift is its ministry to the total good of the church. This applies also to gifts of the spirit which Paul has not mentioned in his Corinthian letter.

There is need for education in the exercise of the spiritual gifts. The ideal is not that the person blessed with the gifts shall become an automaton, having no intelligent part in their exercise, but that his intelligence and experience shall be used as fully as possible, and that he shall grow in power to exercise the gifts for the good of the body.

Questions and Discussion Topics

(1) What are the gifts of the gospel enumerated by Paul in his letter to the Corinthians? What other spiritual gifts are there?

(2) What is the fundamental test of the value of a spiritual gift? Illustrate this from your own experience.

(3) What dangers attend administration for the healing of the sick? How can these dangers be avoided?

(4) What part should the individual play in exercising the gifts of the gospel? Discuss this briefly.

(5) What dangers inhere in the abuse of the spiritual gifts? What protection has been set in the church against these dangers?

(6) Where should the spiritual gifts be exercised most frequently:

in prayer meetings? in daily life? in discharging our specific responsibilities in the church?

(7) In what ways may the effective use of the spiritual gifts be most fully promoted?

(8) Relate examples of the creative use of the spiritual gifts which have come under your observation.

What the Lesson Means Today

We cannot meet the religious demands of today in our own strength. Every member of the church should live in expectation of special blessings which will enlarge his sphere of usefulness.

The greatest source of abuse is the desire for public attention. Every church member therefore should examine himself to see that he is "humble and full of love" for the work.

The gifts are available for the work of the kingdom. Our zeal for these gifts should be a zeal for power to do the work of God.

Chapter XV

THE SCRIPTURES

The lost Scriptures—The open canon—The relation between revelation and Scripture—The authority of Scripture—The Latter Day Saint attitude toward Scripture.

Lesson Thirty-nine

WEALTH GROWS as we take pains to conserve every newly won treasure and make it the means of securing other treasures. This is especially true in the spiritual realm, where the treasure is knowledge of God and of his purposes for humanity. We who live today are to be envied because we have access to the spiritual treasures of many generations, preserved for us by the direction of Divinity and made truly available to us by the inspiration of God in our own lives.

Modern revelation gives us an insight into the nature of Scripture, for in instruction given to men who were later ordained to be apostles, it is stated:

> Whatsoever they shall speak when moved upon by the Holy Ghost shall be Scripture; shall be the will of the Lord; shall be the mind of the Lord; shall be the word of the Lord; shall be the voice of the Lord, and the power of God unto salvation.—Doctrine and Covenants 68: 1.

Scripture is therefore the word of God which carries his mind and will with power unto the salvation of men.

Latter Day Saints believe that the Scriptures include much more than the Old and the New Testaments. Some of these Scriptures have been lost; and others, while not actually lost, are not now available to us. We are told, for example, that in the days of Adam a book of remembrance was kept (Gen. 6: 5, I. V.), and that this book was used in the time of Enoch

(Gen. 6: 47, I. V.). All except such parts of this as were incorporated into later Scriptures has long since been lost. Many other ancient Scriptures have also been lost; such as the prophecy of Enoch (Jude 14), the visions of Iddo the seer, (II Chron. 9: 29) and the Book of Ephraim (Hosea 8: 12). Similarly there is omitted from the New Testament Paul's earlier epistle to the Corinthians (I Cor. 5: 9), his epistle to the Laodiceans (Col. 4: 16), and the earlier epistle of Jude (Jude 3). Even though the Scriptures available to us have been augmented by the marvelous preservation and translation of the Book of Mormon, some parts of this record yet remain to be translated. And, further, we believe that the Scriptures are still not closed, but that the word of God as recognized by the church from time to time becomes part of the record, and a standard of faith and practice.

The idea of the Scriptures is closely connected with the idea of the church. Both emphasize our essential togetherness in our pursuit of spiritual understanding. Both stress the importance and value of accumulated wisdom regarding the things of highest worth. Both illustrate the truth that, in the field of religion, as elsewhere, every man is in some measure dependent on the achievements of his time, and all men come to understanding gradually and together, each adding something to the enlightenment of the yesterdays.

The Scriptures are more than great literature; they bear witness to a great revelation. Jesus indicated this by his own knowledge of the Scriptures and the authority of his personal use, referring back to them repeatedly (Luke 18: 31-33; Matt. 26: 51-54). Even during the forty days after the Resurrection, when time was infinitely precious and only essentials could receive attention, Jesus taught his disciples the things pertaining to the kingdom of God (Acts 1: 3), and showed them that "all things must be fulfilled which were written in the law of Moses, and in the prophets, and in the psalms."—Luke 24: 44-48.

Revelation cannot be fully expressed in words. Words are but tools, and must be quickened by the illumination of the Spirit which shines in the hearts and minds of the readers. Jesus said, "The words which I speak unto you, they are spirit and they are life." This refers, certainly, to the inner meaning of his words. This inner meaning can only be made spiritually luminous as we are enlightened by the Spirit of God. It is impossible to crowd the entire spiritual illumination of the prophets onto paper.

Prophets have always received more than they were able to record, their ability to comprehend the truth having been greater than their power to make that truth known. No man has yet fully expressed what he has learned in the presence of God, so that the record of his inspiring experience always falls short of the spiritual reality. Joseph Smith and Sidney Rigdon testified that God will overcome this difficulty. Speaking in his name, Joseph said: "By my Spirit will I enlighten them, by my power will I make known unto them the secrets of my will; yea, even those things which eye has not seen, nor ear heard, nor yet entered into the heart of man."—Doctrine and Covenants 76: 2.

Revelation, then, is one thing, and the record of revelation is another. The revelation of God which forms the primary experience upon which the Scriptures are built has come to men by dreams, by visions through the visitation of angels, by the voice of the Spirit, and by unusual happenings in the quiet, orderly pursuit of daily life. To record the truth thus received has involved the almost insurmountable problem of injecting spiritual significance into words which have become heavy and soiled in the commonplace traffic of human experience. Paul had something of this in mind when he wrote that Christ

> Hath made us ministers of the new testament; not of the letter, but of the spirit, for the letter killeth but the spirit giveth life. But if the ministration of death, written and engraven in stones, was glorious, so that the children of Israel could not steadfastly behold the face of Moses for the glory of his countenance; which glory was to be done

away: how shall not the ministration of the Spirit be rather glorious?
—II Corinthians 3: 6-8.

It is important that we keep in mind the unique authority of the Scriptures. The prophets of the Old Testament, the apostles of the New, the spiritual heroes of the Book of Mormon, and the prophet leaders of this dispensation are one in their conviction that their messages came from above. Neither their meditations nor their intelligence nor anything else about them fully explains their message. Isaiah, Jeremiah, Ezekiel, and the others each had a sense of special commission. Most of them were unwilling to speak until the burden of the message became unbearable. It is because they recognized the basic fact that the prophets were heralds rather than originators of the divine message that we find Jesus and the apostles using the name of specific prophets only occasionally. Instead they frequently used the expressions, "he saith," or "the Scripture saith," or "the Holy Ghost saith." Paul expressed this point of view quite clearly in writing to Timothy, when he declared that "all Scripture *is* given by inspiration of God" (II Tim. 3: 16). The medium is of secondary importance. The message is of God.

Many collateral evidences tend to confirm us in our conviction that the Scriptures speak with an authority which is of God and to which we ought to give heed. But the greatest evidence of all is the evidence presented by the Scriptures themselves. Our Heavenly Father did not leave the authority of the Scriptures to be attested by the learning of a few people. This witness is borne by the Spirit of God which comes to good people who study the Scriptures in humility and devotion. Such people find that the Scriptures not only harmonize with their own richest understanding of the Spirit and purpose of God, but that the more carefully they study, the more richly are they blessed, and the more their understanding is enlarged.

The central test and proof of the Scriptures lies in their testimony to the divinity of Jesus and his work for humanity. Jesus says, "In the volume of the book it is written of me"

(Heb. 10: 7). Martin Luther asked, "What book and what person?" and then answered his own question, "There is only one book, Scripture; and only one person—Jesus Christ." This is true, even though we understand the Scripture to include more than Luther meant. There is an essential and vital connection between the eternal word of God which was made flesh and the word of God written in the Scriptures. The standard books, the Scriptures, are their own best witnesses. The man who studies the Scriptures with eyes blinded by prejudice and with heart at enmity against God will wonder at the high place held by the Scriptures in the affection of the Latter Day Saint people. But if we can explain our faith without apology, and try only to clear the way in order that the records may speak for themselves, there are yet many good men and women who will be won to faith in God through the inspiration which accompanies the devout reading of these "tracts for all times."

Latter Day Saints are fully abreast of other people in recognizing the unique importance of the Bible as a priceless record of divine revelation. We are true to the fact of history and of experience, however, in pointing out that the testimony of the Bible has been obscured by misunderstanding and misrepresentation. Biblical scholars do not speak with a united voice. Their testimony is divided and confusing. Because of this, our Heavenly Father inspired men living on other continents to write their spiritual experience and to preserve their record for our enlightenment. This record—the Book of Mormon—has now been available for considerably more than a hundred years. Many problems remain which have not been solved. But the passing of the years has brought many corroborating testimonies of the message of this book, and personal evidences of essential spiritual quality are available for all who will give it devoted and careful attention. In addition to these two records, our Heavenly Father has given light in our own day to confirm these narratives, and to add thereto harmonious instruction suited to our present needs.

The Holy Spirit has moved men of spiritual power in every age to write the truth revealed to them in order that this truth might enrich generations yet to come, joining all the generations in one great fellowship of faith and love. That Spirit is still seeking to minister to men. When the man with a burdened heart and an oppressed conscience reads, "Come unto me all ye that labor and are heavy laden, and I will give you rest" (Matt. 11: 28), it seems as if the message is directed to him immediately and as if the Son of God stands near by in personal invitation. The Spirit of God makes the Scripture his living word.

Study Outlines

The Scriptures

Lesson Purpose

To persuade the student to study the Scriptures intelligently and prayerfully so as to become familiar with their fundamental teachings and to interpret them in daily living.

High Points of the Lesson

The Scriptures embody a great revelation. The whole experience of the church is directed against considering the Scriptures as great literature only.

The real values of the Scriptures are only available to those who read them under the guidance of the Spirit of God. Their unique authority is emphasized under such guidance, and is never fully realized without it.

The central message of the Scriptures of today is but an expansion of that available in other dispensations. All Scripture bears testimony that Jesus is the Christ and that men find their truest life with him.

Questions and Discussion Topics

(1) What is Scripture? When did it begin to be written? When is it likely to cease?

(2) What are the major values of Scripture study?

(3) What do we mean by the "standard of Scripture"? Why do we need such a standard?

(4) What was the attitude of Jesus toward the Scriptures? What Scriptures were available to him?

(5) In what sense is revelation greater than the record of revelation? How is this lack made up to the devout student of Scripture?

(6) What is the purpose of the Book of Mormon? Give reasons for your answer.

(7) In what way is the Book of Mormon like the Bible? In what way is it different? Why is the Doctrine and Covenants different in style from either the Bible or the Book of Mormon?

(8) In what ways may we best promote intelligent application of scriptural principles to the problems of daily life?

What the Lesson Means Today

There was no time when the authority of the expert was more highly respected than it is today. The testimony of experts in the field of religion is available for us in the sacred books of the church. It is valueless until it is studied by good people in the spirit of devotion, not an end in itself, but as a means toward fuller life.

The preservation of the Scriptures against vicissitudes of every kind is one of many testimonies of their importance in the sight of God. We cannot afford to treat them lightly. No genuinely earnest Latter Day Saint does.

Chapter XVI

MARRIAGE

The sacrament of marriage—What God has joined —For each other—The family—The safeguards of marriage.

Lesson Forty

I—THE SACRAMENT OF MARRIAGE

WE DO WELL TO MARK THE GREAT EVENTS of our lives in such a manner as to gather up their values and impress them deeply before we move on. Thus the beginning of life is marked by formal dedication to the service of God in the blessing of little children. The completion of school or college is marked by a dignified ceremony to which the young people look forward and from which they date their graduation. Baptism, which ends the life of self and ushers in the life of God, is likewise regarded as a time for deep thought and deep feeling. The consummation of youthful love in a formal marriage ceremony is also wise and significant. It is so closely related to the dignified and yet joyous launching of a new life as to be inseparable from it.

In accord with other religious groups and with the customs of civilized nations, the church, therefore, believes that "all marriages . . . . should be solemnized in a public meeting, or feast, prepared for that purpose" (Doctrine and Covenants 111: 1), and that "marriage should be celebrated with prayer and thanksgiving" (Doctrine and Covenants 111: 2). These statements indicate that while marriage is the primary concern of the participating parties, society has an interest in every marriage, and this interest ought to be freely recognized. In harmony with the nature of the marriage contract and in recognition of this public concern, marriages should not be performed covertly or clandestinely, but in a dignified manner and with the full knowledge of all those who have a right to be informed. It is not essential that the marriage shall be solemnized in church; but it is essential that it shall not be performed in places which are not consonant with its sacred character. Some weddings are frankly unchristian. They make a mockery of what should be a solemn and beautiful sacrament.

As we have already seen, the sacrament of marriage is more than the ceremony of marriage. In a sacramental sense, marriage involves the whole union of husband and wife, a union beginning before an altar of God and continuing throughout the lifetime of the parties. No marriage can persist which is unblessed by the kindly ministries of humor and pleasant concourse, nor will a marriage be truly consummated until suffering and distress have added their somber colors to the pattern of life. But in joy or sorrow, success or failure, marriage is intended to be a sacrament—a living experience in which the common affairs of daily life become the emblems and the indication of a finer spiritual reality, the outward signs of an inner spiritual grace.

There are certain important prerequisites or conditions of true marriage. The first and most obvious of these is mutual affection. This is indicated in part in the statement of Jesus, "What .... God hath joined let not man put asunder" (Matt. 19: 6); for it is the very nature of God to join people together in love. In harmony with the teaching of his Master, Paul wrote to the saints in Ephesus:

> Husbands, love your wives, even as Christ also loved the church and gave himself for it.—Ephesians 5: 25.

and,

> Let every one of you in particular so love his wife even as himself. —Ephesians 5: 33.

This basic condition of an effective marriage is reiterated in the fundamental law of the church given in modern revelation.

> Thou shalt love thy wife with all thy heart, and shall cleave unto her and none else.—Doctrine and Covenants 42: 7.

Such mutual affection is not something to be taken for granted, nor is it the creation of a moment. It has a depth and quality which can only be matured with the passing of the years. To the task of safeguarding the affection of his or her companion every man or woman ought to bring all available intelligence and patience and courage.

A second condition of an effective marriage rises out of this first one. It is indicated in the marriage service:

> You both mutually agree to be each other's companion, husband and wife.—Doctrine and Covenants 111: 2.

One of the old-time elders used to say that he agreed to the requirements of the gospel with the full consent of his faculties. That is what is intended here, for this covenant implies mature consideration on the part of both man and woman. "You both mutually agree" indicates that although friends and relatives may be interested, the right and responsibility of mutual agreement rests on the parties to the marriage. They should not be unduly influenced in exercising this right.

It is essential to such a union as marriage that the parties thereto shall be mature and aware of what they are doing. In relation to the sacrament of baptism, the church has long felt the necessity of insisting that candidates shall have arrived at the age of accountability. In the marriage covenant, a similar requirement is implied. What is involved here is not so much chronological age as the capacity to make the kind of contract involved. One point of view limits this maturity to physical growth. A wider and more socially justifiable point of view extends this to include mental maturity, and says that the parties to a valid marriage must be of sound mind. Should not the church of Jesus Christ teach the importance of adequate spiritual maturity as a prerequisite to the spiritual union of marriage? The spiritual factors in marriage are most important, and a lack of spiritual preparation for what is involved in marriage is the biggest threat confronting many a couple as they leave the church after the ceremony. Such qualities as patience, kindness, forbearance, and self-control should be reasonably matured before marriage.

We must look to religion for the strongest sanctions of marriage. It is part of our duty to see that from childhood those who come under the influence of the church shall be encouraged to take religious views of the responsibility of marriage and of parenthood, views which will enable them to undertake these responsibilities with serious and elevated purpose. It is to religion, more than anywhere else, that we must look to set men free from self-will, from selfish individualism, and to educate them in faithfulness to the basic loyalties of human life.

In a recent article Dr. Howard Chandler Robbins stated:

> It is loyalty, rather than the pursuit of personal happiness or the gratification of personal desire—loyalty inspired and strengthened and directed by personal religion—that furnishes the best basis for marriage and the home, and incidentally, holds the best hope of happiness as well as of permanence. Too many people nowadays are making happiness the first and perhaps even the sole consideration. That aim defeats its own purpose. Happiness is like health; those who seek it too anxiously are generally the last to find it. Happiness and health are both by-products of adaptation to environment; they elude those who pursue them and come unsought to those who put duty and loyalty first. Behind the great upward thrust which led to the institution of the family, there was at all times a generous and sometimes sacrificial thing: parental devotion. Parental love has tempered, chastened, disciplined, and purified the relations of men and women. It has been their common love for their children, and their common care of them, that has made them in some measure patient, faithful, and self-forgetful. In this, the most intimate and exacting of all human relationships, Isaiah's words have been fulfilled, that "a little child shall lead them."

I would like to add one further condition of effective marriage, one which is essentially Christian in its emphasis and point of view and is directly related to the central idea of the incarnation. It is that those who would make a truly spiritual adventure of marriage must have a sane, wholesome, and spiritual concept of the importance of the body. The Scriptures affirm that "the spirit and the body is the soul of man" (Doctrine and Covenants 85: 4). There is no need, therefore, to admit with reluctance the important part that the body plays in rounding out our spiritual lives. The essential greatness of man lies in the fact that in him his spiritual purpose may control all that he does. Until the spirit thus reaches out to every phase of his life, no person is fully Christian.

The hermit of an earlier day assumed that the way of true life lay in repressing all bodily desires and denying all bodily happiness; but instead of promoting the knowledge and glory of God, he succeeded only in making life useless or even disgusting. Yet in spite of the demonstrated poverty of this point of view, there are many people today who still think that the way of life consists in forgetting the body as much as possible in order that the soul may live. Such persons believe they ought to regard with disapproval all physical things, and fail to realize that when God took on himself the body of man he sanctified it forever.

Our life here is an embodied life, and it cannot be fine unless the body is finely tempered. That body is designed as the instrument through which the spirit may find expression. The first essential, no doubt, is to submit it to discipline and so reduce it to the place of a servant. At all cost it must be brought under control. It must be understood, and kept in good health. And if these things be neglected, the life of the spirit is hampered and depressed. But still spirit must express itself through body, and all the wealth of powers with which the body is endowed have significance and worth.—*Men, Women and God,* by Herbert Gray, page XVI.

Latter Day Saints, above all other people, have good reason to be chaste and virtuous. This is entirely possible without ignoring the physical side of the true marriage relation. If mere lust is the vilest thing on earth, then pure love is the most beautiful. And when pure love is a dominant factor in a marital situation, the body is not in this process denied, but is accepted, understood, and made to play its true part.

The foregoing lays the foundation for saying that a true Christian marriage is and ought to be an indissoluble union. When a man and woman assume the relation of husband and wife, their marriage creates a vital social organism, the family, which is the very basis of our social order. This relation is entered into as a matter of contract; but it immediately becomes a status in which each party has an investment and from which neither party has the right to secede. Once it has been entered into, the marriage relation must not be considered from a personal and distinct point of view, but only from the point of view of the new unit which the marriage ceremony has brought into being. A parallel situation occurred in Civil War times in the United States. The southern states claimed that as sovereign states they could secede from the Union if they decided that membership in the Union was no longer desirable. The Federal Government denied this, saying that a sacred obligation had been entered into by the sisterhood of states, and that every party thereto had built a future on the expectation that the other parties would continue to co-operate. It was not possible to go back to where the states had been before the Union was brought into being. Lincoln held to this view through all the dark years of war; and history has vindicated his vision and his understanding. In exactly the same way, the marriage relation creates a new unit in society. The parties thereto are in honor bound to live in and for the new family unit brought into being by their free action.

Psychologists tell us that the greatest menace to well-rounded personality is inner conflict. In the same way the greatest menace to truly happy and successful marriage is division between the parties thereto. Married persons need to sing with new understanding, "awake to union and be one, or saith the Lord, ye are not mine":

For marriage is ordained of God unto man; wherefore it is lawful that he should have one wife, and they twain shall be one flesh, and all this that the earth might answer the end of its creation; and that it might be filled with the measure of man, according to his creation before the world was made.—Doctrine and Covenants 49: 3.

The purpose of marriage is not merely the propagation of the species; but the raising up of godly generations. The only hope of achieving this goal is in building the families of the church on a spiritual basis. This in turn calls for mutual affection, co-operation, peace in the home, and for the exercise of the essentially Christian spirit and self-discipline in love.

Study Outlines

The Sacrament of Marriage

Lesson Purpose

To emphasize the sanctity of Christian marriage and its basic characteristics: mutuality, exclusiveness, permanence.

High Points of the Lesson

The church and society have an interest in every marriage, and this interest ought to be freely recognized. The marriage ceremony gives an opportunity for such recognition.

The sacrament of marriage involves the whole life of the contracting parties, and cannot be properly entered into unless certain essential conditions are present. There must be genuine mutual affection, mature consideration of the contribution which each can make and of the home life which both desire, and an intention that the union shall be permanent.

A true Christian marriage is an indissoluble union. If it is begun in this spirit, the parties thereto will make a genuine effort to live in terms of their common life instead of in terms of their individual desires.

Questions and Discussion Topics

(1) What is a sacrament? Why is it desirable that the major events of life shall be marked by a dignified and sacramental experience?

(2) What interest does the church have in the marriage of two persons? What interest does society have?

(3) Do you believe that persons about to be married must love each other for the marriage to be fully Christian? Why is this important?

(4) What is the meaning of the marriage covenant, "You both mutually agree"? Discuss what this covenant implies.

(5) What is the relation between maturity and the stability of a marriage? Why is spiritual maturity so very important?

(6) Two young people get married with a friendly agreement that if they are not happy they will separate with mutual good feeling. Two others marry with the understanding that theirs is to be a permanent union. Which have the better chance of happiness? Why?

(7) Discuss briefly the importance of religion in the marriage equation.

(8) What suggestions have you looking toward the elevation of standards of marriage within the church?

(9) Think of the most successful marriages you know. On what is their success founded?

(10) What are the characteristics of truly Christian marriage?

What the Lesson Means Today

The Scriptures and traditions of the church unite in emphasizing the sacramental nature of marriage. It is intended to be a spiritual union in which physical things minister to spiritual understanding and power.

The importance of marriage in the life of the church can scarcely be overstated. The elevation of our standards of marriage and the building of the kingdom of God are directly related.

Adequate mental, physical, and spiritual preparation for the mutual adjustments which marriage entails is a major guarantee of happiness and permanence.

There are no substitutes for the basic conditions of successful marriages.

Trial marriages are no marriages at all. Marriage is a spiritual enterprise; its keynote is quality.

Lesson Forty-one

II—THE NATURE OF CHRISTIAN MARRIAGE

The family is the basic social unit. Back of it lie the most powerful biological impulses which Nature has made urgent in order that the race shall persist. These impulses may easily be misdirected. Indeed, the gravitation of sin is felt more strongly at this point than at almost any other, for the social order has been stained by unchastity, and the high spiritual standards which should obtain in regard to marriage and the home have been constantly vitiated by the infiltration of lust. We shall therefore expect our Heavenly Father to have for his children a distinctive message regarding the family and the home.

The Christian standard of marriage was set by Jesus in reply to some questions from the Pharisees. On this occasion the Master laid down the following basic principles:

The union between a man and his wife is even more important than that between a man and his parents.

Married persons belong together and are "no more twain, but one flesh."

What God hath joined together, let not man put asunder.—Matthew 19: 4-6.

No higher standard of marriage has ever been set for any people. All the widely divergent points of view on the marriage question come together at this point: that Christian marriage is designed to be a permanent union and that both the parties thereto, and all Christians having any relation to them, are by the terms of their religion bound to do their utmost to promote the permanence of this union. Just as the physical life of any man is subject to the constant threat of accident and disease, so the spiritual union between a man and his wife is subject to the constant threat of carelessness, insincerity, and infidelity. Maintenance of high standards of marriage, therefore, requires spiritual insight, self-discipline, patience, and hope, such as the gospel seeks to create and develop in the lives of men and women. The Christian ideal of marriage is an ideal for Christian people.

The permanent union of a good man and his wife, which no man must put asunder, is built on the stability of the Christian virtues. No superficial charms can give it enduring quality. Integrity, industry, and abiding affection are vital; and it is altogether too much to take it for granted that God has joined every couple who decide to get married. All such couples acquire social and religious responsibilities by reason of their marriage; but the indissoluble union of a man and his wife contemplated by Christianity imperatively requires a mutual contribution which is quite obviously lacking in many of the marriages of today.

Let us look again, and carefully, at this phrase, "What .... God hath joined together, let not man put asunder." This immediately leads to another question, "Who has God joined together?" Surely in the light of what we know about Christ, we can see that this does not include all who share in the marriage ceremony. Just as the act of going down into the water and coming forth again does not constitute baptism unless accompanied by an inner spiritual change, so also the act of being united in the ceremony of marriage does not initiate a spiritual union unless the spiritual elements which should accompany it are present. The real marriage of which Jesus spoke is initiated by the marriage ceremony, but is accompanied by mutual affection, and, in time, by a definite belonging together; a oneness which it is obviously most iniquitous to dissolve.

In these days of hasty and thoughtless marriages, many people who live together cannot conceivably have been joined together by God. A large proportion of such "marriages" are recognized by the courts to be not marriages at all, and are annulled. Others, which are legally binding, have never carried the sanction of Divinity. Consider, for a moment, the large number of hasty and disastrous war weddings entered into in an atmosphere of personal and patriotic emotion shot through by fear. Consider again the case of clean and splendid women married and thereby immediately infected with a disease of whose very existence they were previously only technically aware. Consider again, the large number of people married for considerations of wealth, position, and safety. God is willing to join together even those persons who marry under these conditions if, recognizing their situation, they join him in strengthening the bonds that unite them and in creating still other bonds. But here is the point: these bonds ought to be created before the marriage ceremony is performed; and persons who embark upon a marital career without such bonds of union between them are not joined by God and run grave risk that they never will be.

Marriage is a spiritual enterprise which can only be made effective by truly Christian people. For others it may be a physical and legal union blessed by mutual affection of the highest possible order, but unless it has the spiritual quality which is achieved by persons who live in the light of Christ, it lacks the full measure of divine sanction and lacks also something of the stability and permanence which was contemplated in its institution.

As will be seen from this line of reasoning, marriage is a great deal more than a physical union. Indeed, while the physical relationship is important, and its importance must not be minimized, it is part of and contributary to the total purpose of marriage. Discussing this question in the British House of Lords, the late Lord Birkenhead once said:

> It seems to me that there can be no doubt as to which is the higher and more important side of marriage. If we think of all that marriage represents to most of us—the memories of the world's adventure faced together in youth so heedlessly, and yet so confidently; the tender comradeship, the sweet association of parenthood—how much more these count than the bonds which nature, in its ingenious teleology has contrived to secure, and render agreeable, the perpetuation of the species.

God brings men and women together for the best possible reasons. He unites those who, by reason of their mutual affections, their cleanness of mind and body, their physical, mental, and spiritual maturity, and the adaption of their personalities to each other, belong together and ought not to be separated. One of the tasks of the church is to promote such marriages, to so prepare and instruct her members that God can join them together as he will, and to so cement these unions that it shall be a sacrilege to think of breaking them.

The ideal set before us in the Christian order of marriage is that of men and women made one by God because of their essential fitness for this union. After the marriage of such persons, they have much to learn and many adjustments to make, but there is hope that their union will grow to be a constantly more fine and precious thing because they have made such a splendid beginning. With such an ideal before them, young people can discuss and prepare for marriage cleanly and intelligently years before the time comes for them to be married. The foundations of decency, understanding, and loyalty can be so well laid as to be fundamental in character and not merely adaptations to the marital situation. Such considerations as money, education, and social prestige can then be properly evaluated, and can be given their right weight in the marital equation without being either ignored or overemphasized. And such absurdities as occur day after day and night after night in the offices of ministers and justices of the peace will be recognized for what they are—travesties on the divine union which God has planned as the ultimate in human companionship and our noblest foretaste of the kingdom of God.

The nature of our modern economic order is such that it tends constantly to postpone the time of marriage. Both on biological and psychological grounds, the arguments in favor of early marriage are overwhelming. Can we not say with assurance that one of the signs of the approach of Zion will be that we shall so reorder society that good people shall no longer be kept apart by secondary considerations after the primary elements of effective marriage have already been developed. Today the question we ask is not, "Are these two physically, mentally, emotionally, and spiritually fit for marriage?" but "Can this man support this woman?" Certainly the partnership cannot be one of irresponsible affection. It must function on a practical basis. But just how practical is it to permit a world order in which purely economic considerations defer marriage beyond the point where it is spiritually desirable? In the long run we shall realize that here, as elsewhere, the hope of Zion is of tremendous importance.

Study Outlines

The Nature of Christian Marriage

Lesson Purpose

To impress the creative spiritual aspects of truly Christian marriage.

High Points of the Lesson

The Christian ideal of marriage is an ideal for Christian people. It can be realized only through the joint cultivation of such Christian virtues as mutual affection, integrity, loyalty.

The marriage ceremony is only spiritually significant if accompanied by an inner union between persons of genuine spiritual caliber. It is difficult to believe that "God hath joined" people who marry for such unchristian reasons as are frequently cited.

Many a marriage has ended in disaster because the parties thereto did not cultivate their mutual affection. Marriage is a high art to which all the intelligence, devotion, and self-discipline of the parties should minister. It requires an exclusiveness which is much more than physical and an inclusiveness which unites husband and wife in every worthy endeavor.

Questions and Discussion Topics

(1) What are the three emphases in the standard of marriage set by Jesus?

(2) Discuss briefly the injunction, "What God hath joined together, let not man put assunder."

(3) "Marriage is a spiritual enterprise which can only be made effective by truly Christian people." Discuss this briefly.

(4) What preparation for marriage is most important? When should it begin?

(5) What changes in the circumstances of marriage may we confidently expect as the kingdom of God is established?

(6) What covenant is made between persons married by Latter Day Saint ministers? Analyze this briefly.

(7) Name some characteristics which seem to you to be vital to a happy and stable marriage.

(8) In what way does the exclusiveness of the marriage covenant minister to the strength of the marital relation? Discuss this exclusiveness briefly on the cultural and spiritual plane.

(9) Should such things as hobbies, ambitions, finances be considered by persons who are about to be married?

(10) What is the importance of religion in the marriage situation? Should this be discussed frankly before marriage or left to take care of itself?

What the Lesson Means Today

The union contemplated through marriage offers such great rewards that we cannot expect to share them without genuine spiritual preparation. It is both foolish, and sinful to rush into marriage heedlessly. The loss of unhappily married persons is threefold: to themselves, to those whom they might have married, and to society.

The ideals of marriage are not ideals to be talked about for other people; they should be worked on in our own lives. It is too late to begin to lay the foundations for loyalty, integrity, mutual helpfulness, and self-discipline when the time for marriage comes. Marriage is an important phase of the total spiritual life: it is best ministered to by healthy, creative, godly living.

III—THE STABILITY OF THE FAMILY

Marriage is essentially a partnership of two to which others may contribute, but into which others must not obtrude. This requirement even applies to the parents of the married parties. Such exclusiveness is not fixed by the fiat of God, but by the very nature of things. It is something that we cannot change, and therefore must recognize, a principle written into the very nature of life itself.

A patriot may have world vision, and his heart may go out to all men, but he nevertheless feels exclusive kinship with his own people. This is natural, and it is to be commended. It is not possible to respect a man whose love for humanity touches everywhere but centers nowhere. A patriot knows that the citizens of other nations also love their own people, and he respects them for it, but he loves his own people; sometimes he may not be proud of them, but he loves them still and is willing to die for them if necessary. Indeed, his love for humanity becomes truly meaningful as he first of all loves those who are nearest to him.

The scientist is similarly exclusive in his interests and affections. So is the adventurer and the author and the artist. In talking of such men and women we say, "he is wedded to his country," or "she is wedded to her music," and we mean that love of country, love of art, love of scientific research, or love of adventure is such a consuming passion that it shuts out every rival from their lives. The wide use of the phrase "wedded" in this sense indicates how fundamental we feel the exclusiveness of married life ought to be. The dignity of marriage requires such an attitude of exclusiveness; lack of this attitude robs marriage of one of its most important characteristics.

This exclusiveness is recognized in the Latter Day Saint marriage covenant. In this covenant the parties to the marriage agree to "keep themselves wholly for each other, and from all others, during their lives" (Doctrine and Covenants 111: 2). There is both a positive and a negative aspect to this promise. First, the husband and wife must keep themselves for each other. Then, also, they must keep themselves from all others, in all matters which should rightfully be shared between them only. Not infrequently the negative part of the foregoing is the only part of the contract to be emphasized. But let it be clearly understood that the constructive aspect of the marriage covenant requires the parties thereto to give their best intelligence and ripest understanding to the problem of happy, mutual adjustment. Evangelist Elbert A. Smith says:

This requires the exercise of patience and mutual confidence and fidelity, and each must so live as to merit the respect of the other, for respect must underlie love. It is a task to be worked at, thought about, stayed with; and it is the most worth-while task in life.—*Marriage and the Home,* page 43.

In a much larger sense than is usually recognized, a husband and wife are required by the very nature of their mutual covenant to seek together those values which will augment their comradeship. Just as marriage is more certainly a spiritual union than a physical one, so the task of living for each other is more certainly a spiritual than physical one. It involves sharing life in its finer elements. It involves the great adventure of mutual understanding so that life can be thus shared. It involves the achievement of togetherness, of unity in point of view and in approach to life.

The intimate association which marriage brings about is of great importance to personality. It is certain that there will be differences in the personalities of husbands and wives. The happiest marriages are those in which the personalities of husband and wife become complementary, the strength of one helping the weakness of the other. This does not just come to pass; it is a major achievement. Honorable compromises in this connection are not signs of weakness but of wise and creative adjustment. Marriage is the acid test of character, and it brings out the finest qualities of character when good people, having entered happily and intelligently on the adventure of life together, are determined to make their marriage work.

The man who is happily married lives for his wife and home under the benediction of God. In so doing he discovers that there is at least one human being who understands, who loves him for his own sake regardless of success and failure, whose patience is truly inexhaustible, and whose compassionate concern is a measure by which he begins to understand the love and forgiveness of God. Where love is, there the ideal state exists in fact; minor adjustments may and will have to be made, but at the heart of things stands an affection which both illuminates and empowers the union. Even when marriage is not entered upon in mutual love, human nature is such that love may yet follow. Good will, a sense of responsibility, and the determination to make the best of things have their reward.

Worldly people regard the exclusive covenant of marriage as something to be resented and avoided. Yet thoughtful and clean-minded men recognize that in its exclusiveness marriage finds its strength. Thus:

> There is a bracing negative aspect to the marriage vow. It commits us more or less irrevocably to forsake all others. It cuts off the freedom to act on the spur of the moment. Unmarried, we are like the riderless horse who allows only for his own height when he ducks under low branches in the forest. In marriage we must choose our path more carefully. But this is just what the vast majority of us need. We need to be fenced into a narrower field than of ourselves we should even find. We need to be harnessed and given a bit of road to cover. In the end we put out more power and win more happiness when our choice is thus restricted and our path narrowed by a promise, given and taken. We get somewhere because we are no longer so free to change our course.—Richard Cabot, M. D., *What Men Live By.*

It is difficult to see how polygamy could ever be considered by persons accepting the doctrine of marital exclusiveness so clearly written in the books of the church. It is even more difficult when we read the word of God that:

> He that looketh upon a woman to lust after her, shall deny the faith, and shall not have the spirit; and if he repents not, he shall be cast out.
> —Doctrine and Covenants 42: 7.

If this means anything, it means that unchastity not only vitiates happy married life, but that it produces such moral decay as to affect every other aspect of life and to make the indwelling of the Spirit impossible. This applies to individuals and to institutions. Any institution which looks with favor upon extra marital relations—and by this I mean such relations whatever their name—and which does not repent, cannot be "the habitation of God through the Spirit."—Ephesians 2: 22.

It is eminently desirable that married people shall have many friends, some of them admitted to an inner circle of intimate affection. Some of these friendships will be based on the usual attractions of social life, and others on mutual cultural interests. Every home will be enriched by such friendships if they are made subordinate to the life and purposes of the home itself. But they must never rival or become substitutes for the spiritual and cultural comradeship which husband and wife ought to achieve together. Even such pleasures as husband and wife do not share with each other should be viewed with understanding by each of them and should be contributory to their mutual affection and understanding.

No one can put down a set of rules for married people, for each marriage is a new creation. Each must be conducted in the power of a new spirit, and not merely according to a prescribed code. And this spirit is the spirit of true religion, affirmative, creative, and affectionate.

IV—THE FAMILY

One of the major reasons why society insists on monogamy and condemns irregular unions lies in the fact that every child has a fundamental right to be brought up by a father and a mother. No society can be strong unless its foundations are laid in family life, wherein men and women co-operate to give the rising generation every possible chance to enter into life nobly. Children have a right to expect the best that the older generation can give, as a foundation on which to build for the future. During the years of infancy, childhood, and youth, they require food and clothing, shelter and education, and the individualized personal care which makes a good home the finest preparation for life which can be made available.

The needs of the children of any marriage constitute one of the major reasons why that marriage should be a union from which neither party may easily withdraw. Since one of the major purposes of marriage is to bring children into the world under conditions which seek to make permanent and stable the gains of civilization and of religion, children yet unborn have an interest in everything that goes into the shaping of family life. For their sakes, marriage must be entered into solemnly and with high purpose, and should be celebrated in a dignified and public service at which the nature of the marital contract is recognized and the social and spiritual obligations assumed are emphasized.

The view of the family as an institution of religion is clearly emphasized in each of the standard books of the church. In the Old Testament and in the Book of Mormon this concept is basic, being the foundation of the hopefulness of the prophets and of their conviction that sooner or later men will be united in creative fraternity. It is significant that Abram was promised, "In thee shall all the families of the earth be blessed" (Gen. 12: 3), that the Book of Mormon tells the story of God's dealings with the great families of the western hemisphere; and that the establishment of the church in these last days combines in one the promises made to the fathers (Gen. 12: 2; Ether 1; Doctrine and Covenants 3: 10, 15; 36: 9). It is significant, also, that the Psalmist, thinking on the mercies of God, sang, "God setteth the solitary in families" (Ps. 68: 6), and that Paul, in contemplating the wonder of the love of God, wrote to the Ephesians of "the Father of our Lord Jesus Christ, of whom the whole family in heaven and earth is named."—Eph. 3: 14, 15.

The Psalmist prayed for godly children, because he saw that his own generation was handicapped as well as blessed by its heritage from the past, and because he looked to the coming of a generation dedicated from birth to tasks too great for his own day. So also with the prophets. These were always picturing the chosen people as having a goal in the distant future, like a husbandman with his vineyard still unplanted or a herald with his message not yet delivered. There runs through the prophecies a strain of penitence and of triumph; penitence because they have not achieved, but triumph because they could pass on their hope to the coming generation to whom they looked for victory. These children of the new day were to be trained in the law and inspired by the vision of the holy city until their hearts were on fire and every unworthy passion and every selfish aim was consumed in the heat of their righteous desire.

It is in such a way that God unites the hearts of the fathers to the hearts of the children. Marriage is a comradeship of affection which fulfills itself in the fruits of this affection. Its great glory is that the mutual constancy of two who love each other is ripened and exalted in the measure and quality of their devotion to their children. It is the children who furnish the incentive to progress, and whose needs constitute bonds that unite their parents long after youth and comeliness have fled.

The family is designed of God to be a center of righteousness in which coming citizens of the kingdom can find an atmosphere congenial to their development. The famous boys' schools in England have certain traditional standards of honor. These form the unwritten law of the schools. On entering such a school, the boy finds himself in this atmosphere and in various ways finds his life shaped by it. The family, likewise, by its standards of honor, is designed of God to be a training school in the righteousness which is of the kingdom. Thus the word of modern revelations states that:

> Inasmuch as parents have children in Zion, or in any of her stakes which are organized, that teach them not to understand the doctrine of repentance; faith in Christ the Son of the living God; and of baptism and the gift of the Holy Ghost by the laying on of the hands when eight years old, the sin be upon the head of the parents; for this shall be a law unto the inhabitants of Zion, or in any of her stakes which are organized; and their children shall be baptized for the remission of their sins when eight years old, and receive the laying on of hands: and they shall also teach their children to pray, and to walk uprightly before the Lord.—Doctrine and Covenants 68: 4.

A recent writer states:

> The cry for social righteousness is a cry for family righteousness. The records of juvenile lawlessness trace back into homes where the family life has broken down. The corruption of the last thirty years in American political and business life has been due in no small measure to the breakdown of standards in the family. The old control of force was largely abandoned, and parents were not adequately equipped to train their children by the power of love and reason.—Ward and Edwards, *Christianizing Community Life*.

The ties which unite us to the good homes that have been and the godly homes which yet shall be, are among the spiritual bonds that attach us to the higher life of the community. "The homing instinct is a spiritual instinct." In spite of the wear and tear of daily life, many a Christian home has sheltered the growth of a Christian family in an unbroken sequence of loving sacrifice. From such homes children have gone out to school and to college over a period of many years, and from the oldest to the youngest, these children have been given continuous material and spiritual support. All of us know of such homes and such families. What greater contribution can be made to the forces which seek to save the nation and build the kingdom? It is in the hope of making such a contribution that marriage must be entered upon with thanksgiving and prayer, as a great stewardship in which God is the major partner, as a great sacrament in which earthly things become the sign and seal of inner grace.

It is because the family is of such crucial importance that the Lord has made provision for a special ministry designed to reach into the homes of the church, in the spirit of love, so as to help both parents and children to achieve a home life which will be a prophecy and a foretaste of the coming kingdom. Modern revelation says:

> The priest's duty is . . . . to visit the house of each member, and exhort them to pray vocally and in secret, and attend to all family duties.
> —Doctrine and Covenants 17: 10.

The church has here a teaching mission of major importance. But this mission cannot be fully discharged so long as it is confined to the ministry of the priests and other officers of the church. Indeed, it is so fully influenced by conditions outside the home that here, again, we have an example of the imperative need for building the kingdom.

The Zionic ideal demands good family spirit and good household management. The Zionic home is a co-operative enterprise, where frugality and thrift prevail in order that the finer things of life can be made available and shared. In spite of the many distractions which our modern world has developed to threaten the sanctity and quality of our home life, the ideal still stands; it is in the Zionic home that our noblest hopes are translated into realities, that our finest dreams take on substance, and that love, joy, and peace become living experiences.

If spiritual insight and fellowship are to prevail, the family must have a definite religious center, and the activities of each succeeding day must fit into a definite spiritual pattern. There was a time when family worship was a potent reality in saintly homes, but in many places family altars have been destroyed and new altars have been erected to strange gods. Enjoyment of the arts, delight in the society of cultured people, and many less noble interests, have crowded family worship into the background. The family altar must be restored to its rightful place. A person whose early life is not enriched by a sense of the presence of God achieved in family worship has lost something precious which can never be fully recaptured.

V—SOME SAFEGUARDS OF MARRIAGE

The stress to which modern marriage is subjected is so great that the wise young man and the wise young woman will safeguard their happiness against all possible intrusion, and will strengthen every possible bond of unity. Wise parents will see that their children have abundant opportunities to meet other young people who will make desirable companions, and who are interested in the work of the church. Mutual affection and common interest in the work of the kingdom, plus the demands of the children, form a threefold cord which is not easily broken.

One of the reasons for the advice of the church that members shall marry within the church, is that the teachings of the church nurture qualities of personal life which make for stability in the home. Within the church also there is unusual opportunity to know the background of one's life partner, and his or her reactions to problems and temptations, to success and failure, to joy and sorrow. The church should see that opportunities for wholesome fellowship are plentiful, and the church member should take advantages of such opportunities pleasantly but with underlying seriousness.

It is a hundred years since the church went on record as favoring marriages with members of the church in preference to marriages between church members and those not in the faith (Doctrine and Covenants 111: 1). The committee on marriage in the home appointed by the Federal Council of the Churches of Christ in America, in its report dated March, 1932, gave interesting support to this century-old attitude. This report states:

Wherever human wedlock is regarded as possessing a sacred character and denotes a conjunction of souls and minds as well as physical union, it becomes apparent that harmony in their religious sentiments is of first importance to those united in marriage. . . . .

Not only for the sake of their own happiness but also for social reasons, for the sake of the stability of the new family created by their union, it is greatly to be desired that there should be agreement in religious faith on the part of those who marry, and it is essential that there should be mutual respect and forbearance. . . . .

It is evident that the problem of mixed marriages is not simple, and that it is not susceptible of easy solution. Religion is a basic interest in human life, and differences in religion, if these are fundamental, may strain a marriage to the point of breaking, especially where they are aggravated by ecclesiastical interference. . . . .

Statistics bearing upon the matter are not adequate, but there is reason to suppose that marriages of this sort are highly unstable; furthermore, that in very many cases they lead either to the departure of both partners from the practices of religion or at least to the abandonment of any attempt on their part to provide for the religious education of their children.

The solution for many of our marriage problems seems to lie in better preparation for marriage. It is so easy to imagine that proper preparation has been made, and then to discover too late that this is not so. Both parents, and ministry ought to make it a point to collaborate in seeing that young people are instructed in the nature of the responsibilities which will come to them at marriage, and in the mutual love and forbearance which successful marriage demands. The marriage service provides that the minister shall address the participants in ways which shall seem wise to him, and this provision points to the wisdom of giving instruction even before this time.

The requirement that marriages shall be solemnized in a public meeting is directed against one of the chief causes of marital instability, hasty marriages performed under the pressure of passing emotion or of fortuitous circumstances, and therefore bereft of the elements of seriousness and of preparation which are a rightful part of the true marriage. It has been found wise, under some circumstances, to publish the announcement of the marriage sometime prior to the ceremony. This practice might well become the invariable custom; the church does well to frown on marriages which lack the dignity that this practice assures.

A further safeguard of Christian marriage lies in the expectation of permanence with which it starts out. The early months of married life are months of compromise and adjustment. Persons who retain the feeling that they are individuals, and that they have rights which they do not share with their companions, find this period extremely irksome. The temptation to refuse the task of renunciation and of adjustment is great. But if there is no thought that marriage is an experiment, that it may be terminated at any time by mutual consent, then these months of adjustment minister to a constantly finer affection. It is not those who have repeated the initial steps of marriage many times who know a great deal about marriage, but those who have achieved marital unity in actual experience, and who have survived the breakers of the early months and have reached the deeper waters lying beyond.

Not all the threats against marriage, however, occur within the first years. During this period, mutual affection may override some rather fundamental differences. But there comes a time when ideals and character and temperament count more and more in the scale of married happiness, and when the transition is made from the joyous adventure of a comradeship of love to the more serious and sober but no less joyous enterprise of family responsibility. Here many marriages come to shipwreck which might have survived if husband and wife had been able to draw on the imperatives of religion, and had found their natural inclinations curbed or reinforced, as might be necessary, in the interest of stable and permanent home life.

Our Heavenly Father does not wish that his representatives shall take upon themselves the business of ordering the lives of his children. He has nevertheless charged the ministry with responsibility for maintaining the Christian character of the home. Affirmatively, the members of the priesthood ought to bring to every home in the church the inspiration of worthy example and of clear-sighted instruction. The influence exercised by the church in the home should be adapted to the problems of the members of the home, and should be given weight through the wisdom and judgment of those who represent the church. The ministry should have such a place of affection and respect in the hearts of the Saints that in times of crises they will be called in and their judgment and advice be sought, and respected when given.

The safeguards of the Christian home are essentially spiritual safeguards. The home may be maintained as a going institution for many lesser reasons, but it can only provide a richly creative and affectionate center of human living if it has a strong spiritual foundation. No home is better for lack of a religious motivation. Any home is a better home when true religion has a vital part in its maintenance.

Study Outlines

The Stability of the Family

Lesson Purpose

To state the belief of the church regarding the nature and purpose of family life, and to review and emphasize some of the major safeguards of marriage and the home.

High Points of the Lesson

The needs of the children of any marriage constitute one of the major reasons why that marriage should be a permanent spiritual union. These needs should be a major influence in placing marriage and family life in a definitely spiritual setting.

The family is designed of God to be a center of righteousness, where rights and duties are considered in an atmosphere of affection. In such an atmosphere the foundations of Zion can be most effectively laid.

The ministry of the church should be directed toward safeguarding the family life for all parties involved. This is most easily possible when husband and wife are both members of the church, and our church-wide endeavor to complete our family circles is of major importance to the families involved as well as to the church.

Questions and Discussion Topics

(1) Give some of the reasons why society insists on monogamy as the rule of marriage. What influence do children have on this question?

(2) Discuss briefly the importance of marriage as a permanent alliance from the viewpoint of the children.

(3) In what way does a serious and dignified approach to marriage in the marriage ceremony promote the happiness and high idealism of the children of the family?

(4) What importance did the ancient prophets place on family life?

(5) Discuss briefly the value of a Christian home as a training school for the work of the kingdom.

(6) In what practical ways may the church strengthen the family life of its members? What spiritual teaching should the church give in this regard?

(7) Discuss briefly the importance of religion as a factor in promoting the stability and quality of the home.

(8) In what ways can parents and ministry co-operate to prepare young people for the responsibilities of marriage?

(9) What obligation does the importance of the family place on the ministry? How can they best prepare to meet these obligations? What ministers are most directly concerned?

(10) What help can the church give to those who are unhappily married?

What the Lesson Means Today

Children have a right to be physically well born. This demands cleanliness on the part of parents at every stage of life. They also have the right to be spiritually well born, and this demands spiritual preparation at every stage of life.

These basic considerations require that marriage shall be an experience shared by Christian disciples, that it shall be initiated in a fitting ceremony, that it shall exist for noble purposes, and that it shall be reinforced by a sense of duty enriched in affection.

Chapter XVII

THE KINGDOM OF GOD

The kingdom in the Bible—The kingdom in modern revelation—The spiritual nature of the kingdom—Stewardship and the financial law.

Lesson Forty-three

I—THE KINGDOM IN THE BIBLE

THE PROPHETS AND SPIRITUAL LEADERS of Israel held before the chosen people an ideal of government which pictured God as living in the midst of his people and administering the affairs of his kingdom with justice and equity. He was to rule in reality because he would first of all rule in the inner courts of life; and would win men to ways of righteousness and justice and brotherhood in the common affairs of daily living. This exalted idea of government is expressed many times in the Old Testament, for example:

> Thus saith the Lord of hosts: Behold, I will gather my people from the east country, and from the west country; and I will bring them, and they shall dwell in the midst of Jerusalem; and they shall be my people, and I will be their God, in truth and in righteousness.—Zech. 8: 7, 8 (I. V.).

The spiritual genius of the Old Testament prophets is revealed in their intensely practical understanding of the nature of righteousness. The Jews had been given a priesthood and certain forms of worship and had been placed under certain religious obligations of a ceremonial nature. But the prophets saw with clear vision that it was the reality behind these things which justified their institution and their continuance. Thus Hosea prophesied, "I desired mercy, and not sacrifice, and the knowledge of God more than burnt offerings" (Hosea 6: 6), and, "turn thou to thy God: keep mercy and judgment and wait on thy God continually" (Hosea 12: 6). In similar vein Amos prophesied, "Seek good, and not evil . . . . let judgment run down as waters, and righteousness as a mighty stream."—Amos 5: 14, 24.

Leadership such as this gave rise to an eager spiritual alertness among the more devout Jewish people. Many of them looked forward to the day when the dominion of God would be extended, until righteousness would be the rule of life even to the remote corners of the earth.

The people who looked forward thus eagerly were not very clear about what they meant by the "kingdom of heaven," or the "consolation of Israel," although there was general agreement that these expressions stood for a new social order founded in righteousness and responsive to divine guidance. Some of the more zealous, for example, interpreted the Messianic hope to mean the founding of an earthly kingdom established by force, if necessary, with its capital at Jerusalem. People of this type wanted to make Jesus king (John 6: 15). Even his immediate followers could not at first understand why the Master refused to use his unique command of force to confound his enemies.

Practically all the devout Jews in the days immediately preceding the coming of Jesus were looking forward to a new day in which they as a people would lead the world in the ways of righteousness. Their idea of righteousness was strangely intermingled with observance of the minute details of the law of Moses; but it was also enriched by the teachings of the prophets and included a strong note of social justice and equity. This anticipation grew stronger as the day of Jesus drew near. Thus Simeon is described as "looking for the consolation of Israel" (Luke 2: 25), and Anna was among those who were "looking for the redemption of Jerusalem" (Luke 2: 38), while Joseph of Arimathaea is commended as one who was "looking for the kingdom of God."

Into such a highly charged atmosphere came John the Baptist preaching the kingdom. There is small wonder that he stirred to their depths the hearts of the most spiritually-minded of his countrymen. He struck a note of vital interest in the lives of those who heard him, and rallied and united those who looked for a new spiritual era led by a new and even greater teacher. He was one of the great pioneers of religious history, and did invaluable service in uprooting the old prejudices and breaking down spiritual barriers so as to prepare the way for the fuller and richer teachings of the Master. But close as John was to Jesus, he did not invest the idea of the kingdom with the wealth of creative significance given it by the Master. John declaimed against wickedness. He cleared away the undergrowth that had impeded progress. He cast up the highway. But the world still awaited the coming of Jesus.

With instant recognition of the value of a phrase which had a history and had gathered to itself the richest ideas and most spiritual aspirations of his people, Jesus took from the lips of John the Baptist the words which had aroused all Judea and the regions round about Jordan, and refashioned them with sovereign freedom. The phrase had a familiar sound to those who heard. It reminded them of the dreams and sacrifices of their national heroes. It reached from their remote beginnings and carried them far forward into the glory of the future where all humanity will own the sway of Jehovah. But it gained new wealth of meaning even as it led them along familiar pathways. It saved them from idle dreaming and called them to immediate and inspired world-building.

The Aramaic word commonly translated "kingdom" means rule or dominion. Speaking literally, therefore, the kingdom of God is the rule or dominion of God. But Jesus never gave a specific definition of the kingdom. Instead, he illustrated its characteristics by many parables and word pictures, the meaning of which becomes clear only as they are studied carefully and in relation to each other.

Probably the reluctance of the Master to give a precise definition of what he meant by the "kingdom of God" arose from his awareness of the limitations of language. Great men always give more expansive meanings to significant words than do smaller men. The "kingdom of God," therefore, meant more to Jesus than his disciples realized, because he knew more of the purposes of God which are to be achieved as the kingdom is extended. So Jesus did not try to convey his message in formal definitions about which men would have been splitting hairs from that day to this. Instead he indicated several lines of thought along which those who were eager to know could discover likenesses to the kingdom of God. He told them that the kingdom is like leaven hidden in a measure of meal (Matt. 13: 33); and like hidden treasure (Matt. 13: 44); like a merchant seeking a goodly pearl to obtain which he would sell all his other possessions (Matt. 13: 45, 46); like growing seed (Mark 4: 26-29); like ten virgins, five of whom were wise and five foolish (Matt. 25: 1-13). None of these parables exhausts the meaning of the kingdom, but all of them contain some germ of truth, understanding of which can be more fully achieved in expanding spiritual experience.

STUDY OUTLINES

THE KINGDOM IN THE BIBLE

LESSON PURPOSE

To discuss the influence of the kingdom ideal in the life of the Jews and its central place in the teachings of Jesus.

HIGH POINTS OF THE LESSON

The prophets were noteworthy for their insistence on the nature of true worship. This was a potent factor in elevating the national character of the Jews and in preparing for the coming of Jesus.

The Jews believed that the coming Messiah would inaugurate a reign of righteousness. Their idea of what would constitute the kingdom was patriotic rather than universal, for they could not think of the blessing of humanity apart from the restoration of the kingdom of David.

Jesus took the central idea of the kingdom and filled it with new meaning. All the teachings of Jesus and of the apostles view men as belonging together and as achieving their full spiritual maturity as members of the body of Christ.

Questions and Discussion Topics

(1) Refer to some of the Old Testament prophecies of the coming reign of righteousness. What were the major emphases in these prophecies?

(2) Did the Jews live up to the kingdom ideal? What was the effect of this teaching on their national life?

(3) What was the teaching of the prophets regarding the relation between worship and social righteousness?

(4) What contribution did John the Baptist make to the kingdom ideal?

(5) What did the term, "kingdom of God," mean when used by Jesus? In what ways did he enrich its meaning?

(6) Why did Jesus refuse to give a precise definition of the kingdom?

(7) In what way is the kingdom idea related to the doctrines of the church?

(8) What aspects of the life of the church, as revealed in the Book of Acts and the epistles of the New Testament, show the influence of the kingdom ideal?

What the Lesson Means Today

The proclamation of the kingdom has been a major factor in elevating the moral and spiritual standards of the church. We must not cease to set high standards because they are not always attained.

Every doctrine of the church should find its fullest expression against the kingdom background, and every ordinance should seek to promote the kingdom purpose.

The best ideals of modern men should be given spiritual significance in the building of the kingdom in our time.

Lesson Forty-four

II—THE KINGDOM IN MODERN REVELATION

On one occasion the disciples of Jesus came to him privately and asked him regarding the sign of his coming and of the end of the world (Matt 24: 3). Part of the answer of Jesus was the promise that "this gospel of the kingdom shall be preached in all the world for a witness unto all nations; and then shall the end come" (Matt. 24: 14). From the beginning of our history, Latter Day Saints have believed that this promise is now about to be fulfilled, and that one of the major tasks of the church is the building of the kingdom of God.

It is highly probable that the instructions given to Joseph Smith and Oliver Cowdery prior to the organization of the church, and particularly after their ordination to the Aaronic priesthood, included a great deal regarding the gathering of the Saints and the building of Zion. It is not only reasonable to suppose this in view of the importance which this topic assumed as the church grew in strength and spiritual power, but it also seems to be apparent from the way in which "the cause of Zion" is mentioned without further explanation in several of the early revelations.—Doctrine and Covenants 6: 3; 10: 3; 11: 3; 12: 3.

In the first months after the organization of the church, the word "Zion" was regarded as being almost synonymous with "church," although even then it was undoubtedly prophetic of the greater church that was to be. At that time Joseph was instructed to devote all his service in Zion, and was promised that to this end he would have strength. In a revelation received in September, 1830, the matter was further elaborated as follows:

> Ye are called to bring to pass the gathering of mine elect, for mine elect hear my voice and harden not their hearts; wherefore the decree has gone forth from the Father that they shall be gathered in unto one place upon the face of this land, to prepare their hearts, and be

prepared in all things, against the day when tribulation and desolation are sent forth upon the wicked.—Doctrine and Covenants 28: 3.

In June, 1830, Joseph had begun an inspired correction of the Holy Scriptures. While engaged in this work, in December, 1830, Joseph and his helper, Sidney Rigdon, received an extract from the prophecy of Enoch which gave great impetus to the movement toward Zion. This narrative relates that Enoch, the seventh from Adam, led the people of God to a land where they were especially blessed of the Lord because of their righteousness. Here the Lord came and dwelt with his people, who were called "Zion, because they were of one heart and one mind, and dwelt in righteousness; and there was no poor among them" (Doctrine and Covenants 36: 2). In the course of time, Enoch and his followers built a city that was called Zion, the city of holiness, which city "in process of time was taken up into heaven" (Doctrine and Covenants 36: 3). Yet the preaching of righteousness continued under the leadership of Methuselah and Lamech, the son and grandson of Enoch, who remained, and whose work was reinforced by the ministering of

angels descending out of heaven bearing testimony of the Father and Son; and the Holy Spirit fell on many and they were caught up by the powers of heaven into Zion.—Doctrine and Covenants 36: 6.

This revelation indicates that the whole course of history was unfolded to Enoch; and that when this early prophet "beheld the Son of Man ascend up unto the Father," he inquired when the Lord would again come to earth. In reply he was assured that in the last days, in the days of wickedness and vengeance and great tribulation,

My people will I preserve; and righteousness will I send down out of heaven; and truth will I send forth out of the earth, to bear testimony of mine Only Begotten; his resurrection from the dead; yea, and also the resurrection of all men; and righteousness and truth will I cause to sweep the earth as with a flood, to gather out mine own elect from the four quarters of the earth unto a place which I shall prepare;

a holy city, that my people may gird up their loins, and be looking forth for the time of my coming; for there shall be my tabernacle, and it shall be called Zion, a New Jerusalem.—Doctrine and Covenants 36: 12.

Under the illumination of these and other prophecies, the Saints turned back to the older Scriptures and read them with new understanding. Gradually, they came to recognize that the idea of personal salvation must give way to the idea of world redemption, and that no man must think of his own salvation apart from the extension of the reign of God into the lives of others. Even in spite of this, the ideal of Zion, as it came to be called, might not have become dominant in the life of the church had it not been for the revelations calling on the Saints to move from western New York into Ohio, and, later, into Missouri, where the center place for the "New Jerusalem" was definitely located. So long as men could think of the kingdom of God as an ideal achievement to be won in some distant future, they could content themselves with an idealistic rather than a practical interpretation of religion. Now, however, with the church committed to the establishment of a literal social order, centering in a specific place, the gospel of the kingdom presented a real challenge. It was a major missionary topic, and attracted many converts whose accession did much to strengthen the ranks of the church.

Various revelations gave considerable light on the principles and procedure of the gathering. There was much to be learned, however, which could not be gained from scrutiny of the revelations only, and which required a certain amount of experience. Just as the Zion of Enoch matured gradually through many years, so the Zion of these days must be achieved by patient continuance in well-doing.

Because the men engaged in the Zionic enterprise in this dispensation were human, they were always subject to the dangers of overemphasis. Some were so eager to win converts that they baptized people who were not genuine Zion-building material. Others were so eager to build the kingdom that they forgot that it is a major missionary project and accordingly failed to maintain their missionary spirit and work. Still others were engrossed in the idea that the building of the kingdom is an intensely practical affair, and they became more concerned about economic and political adjustments than about cultivating the spirit of fellowship, of sympathy, of mutual understanding, and of eager contribution. After a time disaster came, and men and women who had invested all that they possessed in the Zionic enterprise were expelled from the very land where they had expected to build the kingdom under divine protection. Quite naturally they sought the Lord for guidance in this crisis and were told:

There were jarrings, and contentions, and envyings, and strifes, and lustful and covetous desires among them; therefore by these things they polluted their inheritances. They were slow to hearken unto the voice of the Lord their God; therefore, the Lord their God is slow to hearken unto their prayers, to answer them in the day of their trouble. In the day of their peace they esteemed lightly my counsel; but in the day of their trouble, of necessity they feel after me.—Doctrine and Covenants 98: 3.

Yet in this same revelation they were assured:

Zion shall not be moved out of her place, notwithstanding her children are scattered, they that remain and are pure in heart shall return and come to their inheritances; they and their children, with songs of everlasting joy; to build up the waste places of Zion. And all these things, that the prophets might be fulfilled. And, behold, there is none other place appointed than that which I have appointed, neither shall there be any other place appointed than that which I have appointed for the work of the gathering of my Saints, until the day cometh when there is found no more room for them; and then I have other places which I will appoint unto them, and they shall be called stakes, for the curtains, or the strength of Zion.—Doctrine and Covenants 98: 4.

The hope of Zion therefore continued among the Saints; and as the promises of God are being fulfilled and the children and grandchildren of the faithful are returning to build up the waste places of Zion, this hope has been revived until it is now one of the dominant factors in the life of the church and the living promise which inspires and binds together both young and old.

Study Outlines

The Kingdom in Modern Revelation

Lesson Purpose

To show that the kingdom is central to the Restoration Movement.

High Points of the Lesson

Some of the kingdom ideas of the early Saints were crude, just as those of the Jews had been, but the Saints understood clearly that the kingdom was to be built on the basis of self-sacrifice, mutual concern, and joint achievement; and that their doctrinal beliefs and the building of the kingdom were inseparably connected.

The initial endeavor of the Saints to establish the kingdom failed because their philosophy was not yet matched by experience. Yet the hope of the kingdom remained and became a major factor in causing the return of the children and grandchildren of the pioneers under the banners of the Reorganization.

Questions and Discussion Topics

(1) When was the doctrine of Zion first taught among the Saints? What is the relation between the idea of Zion and the other beliefs of the church?

(2) What is the purpose of the gathering to Zion?

(3) What ancient leader was most successful in building a city of Zion? How long did the building take?

(4) What tendencies to overemphasize contributed to the failure of the early attempts at gathering? What spiritual lack was the major factor leading to disaster?

(5) Were the social and political traditions in the United States favorable or otherwise to the Zionic project?

(6) What reception was given to the elders when they advocated a literal kingdom of righteousness under divine guidance?

(7) What promise was given to the Saints regarding the future of Zion?

(8) What lessons are to be gained from the early experiences of the church in the building of Zion? What practices made for success, and what for failure?

What the Lesson Means Today

Every missionary endeavor should be an attempt to win people to a place in the kingdom of God, every family and every branch of the church should be experimental stations in Zionic living, every service should bring the Saints closer to the kingdom.

The goal of the kingdom must influence the methods of church life.

It should not be necessary for us to learn over again the lessons for which our predecessors paid such a great price. We should be familiar with the story of the past and use this as a guide in our present and future efforts.

LESSON FORTY-FIVE

III—THE SPIRITUAL NATURE OF THE KINGDOM

The kingdom of God does not consist of policies or programs, schemes or laws, but of people. The first movement toward the building of the kingdom is therefore to change the minds and hearts and characters of men. As this is done, programs and policies become necessary and important, but until this is done, their significance is entirely secondary. The world is full of movements designed to improve our material comfort without satisfying our underlying spiritual necessities. Of course we want these material needs cared for; but every movement looking toward their satisfaction which does not at the same time satisfy our spiritual necessities carries with it the danger of creating a sense of security which is not consistent with the actual facts. The first step toward the gathering does not, therefore, lie in the construction of a program for society. The first step is in winning men to a personal attachment to Jesus Christ. The best name we have for this first step is conversion.

The change in a man's mind and heart that we call conversion is intensely individual. It is an experience something like the day of judgment, for it requires that a man face his God without pride and without pretense. But the test of the reality of his conversion is its effect on his relations with his fellow men. One of the vital aspects of his own salvation is that he now recognizes his obligation to society by becoming a functioning part of the church. Now he is concerned with policies and programs and schemes and laws, but these are means to an end; and the end is the expression of the love of God which he feels in his own soul, and which urges him to include other people in his plan of life.

It is no accident that the chapter in the Book of Acts which tells of the wonderful outpouring of the Spirit of God on the day of Pentecost tells also how the converts shared their goods with one another. The unfathomable generosity of Christ laid such obligations upon the saints that only self-sacrifice could satisfy their deep feeling. This was no mere unbalanced enthusiasm, for throughout many years of patient obedience the spirit of unselfishness endured. In the first century of the Christian era, need was the only limit recognized in the Christian community. Charity began at home, extending to the place where church services were held and caring for the ministry. Then it extended to the support of widows and orphans; but the sick, the maimed, the weak and the poverty-stricken were never neglected. Harnack's translation of the *Apostolic Constitutions* outlines the work of the deacons of this period: "They are to be doers of good works, exercising a general supervision day and night . . . . they must ascertain who are in distress, and not exclude them from a share of the church funds, compelling also the well-to-do to lay aside money for good works." This spirit continued as long as the spirit of the new evangel continued, and throughout the Dark Ages there are a number of instances where individuals and small groups caught something of the early spirit and gave their lives in service to humanity.

The Christian method of redeeming society, then, is through building the kingdom of God. This kingdom-building begins with the conversion of individual people. It has its root in the change of heart and the uplifting of mind and the redirection of will which we have called the new birth. But while it begins in the heart of the individual, it immediately reaches out so as to include all men. It finds expression in a new order of life in which men live in right relations with their brothers, because they are responsive to the demands of their common fatherhood.

There are two sets of moral qualities which should be characteristic of every Christian. The first set we take for granted. It includes personal morals such as honesty, temperance and truthfulness. We all agree that anyone lacking these or similar qualities has to that degree fallen short of the Christian standard of personal righteousness. The second set of qualities marks the difference between the righteousness of the kingdom and the personal righteousness already mentioned. It has to do with the outgoing qualities of love, self-sacrifice, service, and the like. These qualities are of the very warp and woof of the Christian life and of the kingdom-building experience. If we fail to develop them, we cannot win the approval of Jesus, no matter how correct our private morals may be. Many of the people whom Jesus condemned for their meanness, their unkindness, and their selfishness were people whose private morality was above reproach but who were deficient in outgoing righteousness.

As long as passion, prejudice, fear, and suspicion remain in the underworld of the minds of men, unpurged and unpurified, reason and economic argument will flow over the nations without satisfying their more urgent needs. Trying to cure a nation of spiritual isolationism by passing out information is like trying to cure a man suffering from peritonitis by giving him a new suit of clothes. The only hope is in something that goes deeper than reason and overcomes ungodly passion by a passion for God and for humanity.

As the church takes up the work of the kingdom, she is thereby forced to go to the roots of evil, to attack it at its source, and refuse to be content with halfway measures. So the doctrine of the kingdom means a revolution in methods as well as a revolution in message. Love must be joined to intelligence. Wisdom and righteousness must reinforce each other. And growth in skill must become an accepted accompaniment of growth in grace.

The kingdom of God has to take form, and become concrete, and it is in the earth, in the life of the earth, that we have to express it and so make it real. To refuse to build it here upon earth is to be content with our dreams .... to shirk the cross, to be disobedient to the heavenly vision, and so be damned. Because we build the kingdom on the earth and with it, that does not mean that we build it for earth alone. Once built, it is a thing of beauty and a joy forever to God and man. But it must be built, not dreamt. The only bricks we have are made of clay, so we must use them.—*The Wicket Gate,* by G. A. Studdert Kennedy.

The building of the kingdom of God is the controlling objective of Latter Day Saint corporate life. This kingdom is different from any that has gone before. It will take over the best values of the present world order, such as industry, thrift, and delight in craftsmanship as the Christian dispensation took over the best values of the Mosaic period. But the kingdom is a new creation shot through and through with a new spirit and enlightened by a new understanding. It does not involve merely the association of converted men; but it involves their creative union in the body of Christ.

Study Outlines

The Spiritual Nature of the Kingdom

Lesson Purpose

To emphasize the essentially spiritual nature of the kingdom.

High Points of the Lesson

The tools of the kingdom are more readily available than they have ever been heretofore. The kingdom step needed now is spiritual rebirth.

The great task of Christian men is to break down the distinction between "sacred" and "secular." This will be accomplished when we recognize the high value of material things when used to further spiritual purposes.

The church is frequently referred to in the Scriptures as the kingdom of God. The church triumphant, over which Christ shall reign in person, is also referred to as "the kingdom."

Questions and Discussion Topics

(1) How may modern inventions aid us in building the kingdom? Illustrate your answer.

(2) Contrast the requirements of personal morality and of social righteousness in relation to the kingdom.

(3) What changes should our kingdom ideal make in the methods of church life and activity? Illustrate your answer.

(4) Discuss, briefly, the danger of calling an enterprise Zionic which is not truly of this character.

(5) Which values of the present world order do you think should be carried over into the Zionic enterprise? Which would you like to have eliminated?

(6) Enumerate some of the meanings which have attached to the phrase, "the kingdom of God." How are these meanings related to each other?

(7) In what ways can we eliminate the conflict between "sacred" and "secular"?

(8) In what way can we make our church activities more truly Zionic? What constructive suggestions do you have for improving our kingdom building efforts in the local branch?

What the Lesson Means Today

Improvements in our industrial and social relationships under the kingdom will go hand in hand with improvements in the quality of our righteousness.

Despite the deficiencies of our church organization and life, she constitutes the best guarantee we have of the coming kingdom.

The duty of interpreting our beliefs in Zionic terms still beckons us.

Lesson Forty-six

IV—STEWARDSHIP AND THE FINANCIAL LAW

Early in the experience of the church, the Saints were told, "All things unto me are spiritual, and not at any time have I given unto you a law which was temporal" (Doctrine and Covenants 28: 9). Obedience to the law of God with regard to finances is in many ways the best measure and means of spiritual life. The payment of tithing for example, as a joyous participation in the missionary work of the church, not only marks a man as genuinely concerned about the salvation of his fellows, but also prepares him for further joy in the work of God. All this was anticipated long before the Restoration, and the present practice of the church is identified in principle with what has gone before.

The principle of tithing was known among the ancients and was obeyed by Abraham and Jacob (Gen. 14: 20; 28: 22). It was commanded by Moses (Gen. 27: 30) and re-emphasized by Malachi (Mal. 3: 8). Although the law of tithing evidently has to do with one tenth of one's possessions, it is evident that even in the Mosaic dispensation the spirit in which this tenth was given was of major importance. The writer of the Hebrew letter hints at this when he points out that Melchisedec, to whom Abraham gave a tenth of all that he possessed, was "King of righteousness" and "King of peace."—Hebrews 7: 2.

We have the highest possible warrant for believing that the principle of tithing carried over into the Christian dispensation, for even when the Master denounced the hypocrisy of the Pharisees, he made it clear that they were under obligation to observe the law of tithing. He said:

Woe unto you, Pharisees! for ye tithe mint and rue and all manner of herbs, and pass over judgment and the love of God; these ought ye to have done, and not to leave the other undone.—Luke 11: 42.

Yet, notwithstanding his approval of the principle of tithing, the Master did not teach that our obligation to Divinity can be satisfied by payment of the tithe. On the contrary, he expected the entire life of his disciples to be dedicated to God. He was not content that the rich young ruler should contribute just one tenth of his possessions but told him to give his all (Matt. 19: 21). Zaccheus caught the spirit of Christianity and went far beyond the tithe, and Jesus commended him, saying, "This day is salvation come to this house" (Luke 19: 2-10). The early Christians did not stop with one tenth, but gave out of the fullness of their hearts, as is evident from these reports of Christianity in the first generation:

All that believed were together, and had all things common: and sold their possessions and goods, and parted them to all men, as every man had need.—Acts 2: 44, 45.
Neither was there any among them that lacked: for as many as were possessors of lands or houses sold them, and brought the prices of the things that were sold.—Acts 4: 34.

The apostles, who had been trained under the Mosaic system of tithing, caught the spirit of this larger generosity. Thus, John makes liberality a test of the genuineness of Christian love:

But whoso hath this world's goods, and seeth his brother have need, and shutteth up his bowels of compassion from him, how dwelleth the love of God in him?—I John 3: 17.

James also saw brotherly benevolence as a living fruit of faith. He said:

If a brother or sister be naked, and destitute of daily food, And one of you say unto them, Depart in peace, be ye warmed and filled; notwithstanding ye give them not those things which are needful to the body; what doth it profit? Even so faith, if it hath not works is dead, being alone.—James 2: 15-17.

Paul was eager that what was given should be given freely, "not grudgingly, or of necessity: for God loveth a cheerful giver" (II Cor. 9: 7), but he wanted these gifts to be gathered systematically (I Cor. 16: 1-4). Peter, also, was concerned that there should be no compulsion in this matter, except the compulsion of an inner sense of right. In rebuking Ananias for holding back the price of his land, he said:

> While it remained, was it not thine own? and after it was sold, was it not in thine own power? why hast thou conceived this thing in thine heart? thou hast not lied unto men, but unto God.—Acts 5:4.

These considerations lead us onto a higher plane than that of the Mosaic period, where we can appreciate the word of God in this generation.

Even before the organization of the church, the believers were commanded to "seek to bring forth and establish the cause of Zion" (Doctrine and Covenants 6:3), and Martin Harris, an example to the group, was told, "Thou shalt not covet thine own property" (Doctrine and Covenants 18:3). Within a year after April, 1830, great impetus was given to the gathering by the revelation having to do with the prophecy of Enoch (Doctrine and Covenants 36), which set forth the goal of Zion. This goal was then set before the church, and the Saints were reminded that the poor had complained before the Lord while the rich had been arrogant and self-sufficient, and that this was not pleasing in the sight of God.

After the Saints were established in Ohio, they received the revelation giving the basic law for the church (Doctrine and Covenants 42). In this and subsequent revelations, the following principles of the law of stewardship were outlined:

> The basic motivation of stewardship is love of God and men.
>
> Those who truly love God will remember the poor and consecrate of their properties for their support.
>
> Every man must be made accountable to the Lord as a steward.
>
> A major requirement under the law is the payment of one tenth of one's increase annually.—Doctrine and Covenants 106:1.

> The surplus created by stewards is to be used for the poor and needy and for the extension of the kingdom of God.
>
> Observance of this law is essential to salvation.

As the endeavor to establish stewardships moved forward, further instruction was given indicating the relations of stewards to each other and to the total Zionic enterprise. For example, they were invited to practice intelligent economy so as to avoid waste and free the products of their labor for the highest possible use. This instruction has been repeated as recently as one of the last revelations of the late President Joseph Smith, through whom the Saints were advised to "carry into active exercise the principle of sacrifice and repression of unnecessary wants."—Doctrine and Covenants 130: 7.

It is not possible at this point to enter into a detailed discussion of stewardship. It is well to note, however, the fundamental character of this doctrine in the religious life of the church, and the obligations and opportunities which it conceives as resting upon every member of the church. Stewardships is a spiritual principle and an economic method. As a spiritual principle, it lays on the steward the obligation of becoming profitable to God and to his fellows. As a practical procedure, stewardship introduces a new motivation into industry and economics. It substitutes the service motive for the profit motive and so places the conduct of affairs within the sphere of Christian living. It then calls for efficiency in management, and a sane and businesslike creation of goods and resources and their utilization for maintaining individual and group standards and extending the purposes of Divinity.

Stewardship is a solution to our industrial ills if it is made to work. This requires, first of all, genuine conversion; for stewardship is primarily a spiritual enterprise and its economic fruits are grown only from its spiritual roots. Altruism is the very essence of stewardships; but altruism alone will not make the work of a steward effective. Industry, thrift, intelligence, craftsmanship, management, and self-discipline must all play their rightful part.

Study Outlines

Stewardship and the Financial Law

Lesson Purpose

To show that the practical requirements of stewardship and the financial law constitute a test of our interest in the kingdom and form a basis for the finer achievements which the kingdom should afford.

High Points of the Lesson

According to the doctrine of stewardship, every man is responsible to God for the use of his talents and opportunities. The welfare of every steward is directly related to the welfare of every other steward.

The financial law is an elaboration of the stewardship principle. Obedience to the financial law introduces order, system, and self-discipline, gives wide opportunity to participate in kingdom building, and rescues ideals from dissipation by giving them practical expression.

Questions and Discussion Topics

(1) What do we mean by stewardship? What is the relation between stewardships and the kingdom of God?

(2) What are the fundamental principles of the law of stewardship?

(3) What does a steward undertake to give? What does he expect to receive?

(4) What obligations does the law of stewardship impose with regard to industry, thrift, intelligence, craftsmanship, and management?

(5) Discuss briefly the danger of emphasizing the spiritual aspects of the gospel without relation to its financial obligations.

(6) What is tithing? What is the purpose of tithing? By whom is the law of tithing administered?

(7) Are the financial requirements of the gospel satisfied by obedience to the law of tithing? What further aspects of the financial law apply to the well-to-do members of the church? To others?

(8) Summarize the advantages accruing from willing obedience to the financial law.

What the Lesson Means Today

The basic principles of stewardship can be practiced by anyone who is seriously concerned about building the kingdom. They can be more fully practiced as the Saints gather together and are organized under the direction of the Spirit of God working through the proper officers of the church and kingdom.

We lack many spiritual blessings because of our failure to utilize the privileges of the financial law.

The building of the kingdom has advanced further than some realize. The foundation has been laid in the hearts of many people. There is a widely apparent hunger for kingdom experience, and the way is being prepared.

Chapter XVIII

CONDITIONS OF PROGRESS

The law of agency—The law of intelligence—The law of eternal judgment.

Lesson Forty-seven

I—THE LAW OF AGENCY

WE LOOK AROUND US at the beauty of the earth and the promise of the seasons, and feel within ourselves the stirrings of immortality and eternal life. Then poverty and distress and ignorance and pain mock our high hopes and seem to challenge us to continue to believe. Every newspaper brings fresh evidence of disorder in individual and community life. Drunkenness, crimes of passion, the breaking of treaties, wickedness in high places, graft, war—these are on every hand. If we are to have a philosophy of life, which can be optimistic and encouraging in spite of such facts, this philosophy must not ignore the facts but must face them and discover somewhere in or behind them a promise which overrides their tragedy.

Nothing can justify such a world order as ours but sheer necessity. We can only believe in the goodness of God if we also believe that a godlike humanity is here in process of creation; and that its promise justifies the pain of its creation. This is just what Christian people do believe. With Jesus Christ our Lord we see men as the sons of God in process of growth; we see society as the dim prophecy of the kingdom of our God and of his Christ. "God hath chosen things which are not, to bring to nought things that are."—I Corinthians 1: 27, 28.

The difficulty with the present world-order is that it is organized apart from God. But rebellion against God indicates one thing clearly—that we have the power to rebel. Hence, we have some freedom. We believe that God has given us this freedom in an attempt to make us responsible men. As every parent knows, there are times when children must be permitted to make decisions for themselves, and must be allowed to bear the cost of these decisions. They may be advised, but they must not be coerced. Sometime they must be free to choose, and to suffer, and to grow. This is in the very nature of things. God himself knows no other way to work. If there had been any less costly way in which we might have been fashioned in his likeness, we may be sure that he would have taken it. But our Heavenly Father saw from the beginning that the only way to make us fit for companionship with him was to give us freedom to choose, or not to choose. He saw, also, that the final result—men and women fitted for his companionship throughout eternity—would be worth even the tremendous cost of the intervening immaturity and failure.

If we are to share the life of God, we must share his freedom of action. Agency may therefore be defined as the power of self-determination in the spiritual realm. It is personal responsibility in times of crisis, a responsibility that continues; for choices are not solitary but are linked together into a living chain. We grow only as we are free and know that we are free, and as we realize that this freedom means the power of self-determination.

Effective use of our agency depends on our intelligence. That is one reason for joy in the knowledge that "the glory of God is intelligence" (Doctrine and Covenants 90: 6). No one is free who does not see the choices involved in a situation. If I do not realize that the fork in the road which I am passing is really a short cut to my destination, I am not free to take that short cut. In the same way, if I am not alert enough to recognize the possibilities in a moral situation, then they do not exist so far as I am concerned. Because of this, it is imperative that we who hope to build the kingdom of God shall learn to approach life thoughtfully and critically, cultivating the ability to recognize the situations in which helpful choices can be made, and the strength to make these choices when we see them.

The right of choice belongs to every one of us. If I am to be free to work out my own salvation, my brother must be similarly free. Our freedom therefore must be relative, with restrictions imposed upon the individual for the good of the group. Moreover, we achieve our freedom together. No man is truly free on a desert island, for he must work so hard and live so precariously that all the finer opportunities of life are lost to him. Every energy goes to maintain existence, and culture never becomes a possibility. He is never free to talk with another man, to listen to someone else sing, or to engage in any enterprise which involves partnership. When such a man becomes part of a primitive community, he must give up some of the rights which he had while he lived alone, but in return for this sacrifice he is free to enter into the life of the tribe. This unity with the tribe, at the sacrifice of his personal desires, gives him an opportunity to do many things that he could not do otherwise, but he is still greatly limited. He cannot enjoy the privileges of modern city life, nor travel through the stratosphere, nor be arrested for creating a nuisance among his neighbors by running his radio all night. We modern folk must keep to one side of the road, we must pay heavy taxes, and we must be reasonably quiet when other people want to sleep; nevertheless, we are far more free than our ancestors. Thus we create a paradox: one of the first tasks of any people who would be free is the task of discovering and obeying creative restraints.

An important aspect of freedom appears here. Laws of restraint should prepare for and merge into laws of liberty. Though we may at first keep to the right side of the road grudgingly, because it is the law, we come to do so happily because it makes for speed with safety. Though at first we may do the will of God merely because we bow to his superior power, we must come to do so eagerly because we know that his will is our hope of the fullness of life.

As Phillips Brooks said long ago, many people have crooked souls, which are tied up in the bandages of constraint. As I look through the hospital ward of life, I hear men telling each other when the bandages will be removed from their particular lives. Some expect to be rich, some powerful, some learned. But I wonder how much inner life is now gathering behind their poverty and their lack of great power, and how many who long to be free have strength to be free. Suppose tomorrow all laws of constraint should be repealed, all social penalties remitted, all public restrictions abandoned, until nothing was left but the last legislation of character, would our unshaped lives fall back into shapelessness, or would some of us stand up with strength of our own? Would removal of the compelling force of external authority leave the way open for the glad freedom of an inner authority? Would it?

Agency operates on a constantly higher plane as we become more wise and strong within ourselves. Our freedom is advanced as we live in harmony with our insight into the purposes of life. We do not debate any more as to whether we shall lie or be truthful, be clean or be unsightly, be churlish or be friendly. We choose, early in life, to be honest, clean, decent, and friendly; and we relegate actions of this type to the control of habit. But on the higher plane there is constant need for choosing carefully. The wise man watches himself as though he were in the presence of God. He prays earnestly, searchingly, and frequently. He examines himself in the light of the divine presence. He decides on the course of life which careful thinking, deep feeling, and constant prayer indicate to be wise. Thus only can he find constantly greater freedom.

We can no longer choose to do many of the things that were possible to us years ago. I cannot choose to know about higher mathematics, about medicine, about the beauties of art, or about a thousand other things that once might have been available to me.

You cannot choose many things that were once possible for

you. The sinner, who steeps himself in sin so that it becomes part of him, and spends his life in passion and evil habits, is no longer fully free to choose the higher life. Something must happen to shake him free of himself, so that he is born again, or the hope of a better tomorrow is forever lost to him. If we would be free on the highest plane, therefore, all of us—since we are all sinners—need to avail ourselves of the power of God that makes us free from the habits of the past and enables us to form associations, to choose our environments, and to follow the impulses that lead to real freedom.

Sin is abroad in the world. We are living in a state of sin, in the sense that inducements to ungodliness surround us on every side and have become part of the life we live. None of us is truly free, for all our desires are tainted by the wickedness of the world in which we live and from which we draw our ideas and ideals. Jesus was the only man in the whole range of history strong enough to be free of his environment; and he willed to do the will of God. He was in perfect accord with his Father and was happy in that accord. He is, therefore, our picture of agency at its best. This is what we would want if we were free of the bonds of sin. The wisest course that we can take is to act as though we were free by choosing to be like Jesus. As Tennyson's "In Memoriam," says, "Our wills are ours, to make them thine," and a greater than Tennyson has said, "If the Son therefore shall make you free, you shall be free indeed."—John 8: 36.

Study Outlines

The Law of Agency

Lesson Purpose

To show that true freedom is achieved in intelligent acceptance of rightful responsibility.

High Points of the Lesson

God has laid on us the final responsibility for our salvation. We are free to choose what we will, but must abide by the results of our choices.

Our right of choice is limited by the similar right of other people. God also has rights. The fullest freedom comes when we willingly give God and our fellows their rightful places in our lives.

A wise man learns to practice the restraints necessary to his larger freedom.

Questions and Discussion Topics

(1) Why do we suffer from pain and ignorance and disease? Why does not God abolish these things and so abolish our suffering?

(2) Why is it important that we shall make decisions for ourselves? Do we really choose for ourselves unless we bear the cost of our choices?

(3) "What a man sows that shall he also reap." Is this a promise or a threat?

(4) What considerations determine the choices of a good man? What result always follows such choices?

(5) In what way is my freedom limited by the freedom of my brother? In what ways is my freedom promoted by the freedom of other people?

(6) In what sense is it true that one of the first tasks of any man who seeks to be free is to discover what restraints he ought to obey? Illustrate this.

(7) How do evil habits limit our freedom?

(8) What is the relation between freedom and self-discipline?

What the Lesson Means Today

No man grows by avoiding responsibility, or by accepting responsibility lightly. We grow as we choose to do right and learn more about what is right.

We cannot choose the end without also choosing the means. If we choose to share the mission of Christ we must by that fact choose to carry the cross with him.

No man is free who is ignorant, lazy or wicked. His limitations become his fetters.

Lesson Forty-eight

II—THE LAW OF INTELLIGENCE

It is extremely unfortunate that there have been times when men have set faith and intelligence in contradistinction to each other. Latter Day Saints who are in touch with the spirit of the Restoration Movement, and who are informed regarding the revelations, never make this mistake. Many years ago the word of God came to the church through Joseph Smith: "The glory of God is intelligence, or .... light and truth" (Doctrine and Covenants 90: 6). Ignorance has no program. We can only build Zion as a center from which the glory of God shall radiate to all the world, as we call to our aid "the rich and the learned, the wise and the noble" (Doctrine and Covenants 58: 3). In other words, we must start out with capital, knowledge, wisdom, and godly purpose. As will be seen, intelligence is a major factor here.

The intelligence which modern revelation defines as "light and truth" is certainly much more than mere cleverness. A rogue may be clever, but his cleverness is narrowed down by his selfishness, and he is not truly intelligent. This gives us a hint as to what intelligence really is. Is it not the way of life which takes into account all the known factors in every situation? If a man uses his brain to advance his own interests, as opposed to the interests of the group, it must be that his intelligence is not of a very high order, for he is leaving out of account some of the very factors most likely to promote his own welfare. In this world no man can live to himself alone, and any man who attempts to use his mental powers to outwit his fellows to his own advantage is a crafty man rather than an intelligent one.

Years ago a great many horses wearing blinkers could be seen on the streets. The purpose of these blinkers was to limit the range of the horse's vision so that he would see in front without undue distraction. The price that he paid was that he could not see anything except what was directly ahead of him. Today too many of us wear blinkers on our minds and souls. We look right ahead at immediate things, and pay the price in becoming selfish, callous, and indifferent to the larger areas of life. Whenever we rely on material things only, we have begun to die, for greed eats like a cancer, and materialism is the death of the Spirit.

As we think over the definition of intelligence in Doctrine and Covenants, we realize that intelligent living involves something more than expertness in special fields. It calls for excellence which is in harmony with the total purpose of life. It must not stop at mere knowledge, but must include wisdom also. No way of life is so unintelligent as that which leaves out of account the spiritual forces which determine our destiny. There is no realm in which unintelligence is so costly as in the realm of spiritual things.

Modern revelation assures us that the work and the glory of God is to bring to pass the immortality and eternal life of man (Doctrine and Covenants 22: 23). This marvelous truth is attested in our own experience, for there is a sense in which the glory of any man is in the perfection of his work. If he is a carpenter, then the greatest glory that can come to him is that he shall make a table, a chair, or a window which answers its purpose adequately and beautifully. If he is a teacher, the greatest glory which can come to him is that his pupils shall learn the lessons of life well and shall know how to apply them. Similarly the highest glory that can come to God is that man, his highest creation, shall act according to that divine intelligence which brings light and truth. In the final analysis, the intelligent man is the one who works in harmony with the purposes of God. The forces of the universe are harnessed to his spiritual purpose. No unworthy passion and no moral obtuseness vitiates the keenness of his understanding.

When Oliver Cromwell was about to leave home to take his part in the battle of Marston Moor, he had a quiet talk with his mother, who was a very wise, old lady. Brushing aside the more superficial economic considerations involved in the coming conflict, and trusting her to understand, Oliver said: "What men shall hereafter make of their lives must be between them and God in their own hearts, but today there must be given them the right to live as they most truly may in the light of their own proper character. No king can be against us. He may lead us, but he may not be against us" *(Oliver Cromwell,* play by John Drinkwater). With Cromwell, we say that the intelligent life is that in which men live, as they most truly may, in the light of their own proper character. Such an intelligent life calls to its aid the wisdom of the hand, of the head, and of the heart; and a divine understanding which comes in contemplation of the solemnities of eternity, which are greater than our minds can grasp but which nourish our souls.

So we come back once again to the words and example of Jesus. He is the way. His life embodies the final truth. Here is the supreme intelligence that we shall answer the end of our creation. Head, heart, and hand must each acquire their utmost skill; but life consists of more than these. It must be centered in the eternities. The wise man will demonstrate his wisdom by making every act count toward the enrichment of his entire personality, both for the present and the future. When this occurs, his life will be properly adjusted to that of his fellows. He will see the menace to his own well-being, which lies in his brother's lack; and he will satisfy his brother's need, both for his own sake, and because life and inspiration have conspired to teach him the higher wisdom of brotherhood.

Study Outlines

The Law of Intelligence

Lesson Purpose

To show that members of the church are under a moral obligation to act intelligently.

High Points of the Lesson

Intelligence is much more than cleverness or shrewdness. It involves progressive adjustment to the total purpose of life.

No man is truly intelligent who leaves the spiritual factor out of consideration in planning his life, or who chooses an immediate gain at the price of an eternal loss.

Intelligence is of the heart and of the will, as well as of the head. He is truly wise who thinks most clearly, feels most deeply, and works most devotedly.

Questions and Discussion Topics

(1) What do we mean by intelligence?

(2) Is it true that "ignorance has no program"?

(3) Why are wicked persons described as "lost"?

(4) What is the relation between temperance and intelligence? Between good will and intelligence? Between worship and intelligence?

(5) What is the purpose of our creation? In view of this what are the characteristics of intelligent life?

(6) What did the poet mean by his statement, "It is not wisdom to be only wise"?

(7) What is the relation between knowledge and intelligence? Can an uninformed man use his intelligence effectively?

(8) Which is the more important factor in real progress, keenness of mind or excellence of character? Discuss this.

What the Lesson Means Today

The Zionic enterprise must enlist intelligence of the highest order. This intelligence must be reinforced by such virtues as cleanness of mind and body, temperate feeling and action, etc.

Every man is under obligation to seek light and truth. Real intelligence will not stop at thinking, but will express itself in social action.

LESSON FORTY-NINE

III—THE LAW OF ETERNAL JUDGMENT

At about the time the church was organized, Martin Harris became greatly perturbed regarding the nature of the punishment meted out to sinners after death. He prayed very earnestly about this problem; and one of the early revelations through Joseph Smith gives the answer to his prayer. In this revelation, Martin was told that "eternal punishment is God's punishment" (Doctrine and Covenants 18: 2). Similarly, eternal judgment is God's judgment—the judgment of him who is eternal. When the nature of eternal judgment is stated in this manner, it turns our minds from the idea of duration to the idea of quality, and we note that eternal judgment is righteous, just, creative, and godly judgment.

Eternal judgment, then, is not only an event in the future, but also a continuing process. It is a principle of Christlike life and is the judgment of him who is eternal, even though it is practiced by men. In the British Empire, justice is administered by the authority of the king, and is called "the King's justice." This justice is dispensed by the properly constituted authorities of the kingdom in harmony with the law of the empire, and in the spirit of the empire. In a similar way we can pass the judgment of God on our own acts and contemplated acts. In order to do this, we must scrutinize our own lives as God himself scrutinizes them, and constantly readjust them to his will and purpose. We shall thus anticipate the great day of judgment and prepare ourselves to face that day with confidence and inner joy.

When we consider eternal judgment as the direction and disciplining of our own lives in harmony with the will and Spirit of God, immediately we note how closely this principle is related to the other aspects of effective Christian living. It is related to prayer, for example, for if we are to weigh truly our own acts, as God weighs them, it is imperative that we shall be constantly found in his presence. Here, unimpeded by the petty considerations which so frequently warp our judgment, we can gradually achieve willing responsiveness to his guidance.

In the home, in the school, in the office, in the factory, and in every other field of life our purpose is to develop and to apply mature and creative judgment. I try to teach my children to "see things steadily and to see them whole," and to face the facts squarely, not to be swept away by gusts of passion. The teacher tries to persuade her pupils to use the tools of learning wisely and to develop a fine discrimination and a cultivated judgment. The business man deliberately trains himself to recognize the significant factors in a situation and to decide truly and accurately on the course of procedure required by these facts. The scientist prides himself on his freedom from personal bias. He is willing to sacrifice all his preconceived notions, if he sees that the facts require him to do so. He trains himself to judge accurately every bit of evidence that comes to him, and to relate it to the truths he already knows. The statesman, too, as distinguished from the mere politician, watches international situations from the vantage point of the needs of his country and of humanity and teaches his people to so live that even the stars fight for their cause.

In the still larger issues of life, our essential task is to face the facts, to weigh them carefully, to bring to bear on them all of the wisdom and inspiration that experience, revelation, and devotion can give us, and then to adjust our lives in harmony with our expanding understanding. The task which is hinted in the home, in the school, and in the daily round must be perfected in life. If we are to live successfully, we must judge our own acts without bias, and the acts of our friends without resentment, and must exercise this judgment in self-discipline for ourselves and in constructive helpfulness for others. We cannot do this by ourselves but need the constant guidance of Divinity.

It has been said that law is God's way of loving us, and love is God's way of ruling us. This has been emphasized in modern revelation:

> All kingdoms have a law given . . . . that which is governed by law is also preserved by law . . . . intelligence cleaveth unto intelligence; wisdom receiveth wisdom; truth embraceth truth; virtue loveth virtue; light cleaveth unto light; mercy hath compassion on mercy, and claimeth her own; justice continueth its course, and claimeth its own; judgment goeth before the face of him who sitteth upon the throne, and governeth and executeth all things.—Doctrine and Covenants 85: 9, 8, 10.

There are well-known physical laws which we must respect if we are to live. Fire can destroy life. Water can destroy life. "He that believeth not shall be damned." In the same way there are laws of living together in the moral and spiritual world. There is the law of self-discipline, the law of service, the law of respect for personality, the law of devotion to the best—and he who does not believe in these laws and live accordingly, is thereby damned. This is what condemnation is, that we blunder through life and bark our shins on the laws of life when we ought to be using these laws to guide our conduct and to help us achieve what we want to do. In like fashion, the practice of eternal judgment involves patient study of the laws of eternal life and obedience thereto so that they become our servants and we become free and good.

However solemn it may be to think of our certain and dramatic judgment before the bar of God, it is an even more solemn thought that every day is a day of judgment. If you put your hand into the fire, you are judged and sentenced immediately. Fortunately, as Elbert A. Smith has pointed out, if you have not sinned unto death, but repent, take your hand out of the fire, and put healing lotions upon it, nature immediately begins to forgive you and starts the process of healing. Likewise, if you do a mean and contemptible thing, this becomes part of you just as surely as the burn became part of your physical body. You are judged for your sins now in that you now mark yourself as a sinner. This judgment continues until it is overthrown by the healing forces centering in repentance.

In considering the place and significance of eternal judgment, we must keep well in mind that it is the judgment of God. This judgment has been written, in part, into the nature of things. It is a judgment that we can learn to apply in our own lives. But behind these facts is the larger fact that it is the kind of judgment which God metes out to us. It is not unkind in any sense, nor is it rigid and impersonal, but it is inexorable. It is the judgment which our Heavenly Father passes on us—through the operation of law, through our own understanding and self-discipline, and in many other ways—in order to promote our eternal life. It is the application of the requirements of truth in action to our personal lives. If we are rebellious, it seems brutal, and our attitudes make us constantly more resentful; but if we really desire to learn how to live rightly, we realize that it is patient and understanding. When God judges us, he considers every factor in every situation. He weighs purposes that are unfulfilled as well as those which have come to fruition. His judgment varies according to situations; but it is always directed toward the well-being of the one who is judged, and it is pre-eminently fair.

The old law of an eye for an eye and a tooth for a tooth looks backward. It makes no provision for the betterment of an evil man, and provides no recompense for society. But eternal judgment is related to eternal justice and seeks to make justice prevail. It bears no malice. It looks forward as well as backward. It does not merely enumerate failures and measure exact penalties, but in understanding helpfulness it rewards or punishes according to our needs. It takes into consideration both the individual and the act, ignoring neither and recognizing both. It works to the point where a man becomes possessed of the Spirit of Jesus. If present forgiveness makes for future willingness to be just through the awakening of spiritual responsiveness, then this forgiveness is extended, and the future love of justice is guaranteed.

God is our Father, and with him family relationships are more important than any other. In the family, reward or punishment is not determined by the amount which any member of the family contributes to the whole, but by the spirit and quality of the contribution made. That which is done freely and out of love for the family is much more deeply appreciated than a greater thing which is done grudgingly and out of compulsion. The loving gift of the little child, bought out of his pennies, takes place beside the equally loving gift of the father bought out of his dollars. They are both tokens of love. So it is spirit and quality and purpose that counts. And the judgment that was passed, if we are to practice eternal judgment, must be a qualitative judgment and a spiritual achievement.

Repeated acts of inattention to the spiritual significance of life bring blindness to spiritual opportunity. Evil passions become constantly more powerful if they are not controlled and redirected. By wrongdoing we become constantly less able to discriminate between good and evil, the sensibility of conscience is diminished, and the more we sin the harder it becomes to forsake sin. In the physical organism, habits are built up which are well nigh irresistible; in the moral nature habits just as strong are built daily. This is no trifling matter. There is now immediate and urgent need for us to learn to judge our acts in the light of their consequences, and against the background of eternity, so that cheerfully, happily, with a sense of humor, and yet with an underlying seriousness, we shall extend that judgment into all the interests of our lives.

Study Outlines

The Law of Eternal Judgment

Lesson Purpose

To emphasize the wisdom of judging our own lives as God judges them and of adjusting them accordingly.

High Points of the Lesson

The practice of eternal judgment is a principle of effective living. God judges our physical transgressions instantly, by the operating of physical laws. He judges our spiritual transgressions just as quickly, by the operation of spiritual laws.

Life is a time of crisis. We need to be keenly aware of the eternal importance of the choices we are making.

Questions and Discussion Topics

(1) What do we mean by the principle of eternal judgment? Can such judgment be practiced by Divinity alone, or may we share it? Give reasons for your answer.

(2) Name some aspects of eternal judgment and discuss them briefly.

(3) What is the relation between eternal judgment and prayer? Between eternal judgment and faith?

(4) What is the relation between eternal judgment and the laws of God?

(5) What is the purpose of eternal judgment? What difference does our point of view make in our attitude toward eternal judgment?

(6) How can we learn to practice the principle of eternal judgment? Discuss this briefly.

(7) What is the relation between eternal judgment and the coming Day of Judgment?

(8) In what ways may the church promote the practice of eternal judgment?

What the Lesson Means Today

The Christian life is a thoughtful life. In it progress is achieved by careful scrutiny of our own acts from the viewpoint of God.

Eternal judgment is directly related to worship, for in the act of true worship we abandon all pretenses and strive to see ourselves as God sees us. The church is, therefore, under obligation to make worship a genuinely enlightening experience.

Acts are important, but motives are more important. We must seek out men of good will and arm their good will with understanding, as necessary steps in building the kingdom of God.

Chapter XIX

THE FUTURE LIFE

Immortality—Where are the dead?—The resurrection—The coming day of judgment—The millennial reign—The second death.

Lesson Fifty

I—IMMORTALITY

WHILE WE ARE YET YOUNG, emphasis on immortality and the future life is largely academic, but as we move on into middle age and beyond, we realize that the Christian teaching on immortality is beyond all price. When the death of friends and loved ones arrests us in the midst of our hurried living and forces us to think on the larger issues of life, we are astounded that we did not draw on this source of inspiration and courage earlier in our lives.

Let me say at the beginning of this discussion that our Christian emphasis on immortality is not an emphasis on otherworldliness. We do not have to wait until death to begin the practice of immortality, but we have already begun the life which shall endure through all eternity. There is no thought, therefore, of depreciating the values of this life in contrast with the values of the life yet to come. Life here and hereafter is the same life lived in different environments; the same principles and the same basic laws operate for time and eternity. One of the truths of immortality is that there is no time where righteousness and truth will be outmoded. They belong to the ages.

Life beyond the grave is not an artificial addition to this present existence, but is the natural continuation of life here. If a man is immortal at all, he is immortal now, and full appreciation of this fact deepens and beautifies and solemnizes the meaning of the passing days. So far we are only mastering the alphabet of life; the larger literature of life lies yet in the future. We can work now, laying the foundation and enjoying the opportunities of this present day, and so may begin tasks which will require eternity for fulfillment; and as we do this, we shall find that the assurance of immortality is constantly ripening within us.

Belief in God and belief in immortality stand together. It is not conceivable that our Heavenly Father would call us into existence and dazzle our eyes with a fleeting glimpse of the finer possibilities of life, and then let us perish. We become more and more certain, with every new insight into our Father's purpose for us, that men are essentially spiritual beings whose highest capacities and highest experiences transcend the limits of the world of material facts. We are not born of the earth alone; but are created for eternity, and for this our present life is preparation and part.

No reasonable person gathers the materials from which to make a violin, shapes its body with infinite care and skill until it is ready to send forth sublime melodies of the great masters, and then wantonly smashes this precious creation to fragments. No artist, inspired by a great theme, assembles brush and palette and paint and canvas, prepares a studio with suitable lighting, works with enthusiasm and skill until he has produced a great masterpiece, only to slash it to bits with his knife. It is similarly unbelievable that God will shape our lives at such infinite cost and with such minute care, only to dash his work to pieces at the behest of Death.

Belief in immortality is beset by many difficulties. This is to be expected, for we have had experience of this life only. Our difficulty in believing in life hereafter does not arise from the nature of the case. It is created for us by our ignorance of what lies beyond. From this difficulty we may be rescued by our knowledge that our best Friend has gone on before. In view of the love of God, we cannot doubt that tomorrow holds great promise for his children.

The completely convincing evidence of personal immortality, in the minds of the early Christians, was the Resurrection of Jesus. This is one of the reasons why the apostles gave the Resurrection such a prominent place in their teaching. To these men, who had a vivid consciousness of the fact of the Resurrection, this was a guarantee that in Christ centered the power adequate to their greatest need. So it was that Paul wrote to the Romans:

> But if the Spirit of him that raised up Jesus from the dead dwell in you, he that raised Christ up from the dead shall also quicken your mortal bodies by his Spirit that dwelleth in you.—Romans 8: 11.

Moreover, the life of Jesus, as well as his death, is ground for our assurance of immortality. In the words of Doctor Walter M. Horton, "Faith in the power and justice of God, plus faith in the reality and worth of the soul, equals faith in immortality." Jesus taught that every soul is of individual and infinite worth. Since this is so, then we can trust our Heavenly Father to see that every man's powers are conserved for the achievement of the purpose of God in him, insofar as that man will co-operate.

Man's personality is the flowering of the whole process of development. It is irrational to think that death is the end of personal existence, for if it is then man stands "half built against the skies," a germ, a prophecy of what should be but never can be. But if immortality is a fact, then the human soul, which is so full of beginnings, will some time find opportunity for pursuing these beginnings toward their destined end. It was Victor Hugo who said, "I have not done a thousandth part of what is in me. When I go down to the grave, I can say with so many others, 'I have finished my day's work,' but I cannot, no, I cannot say, 'I have finished my life.'" Many of us feel this very strongly. We know that another day's work will begin in the morning. "My tomb is not a blind alley; it is a thoroughfare; it closes with the twilight, to open with the dawn."

Long ago, when Socrates awaited the poisoned cup that would still his earthly questioning, he spent his last hours discussing the hope of immortality. Some who were there compared man to a harp, and the joys of life to the harmony which the harp gives forth. But Socrates, facing death, insisted that man is neither harp nor music, but the player who may turn from his instrument to a finer one, producing on each the music possible to his capacity. So, today, our assertion of immortality is not an assertion that we are earthly creatures who happen to have achieved immortality, but that we are naturally immortal beings, created to enjoy the music of the spheres; and that we are here a little while until we have graduated from this class into another.

The Bible calls death a departure or a time of "unmooring." Many of us have seen great ships tied to the piers while they are loaded with cargoes brought from many places, but all destined for one port. Then the captain takes the helm, the hawsers are cast off, and the ship heads out to the open seas. This is what takes place when a good man dies. The more we devote ourselves to those things which ought to be imperishable, and which naturally pertain to eternal life, the more certain we become that we are not outward bound, but homeward bound. We are not leaving home behind, but sailing for our home port. With this thought, the spiritual seers of the race have agreed. From Socrates to Tennyson, Browning, Wordsworth, and Emerson, and Whittier, the great poets and dreamers have joined their testimony in favor of immortality. Men divided from each other by race, by time, by civilization, and by temperament are one in their eager anticipation of life beyond the grave. While we may not agree with the details of their points of view, we must be impressed by the unanimity of their basic conviction.

Mere going on, however, is not necessarily desirable. Indeed for some of us to be awakened to the kind of persons that we are, and then to be condemned to live with ourselves eternally, will be the worst conceivable punishment for the kind of life that we have lived. The fact that life goes on, and that we must live with ourselves and our kind, should incline us to righteousness and to missionary fervor. We should build into our spiritual nature that strength and richness which will make eternal life an unending joy; and we should further share with our fellows these insights which inspire us and which can guarantee us their eternal companionship. And, once again, the more we do this, the more sure we are that our investments in righteousness will not fail of fruition.

For one who has learned to forget himself in loyal service to God and his fellows, the sting of death is removed. Such a man faces death as a good soldier. He is so intent upon his life of service, so completely lost in his cause that he has no fear for himself and hardly knows when he is hit. He commits himself to the God whose love has protected him through this life. He accepts without question his transfer from one front to another. He goes forward, expecting to receive and to obey further orders, and knowing that these orders will be rooted in love. "Who shall separate us from the love of Christ? . . . . Neither death, nor life, nor angels, nor principalities, nor powers, nor things present, nor things to come, nor height, nor depth, nor any other creature, shall be able to separate us from the love of God, which is in Christ Jesus, our Lord."—Romans 8: 35, 39.

II—WHERE ARE THE DEAD?

None of us know when or under what circumstances we shall finish our life here. In the long run, it does not matter very much. The important thing is that we shall be ready for death whenever it comes. In order to be ready, as well as from motives of curiosity about something which concerns everyone of us very deeply, it is quite natural that we shall seek to know what lies beyond.

This life is a time of testing and of decisions. Youth is the plastic period during which we make decisions which tend to become fixed in character as the years pass. There is no good reason for believing that the character thus fixed is greatly altered by the incident of death. We, therefore, pass into the life beyond with attitudes set toward good or evil. With an eternity before us, the amount we have learned or the distance we have run does not matter so much as the direction in which we are going—the quality of our manhood.

This life is important as the time during which we determine the trend of our development in time and in eternity. It is a period of probation, even for the heathen (Rom. 2: 14-16). Those of us who have sinned against a great light will go into the hereafter stunted and dwarfed. Those of us who have lived up to the best we have known will be ready for future knowledge and power and will receive it.

The Scriptures declare that when death overtakes us, the body is separated from the spirit, and the spirit of the righteous enters paradise, a place of happiness and rest. Jesus promised the penitent thief that they would be together in paradise immediately after their death (Luke 23: 43). Evidently, paradise is a desirable place of rest, for Paul wrote to the Philippian saints that he was torn between two desires, the desire to preach Christ and the desire to be with him (Phil. 1: 23). The fact that paradise is the abiding place of our friends will add to our joy there, and this is augmented by the thought that there we may meet the great men of other years, and may share with them the harvest of the ages.

The expectation of reunion in paradise with those who have preceded us may well be one of the major factors helping us to overcome the fear of death. I once spent one of the happiest hours of my life in conversation with a dear friend who was suffering from cancer. She knew that she would die shortly, and that the interim would be a time of great pain. Knowing something of my distress and of my reluctance to talk with her frankly about her condition, she herself opened the conversation. After a passing allusion to the immediate future, she referred with the utmost confidence and joy to the friendships she expected to renew on the other side and of new friendships which she wished to establish. With simple faith she said, "I always felt that I wanted to know Brother Joseph even more intimately than I did, but he was so busy that I feared to intrude. Now, after I have greeted my husband, I must seek him out and talk with him about many things that have troubled me. And, maybe, in God's good time, he will literally take me to Jesus.' " I have never seen courage so sublime, faith so unwavering, reason so clear, or life raised to a higher point of beauty and sweetness than on that bed of pain. If I had no other reason for believing, this experience would convince me that there is, and ought to be, rich and enlightening communion with "the general assembly of the church of the Firstborn."

In this place of conscious rest and peace, the righteous dead remain with opportunities for learning more of the principles of truth under the best possible instruction. It is not difficult to believe that in paradise those who have achieved refinement of spiritual character in this life minister to their less advanced brethren; and that they have rich opportunities for sharing their understanding and experience. Yet they look on their long absence from their bodies as a bondage (Doctrine and Covenants 45:2), and know that it will not be possible to express fully the good that they have learned until the spirit and the body are reunited and they again become living souls, eager to respond to the will of the Master with a body adapted to their needs and the quality of their ministry.

We believe that the spirits of the wicked go to a place of restraint and punishment called hell. There is no necessity for restraining those who are unconscious, and the fact that the spirits of the wicked are in the "prison house" implies both that they are capable of feeling and are in conscious suffering.

We shall do well to rid ourselves of two popular misconceptions concerning hell. The first is that hell is simply a place of torment. This is not true. It is a place in which men are capable of learning and of changing their attitude toward God and his work. It was for this reason that Jesus himself visited this prison house and preached to those who were incarcerated there (I Pet. 3: 18-20). There is no reason why they should be visited and instructed by the Master unless it was possible for them to respond to his preaching and in time to be liberated from their place of restraint.

The second misconception is that those who are confined to hell must remain there forever. This is directly in conflict with the teaching of the New Testament. The word of his resurrected Lord came to John:

> I am he that liveth, and was dead; and, behold, I am alive forevermore, Amen; and have the keys of hell and of death.—Revelation 1:18.

John looked forward to the time when:

> The sea gave up the dead which were in it; and death and hell delivered up the dead which were in them.—Revelation 20: 13.

The Apostle Peter was particularly aware of the opportunities of life beyond the grave; and it is through him that we learn about the ministry of Jesus to the disobedient dead. If Christ preached to dead men who were once disobedient, then here is warrant for believing that there is nothing in the event of death which changes his attitude toward us. The opportunities of this life may be gone beyond recall. But though we may never recover the ground we have lost, our Lord will help us, even in hell, if only we will turn to him. If any man is eternally lost, it will not be because God hates him, but because he is utterly rebellious and willfully chooses to continue in the way of sin, which is the way of death.

In the nature of things, wicked men must go to this prison house. To believe otherwise is to permit our sentimental concern for them to blind us to the facts of revelation and the requirements of morality. Hell has been called an asylum for the criminally insane. It is all of that. It is a place of restraint where it is possible to learn and where, having learned, it is possible to repent and prepare for the judgment and for the life which lies beyond.

In one of his most famous passages Canon Farrar says:

> Shall nature fill the hollows of her coarse rough flints with purple amethyst; shall she, out of the grimy coal over which the shivering beggar warms himself, form the diamond that trembles on the forehead of a queen; shall even man take the cast-off slag and worthless rubble of the furnace and educe from it his most glowing and lustrous dyes—and shall God not be able to make anything of his ruined souls?

Hell is the furnace in which these ruined souls are recast. Because they are living people, who have become what they are by the lives they have lived, the process is painful. There are no anaesthetics for moral surgery; but it can still be effective if there is moral co-operation. Hell is our last chance of such co-operation.

The difference between paradise and hell is so great as to urge us to make every effort to qualify for the former. This is not merely because of our fear of punishment. Perhaps one of the most disturbing thoughts in relation to hell is that those who are confined there are thereby condemned to live with people whose standards they may have despised, but whose conduct they have emulated. The inhabitants of paradise and of hell are two distinct types of people; those who are seeking to obey the will of God and those who are still in rebellion. Between them necessarily there is a great gulf.

Study Outlines

Immortality

Lesson Purpose

To show the wisdom of living in view of the totality of life, both here and hereafter.

High Points of the Lesson

Immortality has already begun, for we are now shaping our lives for eternity.

Mere continuity of life is not desirable unless it is enriched by comradeship with desirable persons in desirable tasks.

Character is not changed by death, except that freedom from the body may free us from the physical pull of some habits which we would like to abandon.

Questions and Discussion Topics

(1) When does immortality begin?

(2) On what grounds do we believe in the immortality of the soul? Mention typical arguments which confirm this belief.

(3) Who is the greatest argument for immortality? In what way is the life of Jesus connected with our hope of immortality?

(4) What assurance of immortality rises out of our belief in the power of God? What assurance rises out of our conviction of the worth of the soul?

(5) What happens to the body when we die? What happens to the spirit?

(6) What do we mean by paradise? What is the purpose of paradise?

(7) What do we mean by hell? What is the purpose of hell? Must a person consigned to hell remain there forever?

(8) What is the significance in your life of your belief in immortality?

What the Lesson Means Today

Death is inescapable, and may be imminent. Those who are wise with the wisdom of the ages make this life minister to eternity.

Quality is supremely important against the background of eternity. But sinful men can only achieve genuine quality under guidance, for the blindness of sin prevents us from seeing clearly. We shall be wise to accept the standard of values set by Jesus, and to incorporate these values into our lives for time and eternity.

Lesson Fifty-one

III—THE RESURRECTION

One of our most interesting and persistent legends is the story of the "Wandering Jew." According to the story, the Jew had been condemned by Jesus to live until his return, and he is depicted as weary of mortality, all his friends of an earlier day long since passed on. He sees every generation fearing death, yet he is utterly tired of life and seeks only release. We say this is but a story. Suppose it is; but let us for a moment put ourselves in the place of the wandering Jew. What a burden mortality might become. Not merely the multiplying of pain and physical maladjustments, but the long-continued presence of a living spirit in a decaying body. No one wishes to continue to live without the full and growing vigor of intellectual life, or to exist, physically alive, and incapable of further development.

Here, then, is a practical situation. What we really want is to live and to grow in wisdom and in understanding, to cultivate the arts and graces of life, and to achieve the refinements which make life beautiful; but we want this to be accompanied by perennial youth and by stalwart vigor. Has the gospel of Jesus Christ any answer to this need? I believe that it has.

Natural death is a cessation of the ability of the body to correspond with its environment, and, because of this fact, it includes a separation of spirit from the body (James 2: 26; Eccl. 12: 7). We believe that through the work of Jesus Christ there is to come a day of resurrection, when the body and the spirit will again be united and by that union the soul will be restored to full vigor of expression.

Our bodies are given us for a definite purpose. Their union with our spirits is necessary in order that we might receive the fullness of joy. But this fullness of joy is only possible when the intrusion of death can no longer interrupt our best work. In this life, where the body and spirit are not inseparably connected but may be separated at any moment, any work we attempt is subject to frustration by the caprice of death. Our major works of art, like the cathedrals, have to be left to others for completion; our ideals of freedom and justice are never expressed in their fullness but must await the contribution of future generations. But in the resurrection the spirit is joined to a body which is ultimately suited to its needs; and the fear of death is removed from all but those who are utterly rebellious. The achievement of this inseparable union constitutes "the redemption of the soul" (Doctrine and Covenants 85: 4-6), and gives us promise of sharing in the creative work which properly belongs to "the power of an endless life."

Such a reunion of the spirit and the body, inseparably connected, was first achieved by Jesus. It is true that he himself had brought back to life the son of the widow of Nain, the daughter of Jairus, and Lazarus, his friend; but each of these three was still subject to death. Their restoration to life was merely an extension of their mortality. Each of them had to die again. When Jesus rose, he became "the first fruits of them that slept" (I Cor. 15: 20), the first born from the dead (Col. 1: 18), and "the first begotten of the dead" (Rev. 1: 5). It is in this sense that the resurrection is to be understood. It is not merely a restoration to life. It is a guarantee of security in life; and of the opportunity to function through bodies fitted to our spirits.

The exact nature of the body with which we shall rise is not known to us, although revelation gives us a number of hints. Paul says that this body shall be changed until it shall become like the body of Christ (Phil. 3: 20, 21), that God shall give us a body according as it pleases him (I Cor. 15: 38), that the body with which we are raised will be one of "incorruption," "glory" and "power" (I Cor. 15: 42, 43). Perhaps an even clearer statement of the significant facts is that of John:

> Beloved, now are we the sons of God, and it doth not yet appear what we shall be: but we know that, when he shall appear, we shall be like him; for we shall see him as he is.—I John 3: 2.

One of the limitations of our present way of living is that because of the evil habits which have become part of our bodies, our understanding and our insight are impaired. If we are to "see him as he is," it will not be just a matter of intellectual understanding, but of insight based on righteousness which has purified our whole selves, both body and spirit.

In view of the differences between men it is not surprising that we find the Master teaching that the resurrection from the dead, though universal, is not simultaneous. When Christ shall appear, he will first redeem those who are ready to be entrusted with bodies suited to the needs of their spirits and secure from the threat of dissolution. Then, after an extended period, those of lesser quality who have had their extended opportunity to learn the lessons pertaining to immortality will in turn come forth and will receive bodies suited to their spiritual stature (I Cor. 15: 22, 23, 39-45, 52-57; Doctrine and Covenants 76; 85: 4, 6).

In the day when all things be made new, the earth itself will be transformed so as to become a fit dwelling place for those enlightened by the presence of the Father (Rev. 21: 1-5). "For this intent was it made and created, and for this intent are they sanctified" (Doctrine and Covenants 85: 4). In this perfectly adapted environment, therefore the righteous will live without fear, and will build toward perfection unmolested by the intrusion of death.

At the resurrection, we shall all be assigned to our respective places according to our works. Our destinies will not be determined by the arbitrary decree of Divinity, but by own natures. Every man will be raised "in his own order," or according to his own nature. Everyone will be quickened by the glory for which he has prepared, and those who enjoy a lesser glory will do so because they "were not willing to enjoy that which they might have received."—Doctrine and Covenants 85: 6.

The purpose of our Heavenly Father in our creation is to prepare us to associate with him and to participate in his creative handiwork. In order to share in such a work, we must be free, so that we participate by our own choices. Whenever we yield graciously to the beckoning of God, therefore, and learn his laws and continue in his ways, he builds constantly towards this ideal in our lives. For a time in this world, we are sent to school to learn the lessons of mortality. When these lessons are learned and we are prepared for the next grade, we are promoted by the Angel of Death. Then, having continued to learn in the period of consciousness between death and the resurrection, we are ready to take bodies fitted to our further growth. With eternity before us, we go forward in the likeness and under the tutelage of our Father.

Some are not willing to respond to the challenges of the abundant life. Although these refuse to pay the price of greatness, God continues to love them and to create out of them the best kind of persons that they will permit themselves to become. They, too, are graduated by death. They, too, go to receive further schooling in preparation for further life. As they become ready, they, too, are clothed with bodies suited to their needs. Only those who deliberately choose separation from the Father are finally excluded from his presence in what is known as "the second death."

So far we have been busy thinking through to the point where we realize what future is fitting for persons created with the glorious possibilities which have been given to men. But we do not have to rely on conjecture. In his own resurrection, Jesus has confirmed our highest expectations. The reunion of the spirit with the body, which only God can guarantee has already been accomplished. What we have been discussing is, therefore, not theory but fact. With growing gratitude, we realize that the life of Jesus is the prophecy of our own lives. He is our great elder brother, the pioneer of experience, who has gone before us both in the way of mortality and in the experiences of immortality. He who died and rose again brings to us, as one of his greatest gifts, the guarantee that we shall rise from the dead and shall live with him.

Death is a great adventure; but it is one in which the pioneering has been done before us. The man of faith must face it, not as Columbus faced his first voyage from the shores of Spain, but as those intrepid adventurers who followed him. He has little knowledge as yet of what lies across the dark vistas, but he knows that the way has already been traversed by one of his own kind, and that the promised land lies beyond. He knows, too, that the Columbus of our faith has not made the journey and passed on, but that he waits for us and lights our way.

The resurrection of Jesus is a fact and a prophecy. It is also a demonstration of a vitally important principle of the gospel, the principle of resurrection.

As we have already realized, our bodies are both aids and hindrances. They are aids when they prove fitting instruments for expressing our spiritual purpose. They are hindrances when the blindness and evil habits of the yesterdays, embodied in us, deter us from our highest purpose. This is what Paul had in mind when he wrote:

When I would do good, evil is present with me. For I delight in the law of God after the inward man. But I see another law in my members, warring against the law of my mind, and bringing me into captivity to the law of sin which is in my members. O wretched man that I am! Who shall deliver me from the body of this death?—Romans 7: 21-24 (See also Inspired Version.)

There is a sense in which we are "dead in trespasses and sin," separated from God by our inherent blindness and waywardness. Being dead, we can do very little about the business of living. Help must come from above. And for such as are thus bound in the chains of sin, there does come a promise of deliverance and a guarantee of power for new life. He who raised Christ from the dead can and will quicken our mortal bodies, so that we will walk with him here and now in newness of life.

Study Outlines

The Resurrection

Lesson Purpose

To show that it is scriptural and reasonable to live in hope of the resurrection, when the soul is redeemed by the reunion of the spirit and body.

High Points of the Lesson

The body is a necessary instrument of the spirit. So long as the spirit is threatened with severance from the body, we cannot receive a fullness of joy. It is the purpose of our Father to confirm us in the possession of bodies suited to our spiritual stature.

Death is a minister of love who prepares the way for our resurrection.

Every man will be raised in his own order. The true followers of the Master, and the honorable men of the earth, will come forth in the first resurrection. Others will be raised after a further period of preparation and instruction.

Questions and Discussion Topics

(1) What is life? What is death?

(2) With what bodies shall we be raised from the dead? Where shall we live?

(3) Why is it important that the spirit shall be inseparably connected with the body?

(4) Why were not our spirits and bodies inseparably connected from the beginning?

(5) Who will come forth in the first resurrection? Why?

(6) Who will come forth in the second resurrection? What is the purpose of the delay in their reincarnation?

(7) What do we mean by the terms "celestial glory," "telestial glory," "terrestrial glory"?

(8) What value does the church's teaching regarding resurrection have for our present life?

What the Lesson Means Today

The spirit and the body depend on each other to a large degree. Genuine Christianity requires that we shall care for our bodies as the temples of God.

Resurrection is a principle as well as a fact. We can prepare for celestial glory by living the celestial life. The order of our resurrection is being determined by our daily life now.

LESSON FIFTY-TWO

IV—THE COMING DAY OF JUDGMENT

Hell-fire preaching is out of date. We are learning that you cannot frighten people into goodness. Persons who turn from their wrongdoing because they are afraid are not good; they are just cowed. But if the church has outgrown the appeal to fear, she has not outgrown the appeal to serious consideration of the facts about life and death. The preaching of judgment, therefore, has an abiding place in the Christian program. Moreover, all the providences of God are for our good; and if we approach our study of coming judgment with this in mind, we shall find that here, as elsewhere, God is moving in love toward our salvation.

It is evident that a preliminary judgment takes place at death. When we die our bodies go to the grave and our spirits return to God (Luke 23: 43ff.). The man who has spent himself in accumulating wealth or power has judgment passed on his way of living by the very fact that his material assets are stripped from him, and the real man enters into the life beyond puny and weak and spiritually undernourished. Similarly, the man who has become strong in the powers and abilities which survive, moves immediately into a richer life than those who are not so prepared.

In addition to this judgment which takes place at death, reason and the Scriptures point to the coming of a great time of judgment when all men will be rewarded or punished according to their deeds. Thomas à Kempis has pointed out, many years ago, that this double judgment is an echo of our dual nature. "Every man," he says, "is an individual person and also a part of the human race. Hence he must undergo a double judgment: One immediately after death, when he receives award individually; the other that which he must undergo as an integral part of humanity." It is this general judgment that we wish to discuss in this chapter.

There are few subjects concerning which Jesus speaks more frequently or at greater length than the judgment. Indeed in the mind of Jesus judgment is the necessary resultant of the nature of God. Jesus repeatedly emphasized the importance of choosing the right and avoiding the wrong. The thought of the coming judgment follows naturally. A day shall come in which the injustice of the world will be righted, and men will be rewarded according to the demands of justice, by One who sees beyond our acts to the purpose behind them.

Many years ago I read the story of a dream. It ran something like this:

I thought, in my dream, that I was one of a great number of people moving urgently toward a point where a small crowd had already gathered. I noticed, to my surprise, that all kinds of people were on their way. There were no horses, and no cars, but every man and woman walked purposefully in the same direction. At last we arrived, and I had time to whisper to my neighbor, "Why are we all here?" "Hush," he said, "and listen. Don't you know it's Measuring Day?"

It was not long until we had all arrived, and a man, who appeared to have been waiting for us stepped forward and stood beside a rather tall standard which was clearly marked so as to show various heights. This man explained quietly that today was measuring day and that everyone was required to be measured. Nothing was said about the order in which the proceedings should be carried out. Indeed, the person in charge seemed to want us to co-operate as fully as we would. One thing, however, was certain; everyone there, man and woman, old and young, rich and poor, famous and unknown, stood that day on a basis of equality. Everyone must be measured.

At first it seemed that no one was willing to go forward. After a time, seeing the hesitation of the people around, one of our best-known men, and a man whom I had always greatly admired, said, "Well, it has to be done, and I guess I might as well lead the way." With that he stepped forward. Then a strange thing happened. As he stood out from the crowd, he seemed to be thinner and smaller and more shrunken than I had ever before known him to be, and, to my astonishment his appearance seemed to grow worse the nearer he went to the standard. I could hardly believe my eyes, but he actually was shrinking perceptibly with each step he took, and when he finally stood beside the standard, it was only with the greatest difficulty that he reached up to one of the lower markings. The one in charge gravely noted the measurement in a great book, and my important friend came back to join us. As he returned he resumed his usual proportions, but I could see that something had happened inside him. Something of his old assurance was gone.

As I watched my discomfited friend, I noted a stir on the other side of the crowd, and there soon emerged a man everyone recognized as the most persistent public opponent of the man who had just been measured. This second man started out with just as much assurance as the other had displayed, but the same thing happened to him and he, too, seemed to shrink before our eyes. Once again it was only with the utmost difficulty, standing on his toes and stretching up to his full height, that he was able to reach even one of the lower marks. As he retreated, shamefacedly, I heard someone behind me whispering, "It is rather absurd of him to try to make himself out to be more than he actually is. That standard measures you just as you are."

After this there was quiet for a long moment. No one seemed willing to submit to measurement when two such prominent men had failed so ignominiously. The person in charge smiled then toward a man not far from me and said, "Will you not lead the way now, please?" At the word, this man stood forward. I noted that he was about average size and not specially distinguished by his dress or appearance, except for one thing; his face radiated intelligence and kindliness. As I looked at him, I became aware of a quiet vigor wedded to a kindly good humor. Without comment the man moved forward, and as he went he grew before us. There was no pretense, no stretching so as to obtain a high mark; just a quiet and willing submission to the test. Without any of the efforts so apparent in the two who had preceded him, he far outreached the mark which they had attained. I thought to myself, "I would like to meet that man," but before I could do anything about it, I heard the person calling my name and saying, "Will you not come forward now, please?"

This story is simplicity itself. There is no attempt to portray the majesty of God or the awe which all must feel in approaching his presence. There is no indication of the clear insight upon the part of the people to be judged, which will make them recognize that the judgment passed on them is just and right. There is no consignment of each man to the life which he has merited by the character which he had achieved. The story, nevertheless, brings out two or three basic facts about the great judgment: It is inevitable and cannot be escaped; it is impartial and will be passed on all men without regard to their reputations or pretentions; it is unerring, piercing through shams and pretenses, ignoring the undue modesty of simple people whose work has never before been recognized.

The more we think of the Christian doctrine of judgment, the more necessary it seems to be. In any well-ordered system the punishment corresponds with the crime, and reward with right doing, or the system itself is irrational. As we have seen, our fundamental faith is that this world was intended to be a school in which men can come to know and love God. The laws which govern the life of the universe are paralleled by laws which operate in human life and which are just as irresistible. This is just another way of saying that judgment is inescapable. It is tied up with the system of life. The inevitability of judgment is both a warning and a promise.

President Joseph Smith was very fond of saying that he did not wish to "scrape into the kingdom," but that he hoped to merit an "abundant entrance" into the presence of God. Those of us who have read Vachel Lindsay's poem on "General Booth Enters Heaven," will understand better what President Smith meant. The basis of judgment will be the kind of life we have lived, and the kind of character we have achieved. We shall be judged according to "the deeds done in the body." Destiny will be determined by the character which we have developed; we will be quickened by the glory for which we have prepared. Those who enter into a lesser degree of life will do so because they were not "willing to enjoy that which they might have received" (Doctrine and Covenants 85: 6). Every man will be "raised in his own order" (I Cor. 15: 23), and while this applies primarily to the resurrection itself, it applies also to the judgment which will be passed on us at that final day.

If we agree that the stability of the moral order requires that good shall be rewarded and evil shall be punished, and since this does not occur in this life, there must be a final judgment where it does happen, we are immediately confronted with a second important question, "Who shall be the judge?" Evidently whoever does the judging must be impartial, but he must also be sympathetic. He must understand both the persons to be judged and the real significance of the reward or punishment. Who measures up to this requirement but Jesus? He knows the full story, and he sets the same value on men and women as he did when he was here. We believe, then, as reasonable people, the scriptural teaching that we are all to be judged by the One who loves us best, and who is most concerned about our eternal destiny.

Jesus is both the judge and the standard of judgment. The character and personality of Jesus are the ultimate standards for humanity; and we must be judged by our approximation to these standards. Business men like to apply a pale shadow of the standard of Christ to applicants for employment, asking searching questions about honesty, integrity, and dependability. On the day of judgment, we shall confront the living standard; and though we may not measure up very well, there will be no appeal for us or against us. The Judge will know; we shall know both that he knows the facts and their significance, and that he is judging us fairly and accurately.

Reward and punishment are in the nature of things. They are not arbitrarily attached to acts with which they have no particular connection, as is sometimes the case in human courts of justice. We are not called before the judgment bar of God and sentenced to pay a fine or to spend so many years in prison, in accordance with some arbitrary standard which has no relation to the kind of person we are. What happens is that opportunities are given us or withheld from us in accordance with our essential nature, and we are required to associate with persons of our own caliber, persons who have chosen to live on the same level of life we have chosen. The rewards and punishments of Divinity are the working out in us, through law, of the consequences of the way of life which we have chosen.

The Apostle Peter wrote that the saints of his day lived by virtue of certain "great and precious promises" (II Pet. 1: 4). Surely one of these great and precious promises was the assurance of vindication in the great day of judgment. We may have similar assurance, and look forward with confidence to the commendation: "Well done, thou good and faithful servant; thou hast been faithful over a few things, I will make thee ruler over many things; enter thou into the joy of thy Lord" (Matt. 25: 21). Not in the spirit of fear, therefore, but as those who face the necessities of moral control being ordained of God, let us live happily and in full expectation of the coming day of judgment.

STUDY OUTLINES

THE COMING DAY OF JUDGMENT

LESSON PURPOSE

To state clearly the fact of the coming judgment, to indicate the basis of judgment, and to emphasize the importance of living in view of the judgment.

HIGH POINTS OF THE LESSON

Since God presides over the destinies of humanity, the day must come when inequalities will be righted, and each man shall enter into his own proper place.

When Jesus assigns us to our eternal destiny, he will not judge as one who is untouched by our infirmities, but as one who has shared our life.

The doctrine of the judgment is not a threat to frighten us into right doing, but a promise to assure us that righteousness shall not fail of its reward.

QUESTIONS AND DISCUSSION TOPICS

(1) What preliminary judgments do we all undergo? What is their purpose?

(2) What are the characteristics of the great Day of Judgment?

(3) What do we mean when we say that God is an impartial judge? When we say that he is just?

(4) Will the judgment be primarily a matter of bookkeeping or of assessment of character? Discuss this briefly.

(5) What pre-eminent qualifications does Jesus possess as the judge of all men?

(6) Is divine punishment always remedial? Discuss this briefly.

(7) What is the present practical significance of the doctrine of judgment?

(8) What is the relation between mercy and justice in the final judgment?

What the Lesson Means Today

The judgment of God is clear-sighted. It pierces behind acts to motives, and yet recognizes that good intentions are not enough. In view of this our false pretenses and affectations seem very trivial.

Nothing really matters but actual goodness. As we look back on our lives from the vantage point of the throne of God, how topsy-turvy our present standard of values will seem. Why do we not adjust it now?

Lesson Fifty-three

V—THE MILLENNIAL REIGN

The preaching of "this gospel of the kingdom" in all the world and the gathering together of the righteous will immediately precede the return of our Lord and the beginning of his personal reign on earth. This is the clear teaching of the Scriptures, and becomes more and more apparent as we try to look into the future in the light of our knowledge of the past. The personal and visible return of the Lord Jesus Christ, the resurrection of the just, and the inauguration of the period of righteousness and co-operation referred to in prophecy as the millennium, or the millennial reign are so near at hand that the intervening period was called "today" a hundred years ago. The Lord said:

> Behold, now it is called today until the coming of the Son of Man, and verily it is a day of sacrifice, and a day for the tithing of my people.—Doctrine and Covenants 64: 5.

The Prophet Enoch foresaw many of the events of these last days, and a partial account of his vision has been preserved for us in modern revelation. This record says that the city of Zion, the New Jerusalem, will be built in the last days; and that righteousness and truth will "sweep the earth as with a flood" to gather out the elect from the farthermost parts of the earth to a place where they can prepare for the return of Jesus. The prophecy continues:

> Then shall you [Enoch] and all your city meet them there, and we will receive them into our bosom, and they shall see us, and we shall fall upon their necks, and they shall fall upon our necks, and we shall kiss each other and there shall be my abode, and it shall be Zion which shall come forth out of all the creations which I have made, and for the space of a thousand years shall the earth rest.—Doctrine and Covenants 36: 13.

During this millennial era, even the enmity of man and beast will cease, for "the wolf also shall dwell with the lamb, and the leopard shall lie down with the kid, and the calf and the young lion and the fatling together; and a little child shall lead them . . . . for the earth shall be full of the knowledge of the Lord, as the waters cover the sea" (Isa. 11: 6-9). We are also told that Satan will be "bound," having no power over the righteous (Rev. 20: 2).

The triumph of the righteous will be so complete that there will be no wicked among them (Doctrine and Covenants 28: 2). Under these conditions the Master will not just visit the earth occasionally, but will actually "dwell in righteousness with men on the earth a thousand years" (Doctrine and Covenants 28: 2). The life of the race will be one of righteousness and peace, with men working under Christ, according to their several abilities, in administering the affairs of men (Luke 19: 17-26). In many ways the situation will be comparable to that in the Zion of Enoch's time, and to the period of Nephite righteousness following the ministry of Jesus on the American continent (4 Nephi 14-26).

Among the resurrected dead who are on the earth at this time will be many who yet remain in mortality. Yet the significance of earthly life will be so different by reason of the outpouring of the Spirit of God, the presence and companionship of the righteous of all ages, and the personal guidance of the Master, that many of those born during this period will partake of the spirit that prevails, and it will not be necessary for them to go down to the grave in death, but they "shall be changed in the twinkling of an eye."—Doctrine and Covenants 63: 13.

Before the millennium begins, the earth will be cleansed of much that is corrupt and vile. It is not clear just what degree of perfection must be attained by those who are permitted to remain; yet the various prophecies indicate that many will remain in mortality who are not yet members of the church and professed followers of Jesus Christ. The Prophet Zechariah, for example, makes it clear that some will be left from among those who previously fought against Jerusalem (Zech. 14: 16-.

19). The wicked will be destroyed, yet there are many among all nations who are not wicked in the sense in which the word is here used. They may have partaken of their worldly environment, yet may not have been persistent and malicious in their opposition to the things of God. There will be enough in this class left to constitute "many nations," and they will say,

> Come, let us go up to the mountain of the Lord, and to the house of the God of Jacob; and he will teach us of his ways, and we will walk in his paths; for the law shall go forth of Zion, and the word of the Lord from Jerusalem.—Mic. 4: 1-4.

These nations will learn and Christ will judge among them, and they "shall beat their swords into ploughshares, and their spears into pruning hooks." They shall learn war no more, but peace and righteousness shall prevail, and "they shall sit every man under his vine and under his fig tree; and none shall make them afraid."

Among those participating in the first resurrection will be righteous men whose glory is compared to the sun, and who will be clothed with celestial bodies, together with the "honorable men of the earth" (Doctrine and Covenants 76: 6), who have not merited the full glory of the celestial kingdom, but who have been given bodies of the terrestrial order. All of these, secure from the ravages of death and strong in the character developed on earth and matured in the period between death and the resurrection, will share the life of the millennium under the personal guidance of Jesus, and will minister to those who are yet mortal and who have not yet achieved spiritual maturity.

The hope of the millennium is the hope which lies near to the heart of all the people of God, as a demonstration of righteousness under the immediate and visible direction of Divinity and without the blinding hindrance of sin. It is not possible to imagine the exact conditions of that day. Indeed, there is no profit in so doing; but there is great profit in the assurance which the millennium brings to us. It is the assurance that though death may intervene, yet the righteous shall have an opportunity to work and worship together under the guidance of Jesus. Much of the curse of sin will be removed. There will yet be much to learn, but children will "grow without sin unto salvation" the conflict between man and beast will have passed away, and

> New arts shall bloom of loftier mold
> And mightier music thrill the skies.
> And every life shall be a song
> When all the earth's a paradise.

The Scriptures tell us that the millennium will continue for many years, but that finally Satan will be loosed for a little season, and will resume his work of deception. This is an important illustration of the fundamental nature of our agency. Even in the millennium, we will be free to choose our way of life. Satan is not bound or loosed according to a calendar of events predetermined in heaven, but according to the righteousness or unrighteousness of the children of God. When Satan is bound, it will be by the power of God made manifest in the godliness of his people. And when he is loosed, it will be because men have again yielded to the blandishments of evil.

But the Scriptures also tell us that although men will again rebel against God at the close of the millennial era and will increase in wickedness and fight against Zion until the end of the world, there shall then "be a new heaven and a new earth; and they shall be like unto the old save the old has passed away, and all things have become new."—Ether 6: 8, 9; Rev. 21: 4, 5.

VI—THE SECOND DEATH

In the great judgment which we have already considered every man will receive justice at the hands of his Creator. It is one of the basic aspects of our belief that here, at least, men will be rewarded or punished according to the deeds done in the body. Careful reading of the Scriptures, and particularly the marvelous revelation given Joseph Smith and Sydney Rigdon in this connection (Doctrine and Covenants 76), shows us that it will be possible for the vast majority of those judged to receive a reward of some kind, the glory of the sun, the glory of the moon, or the glory of the stars (I Cor. 15: 41, 42). There will, however, be some who will not be fitted for any degree of glory; as it is written, "He that is unjust, let him be unjust still; and he that is filthy, let him be filthy still" (Rev. 22: 11). These are known in Scripture as the "sons of perdition," and the judgment passed on them is called the second death (Rev. 21: 8).

Eternal life consists in knowing God and his Son Jesus Christ. The second death is therefore best described as complete separation from God and from his Son Jesus Christ. This does not necessarily mean that those consigned to this second death will lose all knowledge of Divinity, but it does mean that they will lose all response to the kindly ministries of Divinity. Many years ago Paul wrote to the Romans:

> To whom ye yield yourselves servants to obey, his servants ye are to whom ye obey; whether of sin unto death or of obedience unto righteousness . . . . for the wages of sin is death; but the gift of God is eternal life through Jesus Christ our Lord.—Romans 6: 16, 23.

Those who shall have part in the second death shall have chosen to obey Satan and shall have persisted in this choice and therefore shall have been consigned to his domain.

Our understanding of the fatherhood of God carries with it expectation of his infinite readiness to forgive men. There is no limit to the number of times that our Heavenly Father will accept our repentance and encourage us to begin again. As long as we are capable of returning to him, he will be willing to receive us. The time may come, nevertheless, when our Father will be driven to reject some of his sons. Every man will have the fullest opportunity of knowing God, and of making his peace with him in this life or beyond it. But if a man persists in refusing his spiritual opportunities and sins against the light until he finally destroys all the good that was in him, and takes evil to be his good and Satan to be his god, what can be his final end but to be banished from the presence of the Father? (See Charles Gore in *The Creed of the Christian.*) This does not mean that there is a point at which our Heavenly Father becomes vindictive. But it does mean that sin carries its inexorable penalty of death.

The prophets and seers of every age have evidently held this second death in unabated horror. The ancient American prophet, Samuel, warned his hearers against it:

The resurrection of Christ redeemeth mankind, yea, even all mankind, and bringeth them back into the presence of the Lord; yea, and it bringeth to pass the conditions of repentance, that whosoever repenteth, the same is not hewn down and cast into the fire; but whosoever repenteth not, is hewn down and cast into the fire, and there cometh upon them again a spiritual death, yea, a second death, for they are cut off again as to things pertaining to righteousness.—Helaman 5: 71-73.

Both reason and revelation therefore teach us that there is a place of punishment more to be dreaded than death or hell. The writer of the Hebrew letter said:

He that despised Moses' law died without mercy under two or three witnesses; Of how much sorer punishment, suppose ye, shall he be thought worthy, who hath trodden under foot the Son of God, and hath counted the blood of the covenant, wherewith he was sanctified, an unholy thing, and hath done despite unto the Spirit of grace?—Hebrews 10: 28, 29.

Perhaps the clearest teaching of the Scriptures, however, is to be found in a revelation received at Kirtland Temple:

Thus saith the Lord, concerning all those who know my power, and have been made partakers thereof, and suffered themselves, through the power of the Devil, to be overcome, and to deny the truth, and defy my power; they are they who are the sons of perdition, of whom I say it had been better for them never to have been born; for they are vessels of wrath doomed to suffer the wrath of God, with the Devil and his angels, in eternity, concerning whom I have said there is no forgiveness in this world nor in the world to come; having denied the Holy Spirit, after having received it, and having denied the only begotten Son of the Father; having crucified him unto themselves, and put him to an open shame: these are they who shall go away into the lake of fire and brimstone, with the Devil and his angels, and the only ones on whom the second death shall have any power; yea, verily, the only ones who shall not be redeemed in the due time of the Lord, after the sufferings of his wrath; for all the rest shall be brought forth by the resurrection of the dead, through the triumph and the glory of the Lamb, who was slain, who was in the bosom of the Father before the worlds were made . . . . they shall go away into everlasting punishment, which is endless punishment, which is eternal punishment, to reign with the Devil and his angels in eternity, where their worm dieth not and the fire is not quenched, which is their torment, and the end thereof, neither the place thereof, nor their torment, no man knows; neither was it revealed, neither is, neither will be revealed unto man, except to them who are made partakers thereof; nevertheless, I, the Lord, show it by vision unto many; but straightway shut it up again; wherefore the end, the width, the height, the depth, and the misery thereof, they understand not, neither any man except them who are ordained unto this condemnation. And we heard the voice saying, Write the vision, for lo, this is the end of the vision of the suffering of the ungodly!—Doctrine and Covenants 76: 4.

There is no need to dwell at length on this theme, except to note that the second death is but the working out on the negative side of principles which bring great happiness to many. The agency which, rightly used, will enable us to stand unashamed in the presence of God will cause us to be separated from him eternally if we abuse it; but we shall not be utterly cast out until we have known something of the testimony of the Spirit. If we know the truth and deliberately and persistently choose evil, we can never enjoy the presence and blessing of Divinity, worlds without end.

Study Outlines

The Millennial Reign and the Second Death

Lesson Purpose

To epitomize the teaching of the Scriptures regarding the millennial reign and the final destiny of the unrepentant.

High Points of the Lesson

The visible return of the Lord Jesus Christ and the resurrection of the just will inaugurate the millennium.

Among the resurrected dead who live during the millennium will be many others who yet remain in mortality.

After the close of the millennium, the little season when Satan will again be loosed, and the second resurrection and judgment, a small number who continue to be rebellious will be assigned to the second death. Abuse of their agency will bring eternal separation from Divinity.

Questions and Discussion Topics

(1) What do we mean by the millennium? What great events will precede it? When will it begin?

(2) What ancient prophets foresaw the millennium? What characteristics of the millennial reign did they emphasize?

(3) Describe, in a general way, conditions on the earth during the millennium. Who will inhabit the earth at that time?

(4) What will happen to those born during the millennium?

(5) What does John the Revelator mean by his statement that Satan will be "bound" for the period of the millennial reign?

(6) Describe conditions on the earth during the little season which succeeds the millennium.

(7) What great events do we expect to follow the "little season"?

(8) What do we mean by "the second death"?

What the Lesson Means Today

The millennial reign will take place here. This fact should rescue us from despising the opportunities of our present life.

In the days to come mortals and immortals will live together on the earth and children will grow up and be changed from mortality to immortality in the twinkling of an eye. In view of these statements we should not fear the transition of death.

The awful picture of the second death is a vivid illustration of the terrible consequences which inevitably follow our abuse of our agency. There is no tragedy so great as the misuse of powers given us of God for the building of his kingdom.

Chapter XX

THE CHURCH OF JESUS CHRIST

The authority of the church—The importance of church membership—Necessity of the church of the restored gospel—Indispensable functions of the church in society.

Lesson Fifty-four

MEN BELONG TOGETHER RELIGIOUSLY as well as in every other way. We may and do have religious experiences in which we stand alone in the presence of Divinity. But our friends or our enemies surround as before we go to the mountain of contemplation, and await us when we return. God has so ordered our lives and our spiritual growth that we belong together both for learning and for serving. There are many good men who do not recognize this, and so do not belong to any church, but there are no good Christians who are not church members.

In the light of experience and of reason and of the clear teachings of the Scriptures, he who desires to serve the Master will do well to become a member, that is a functioning part, of some church body. But in spite of the modern trends toward church union, all churches are not equally acceptable. In the Mosaic dispensation, the service of God in life and worship under divine guidance was held to be so important that the children of Israel were separated from the surrounding nations with the utmost rigor. Jesus felt that the church was so important that it must not be contaminated in any way by infiltration from without. He said: "I will build my church" (Matt. 16: 18), and refused to recognize as members of this church any but those who were truly born again. The apostles caught the Master's concern about this matter; and we find Paul writing to the Galatian saints:

Though we or an angel from heaven, preach any other gospel unto you than that which we have preached unto you, let him be accursed. As we said before, so say I now again, if any man preach any other gospel unto you than that ye have received, let him be accursed. For do I now persuade men, or God? Or do I speak to please men? For if I yet pleased men, I should not be the servant of Christ. But I certify you, brethren, that the gospel which is preached of me is not after man. For I neither received it of man, neither was I taught it, but by the revelation of Jesus Christ.—Galatians 1: 8-12.

John wrote in similar vein:

Look to yourselves, that we lose not those things which we have wrought, but that we receive a full reward. Whosoever transgresseth, and abideth not in the doctrine of Christ, hath not God. He that abideth in the doctrine of Christ, he hath both the Father and the Son. If there come any unto you, and bring not this doctrine, receive him not in your house, neither bid him God speed.—II John 8-10.

The exclusiveness here revealed is not harsh or narrow. It is required by concern for truth and righteousness. If one takes religion seriously enough to believe that it makes a difference to character and conduct, it is impossible not to discriminate in some fashion in favor of religious organizations which exhibit fidelity to the Master and function with intelligence and ethical soundness. All Christians agree to this by fact of their Christianity. Without considering themselves guilty of bitterness, hatred, or bigotry, Christian people testify by the fact of their faith that Christianity is better than Judaism or Mohammedanism or Buddhism. In like fashion Latter Day Saints testify that the church of Jesus Christ offers more for the spiritual well-being of individuals and of mankind than any approximation to this church can do. And this seems to us to be reasonable, since we believe that God seeks to guide his people directly, by the spirit of revelation; and that he is represented on the earth by a priesthood, prophetically guided, whose only claim to distinction is that they represent him.

The Restoration Movement began in an affirmation that existing creeds were wrong. During the years which have elapsed since that time, the various Protestant Churches have agreed with this judgment, and have shown their agreement by making changes in their fundamental statements of belief. The historic creeds, of course, have not been changed; but the attitude of religious people toward these creeds has changed very perceptibly. Yet the statement of Joseph Smith cannot mean that there was no good in the various religious groups. Does it not mean, then, that the church of Jesus Christ is a living creation, drawing life from heaven and living for Christ; and that creeds which do not reflect this are necessarily wrong? There are many good people in the world, and many religious organizations which render a valuable service to society. But the church of Jesus Christ is intended to be more than a religious organization. It is intended to be a divine creation, filled with the Spirit of God and functioning in love.

Many good people find this position extremely distasteful, since they feel that it is narrow and bigoted and inconsistent with our modern tolerance. Yet it is the position taken by the vast majority of churches. The Roman Catholic Church, for example, believes just this, and refuses to recognize the authority of any of the Protestant Churches. The Greek Catholic Church takes the same fundamental position, although she is more willing to recognize the authority of some national churches, such as the Church of England, than is the Roman Catholic Church. Truly, great strides toward church union have been made during the past quarter of a century, and further developments are just over the horizon. But wherever the church is regarded as the divinely organized and empowered society of the redeemed, the distinctively importance of truth is still recognized as a valid reason for distinctive organization and worship.

If we admit that it is like God to commit his truth to one people, and to choose first those who choose to do his will, then the way is open for recognizing the rightness of the position of the Saints. This is particularly true when we recognize that the faith committed to the Saints is not a body of truth, circumscribed and defined, which was designed to be taught from age to age without elaboration or variation; but is rather a spirit of life and revelation and understanding, which keeps men true to the faith of yesterday and also guides them in the way of truth as this revelation opens before them.

The status of the church before God is not to be determined on the basis of history, or of material resources, nor even of great learning. If this had been the basis of determination, then, instead of founding a new spiritual order, Jesus would have sought to revivify Judaism or the most promising of the pagan religions. Acceptance with God depends, rather, on ideals and spirit and germinal power. Not what a man is, but what he may become, commends him to God. In the same way, it is not the visible power and promise of any group, but the quality of its inner spiritual life, which determines its destiny. It was in view of this fact that Jesus reassured his disciples, "Fear not, little flock, for it is the Father's good pleasure to give you the kingdom."—Luke 12: 32.

We do not believe that the church of Jesus Christ as now organized among men is perfect. Indeed, our solemn affirmation of the truth and importance of the gospel of Christ is made in utter humility, and with deep consciousness of our shortcomings. What is here set forth is not stated boastfully, in evidence of our distinctive goodness, but gratefully, in testimony of the enduring love of God. It is a challenge rather than an accomplishment; but it is also an indication of the lines along which accomplishment is to be won.

The church of Jesus Christ has spiritual resources which are indispensable both for the eternal well being of the individual and for the present and future salvation of society; for the church is different from all other institutions in that she ministers to deeper needs than any others. The church can guide the individual in escaping from despair and selfishness to a joy that endures even through pain. She can build society in which injustice and strife give way before righteousness and peace. She can lead the world into truly abundant life for every age and race.

The church justifies her calling as the "pillar and ground of the truth," (I Tim. 3: 15), by providing a center of creative faith. This is first of all faith in Jesus Christ as the Son of God and the author and crown of our salvation. From the beginning, the message of the church has been, "Hear ye him." To him the Holy Scriptures, the Book of Mormon, and the revelations of the Doctrine and Covenants bear joint witness. The priesthood are his ambassadors. Their message is his message. Such doctrines as the church teaches derive their life and power from Jesus the Lord. They give no mechanical guarantees of salvation, but lead always to him. The life and power and spiritual quality of the church are derived. They belong primarily to the Master of us all, and have place in the church only so long as it remains in fact, as well as in name, the Church of Jesus Christ.

Again, the Church of Jesus Christ offers to the world an inclusive spiritual objective. What is the task of the church? Fundamentally it is to teach the gospel of Jesus Christ, to transmit the moral ideals and spiritual power which come from him. This is not the transmission of a closed and completed faith, but the transmission of life. This church purpose is achieved as individual men and women are stimulated and made secure by a sense of comradeship in the greatest cause of all time. The church of Jesus Christ, therefore, offers the world the vision and the goal of the kingdom of God, in which men are brothers, because they are first of all the children of God.

Never before in the history of the world has religion been so important in the lives of men and nations, or the absence of the spirit of brotherhood so tragic. The machinery of the kingdom is ready to our hands, and new and improved machinery is being built every day. Time and distance and the barriers of language are being annihilated, and the world is truly becoming a neighborhood.

A house divided against itself cannot stand; nor can a world divided, as is our present world, into races that despise one another, nations that fear one another, and groups that distrust one another. A world which economically has become a neighborhood must spiritually become a brotherhood if civilization is not to give way to chaos."—Ernest Fremont Tittle, in *What Salvation Can the Church Offer Today*.

The church also offers us a guarantee of forgiveness. It is only when we come face to face with Jesus Christ that we realize what a heavy burden of sin we carry. Lives are warped and misdirected and enfeebled which might be strong and vigorous and great. Think how much of the potential power of this world, which might be directed toward the building of the kingdom, is dissipated through hate and lust and greed! How adroit men are in "getting in on a good thing," or in refusing to share their gains with others, and how much this adroitness costs! In the face of such waste, the church proclaims the love of God and leads men into the presence of Divinity. There, realizing the tremendous price which God has paid that we might come to understanding, men are daily being moved to hunger for righteousness, and are being received into the church through repentance and baptism, being saved through working at worthy tasks. Men are not forgiven by themselves, but in the process of being built into the working force of the kingdom of God.

From time to time the church is tempted to leave her high mission and to become just another social agency, for many who do not fully sense her essential task think that the final purpose of the church is remedial and reclamatory social service. But, in spite of this danger, the church persists in her central ministry of worship. By this I do not mean the organization of services of worship, but the maintenance of opportunities and inducements to meditation and prayer, the opening of the soul to the light and power of revelation.

If the church were only a shrine, a sanctuary, a place to worship and adore God, a place where God is quietly but firmly taught and the knowledge of him kept alive, like a never dying flame, that alone would justify the church. Worship is the big thing. We must not forget that. When a man goes away from the church he must feel that he has seen God, that God has touched him; God is vital.—John R. Ewers, in *The Value of the Church*.

Such worship as the church inspires carries forward a constant process of re-creation, which reaches beyond the sanctuary and enriches and ennobles every common task. Because the worship of the church ministers to a great soul hunger, and causes men to consider "righteousness and temperance and judgment to come," it reaches out also to satisfy physical and economic needs which otherwise go unsatisfied. Banks, mills, schools, and houses do not make a city. Life is more than machinery. A spirit and a purpose and a soul are needed, and to these the church ministers.

Finally, the church offers an inspiring glimpse of the life that is yet to be. We believe that we are but a colony of heaven, that the day will yet come when Christ the Lord shall reign over us in person. The spirit and the body will be brought together, free from the threat of death, and will be able to participate in the creative tasks of eternity. Eye has not seen, nor ear heard, nor has it entered into the heart of man what great things God has prepared for his children. Yet we know that the greatness of his love guarantees to us the opportunity of comradeship with the heroes of every age in tasks which shall employ our noblest powers, and which shall lead us to progressive understanding of the divine purpose, which is that we might enjoy constantly richer communion with our Heavenly Father, through Jesus Christ, our Lord.

Study Outlines

The Church of Jesus Christ

Lesson Purpose

To emphasize and justify our belief in the distinctive importance of the gospel recommitted to earth in the Restoration.

High Points of the Lesson

Religious exclusiveness is demanded by a high regard for the truth. In the final analysis the only salvation lies in being right. Good intentions are important, but only as they lead to the truth.

In view of the nature of the Christian enterprise, it is difficult to see how any religious organization can expect the full approval of Divinity without providing in its structural organization for divine guidance.

As the "pillar and ground of the truth," the church should provide a center of creative faith, an exclusive spiritual objective, a ministry of forgiveness, a shrine of worship, and an inspiring hope for the future.

Questions and Discussion Topics

(1) Refer to the teachings of the Scriptures regarding the exclusive nature of the church of Jesus Christ.

(2) Do any other Christians share this belief in religious exclusiveness?

(3) Has history justified Joseph Smith's affirmation that the creeds were wrong? Give reasons for your answer.

(4) What facts determine the status of the church before God?

(5) In what sense does the church provide a center of creative faith? In what ways can the ministry of the church in this regard be improved?

(6) Discuss, briefly, the inclusiveness of our Zionic objective. In what sense is this objective also exclusive?

(7) What part can the church play in bringing men to forgiveness?

(8) What is the purpose of the worship of the church? What is the test of its effectiveness? Why is it important?

What the Lesson Means Today

Our claim of exclusive spiritual enlightenment carries with it corresponding responsibility. Such a belief, if held firmly, releases tremendous spiritual power, but it also entails tremendous spiritual responsibility.

The church is yet in the process of becoming. Her power can be augmented only as members of the church live in the light of the truth.

In every age the gospel has carried a message which worldly men found incredible: that a man crucified between two thieves was the Son of God, that a group of obscure men would build his kingdom, that men chosen of God have returned to earth to reconfer the authority of priesthood and to link the dispensations together in the name of Christ. Yet the spirit of conviction has always accompanied a straightforward declaration of the message. It always will.

Study Outlines

Lesson Fifty-Five

Belief and Life

(Review)

Lesson Purpose

This lesson may well be devoted to a review of some of the major positions taken in this book. Any method which commends itself to the teacher may be followed. One possible method is to assign statements for brief discussion in the class period. The following is a list of possible topics:

Possible Discussion Topics

"I believe in God, the Father, Almighty."
"God is a spirit, and they that worship him must worship him in spirit and in truth." (See John 4: 24-26 I. V. for a better rendering.)
"I am come that they might have life, and have it more abundantly."
"By my spirit will I enlighten them."
"As my Father sent me, even so send I you."
The church is "the pillar and ground of the truth."
"The wages of sin is death."
"The gift of God is eternal life."
"The spirit divideth to every man severally as he will."
"My word shall not return unto me void, but it shall accomplish that whereunto it was sent."
"This do in remembrance of me."
"I saw another angel, flying in the midst of heaven."
"The glory of God is intelligence."
"Remember the Sabbath Day to keep it holy."
"Though I, or an angel from heaven, preach any other gospel . . . . let him be accursed."

FUND.—12